Roll of Ho

The story of hundreds of Leek men
who fell in the First World War

Written and researched by
C. W. Sheldon

Dave,
Hope you enjoy the book.
Thanks for your help.
Chris

THREE COUNTIES PUBLISHING (Books) LIMITED

Published by

Three Counties Publishing (Books) Limited

P.O. Box 435 Leek, Staffordshire England, ST13 5TB
telephone 01538 380910 fax 01538 382204
email: tcpbooksltd@aol.com

ISBN 0 9544080 - 3 - 9

Typeset by Clermont Ferrand Int. Staffordshire, England
and Printed by Biddles Limited, King's Lynn, England

'Roll of Honour'

The untold story of the hundreds of soldiers, sailors
and airmen from Leek who gave their lives
during the First World War.

"I see by the Leek Post that Leek has
lost a few more men. My word, our
little town has suffered and no
mistake"

Private Harold Plant, aged 18, in a
letter to his parents at 51, Picton
Street, Leek, seven weeks before he
was killed in action on the Somme,
September 1916.

Contents

Preface

When I published my first book, 'In Name Only', two years ago, I was amazed at the response I received from its readers. The book told the story of the Leek servicemen who died during the Second World War. For some, the book revived treasured thoughts of an old friend, for others it invoked sad, but proud memories of a lost loved one. For many, the book is a source of reference and has even accompanied groups visiting war cemeteries in France and Belgium and helped them to identify particular graves of local servicemen. Copies have been sent to far-away countries such as South Africa, Canada and Australia where former Leek residents live. But, for whatever reason you possess a copy of 'In Name Only' (if indeed you do), perhaps the most important aspect is that it will remain a permanent and detailed tribute to those who gave their lives, not only for now, but also for future generations.

Much the same can be said about 'Roll of Honour' although, of course, there are very few people around now who can remember back, even as children, to the Great War. Surely though, it is only right that all the hundreds of Leek men and boys who died during that shocking conflict should be similarly remembered? Sadly, their story cannot be told in as much detail as I would have liked. Families have faded out, dusty and yellowed photographs of once-proud soldiers have been lost or discarded, historical records are often incomplete or unreliable. Nevertheless, the best has been done over a three-year period of research with the available information and material. One in ten of the servicemen listed on the Monument cannot even be identified with official, or unofficial, records. Whilst I found that the most exasperating and frustrating part of my research, it does at least reinforce the certainty that this book needed to be researched and written before it was too late altogether.

It is inevitable with the passage of time that a few of the details relating to the fallen may contain inaccuracies but hopefully these, if any, should only be of a minor nature. For example, I may show a man as aged 22 and working at Wardle and Davenports. If someone can produce evidence that he was in fact 26 and worked at Leek Railway Station then I will apologise! Whilst I have tried to be as accurate as possible, many of the details available cannot be fully validated as much as I would have liked. Just occasionally, there are discrepancies in official records over the date of a serviceman's death. In those instances, and they are very few in number, I have used the date recorded by the Commonwealth War Graves Commission unless I have irrefutable evidence (such as a death certificate) to show otherwise. The reader will understand, I feel sure, that if I had set out to guarantee 100% accuracy of <u>every</u> detail in this book, I would have given up the project many months ago and this tribute to the fallen would never have been published. I hope that I have managed to create an informative, interesting and permanent record of the fate of most of those who fell and to put real people behind the long, tragic list of names on the Nicholson War Memorial in Leek.

Finally, my heartfelt thanks goes out to all the people who have helped make this publication possible. In particular, I am indebted to Mark Bibby, John Crosby, David Irving, Malcolm Sperring-Toy, Ray Poole, Brian Podmore, Pam Webb and David Baldwin for their valuable assistance. I am equally grateful to my nephew, Paul Sheldon, for his technical problem-solving abilities and my wife, Lynette, for her patience.

Chris Sheldon, Leek, December, 2003

Foreword

Leek Historian, Ray Poole.

On Armistice Day, November 11th, 2002, I was privileged to be present at the Remembrance Ceremony at the Menin Gate in Ypres. It was an impressive and moving occasion, greatly enhanced by the presence of three of the ever-decreasing number of surviving First World War veterans. Their combined ages totalled 311 years, and to hear the words: *"TO THE FALLEN"* spoken by one of these veterans in a clear, firm voice which resounded round the arches of the Menin Gate was an unforgettable experience.

As I mingled with the crowds in Ypres I was conscious of the fact that we were surrounded by a great crowd of unseen witnesses - the 54,896 casualties of the fighting in the Ypres Salient who have no known grave and whose names are inscribed on the panels around the Menin Gate. The thousands of names include a number of Leek men and more can be found on other memorials and in military cemeteries in France, Belgium and even more distant corners of the world. Names on war memorials are always evocative; behind each one is a story, often of great bravery, a supreme sacrifice and a family torn apart by sorrow.

I was also conscious of being part of a universal act of remembrance, as, simultaneously with the ceremonies in Ypres, similar events were taking place at the Cenotaph in London, and, of course, at the Nicholson War Memorial in Leek. A visitor to Leek may be unaware of the town's fascinating history and the close-knit community within its confines, but he can hardly fail to notice this striking reminder of the past, known to local people as 'The Monument'. If he pauses to look at the weather -beaten brass plaques on the walls of the 90 foot high memorial, he will see that it was built in 1925 by Sir Arthur Nicholson, a wealthy silk manufacturer, in memory of his son, Lieutenant Basil Lee Nicholson and 418 other sons of Leek who died in the Great War of 1914-18. What he cannot know, as he gazes at the long list of names that have adorned the Portland Stone memorial for three quarters of a century, is who these local lads were. Many of them would be workers in the local silk industry, for which Leek was famous; they would have families, wives, sweethearts. Where did they die? Was it on the Somme, the fields of Flanders or that dreadful place with the name so emotive of all the horrors of the war, Passchendaele? For the first time, the story behind those tragic names is told in Chris Sheldon's 'ROLL OF HONOUR'.

I am honoured to be associated with this splendid piece of work. Leek people are proud of their town's history and this is a vital part of it. In undertaking the immense task of research to tell these stories, Chris has done a great service to the town. As ever, many local people have given their time and help unselfishly in granting interviews with the author and making available precious family photographs and memorabilia.

This book deserves to take its place amongst the growing list of literature on the First World War, and, as Remembrance Sunday comes round each year, it will help to make the names of the fallen even more meaningful each time we hear those traditional words:

"WE WILL REMEMBER THEM".

Ray Poole, Leek. April, 2003.

"Off to war with a smile"

The soldier of 1914 and 1915 was keen
to get into the action before the war was
over, but little did he know what lay ahead.

The smiling face of this young volunteer,
photographed in the garden of his Buxton
Road home, tells its own story.

Harry Billing was killed in action on the
first day of the Battle of the Somme in
July, 1916. He was 20 years old.

I. Billing

The Nicholson War Memorial, Leek

The words carved in the lintels of the clockface at the top of the structure are all placenames representing battles or actions in which the Leek Battery was involved between 1915 and 1918. The memorial was erected by Sir Arthur Nicholson whose son, Lieutenant Basil Lee Nicholson, was killed in action whilst serving with the Battery in 1915. The placenames, and their locations, (**Hooge, Loos, Ypres, Lens, Gommecourt, Somme, Bellenglise, Ramicourt, Bohain,**) can all be found within the text of this book.

Introduction

The Great War of 1914-18 took its dreadful toll on Leek and district as it did across the rest of the country and, after it was all over, memorials to the dead sprang up in towns and villages everywhere. Possibly the largest memorial in England is the Nicholson War Memorial in the centre of Leek, built in 1925 by wealthy silk manufacturer Sir Arthur Nicholson whose son was killed in the war. The names recorded on the 'Monument', as it is known, number 420.

'Roll Of Honour' tells the story of those soldiers, sailors and airmen who never came home. Or more accurately, it records the *known* details and fate of the *majority* of those listed on the two large brass plaques and sets their story within the context of the war. Inevitably, with the passage of time, it has not been possible to positively link some of the names with servicemen on official records. Regretfully, 40 of the names have therefore had to be relegated to an appendix at the rear of this book instead of taking their rightful place within the main body of the text. With the passage of time, over 85 years since the Great War ended, I hope I may be forgiven for not finding and identifying these unfortunate souls. When one realises the sheer volume of people who lost their lives, it is perhaps not surprising. For example, over 3,400 Johnsons died, over 2,800 Robinsons and a staggering 13,800 Smiths!

(Author's Collection)
*One of two lists of the fallen on the
Nicholson War Memorial*

Great reliance has been placed on the records of the Commonwealth War Graves Commission, Regimental Histories and War Diaries, the publication of 'Soldiers Died in the Great War', the Leek Post and the Leek Times of the war years and other authoritative publications. As in my earlier book, *'In Name Only'*, local people have again given their help willingly, although, of course, much of the available information has been understandably patchy. In some cases, though, I have been lucky enough to find descendants who have done their own research into a fallen relative, or have kept photographs and letters sent from the front. That has made a very hard task somewhat easier and I am very grateful for all contributions, no matter how large or small they may have been.

This is the first time that an attempt has been made to record the story of <u>all</u> the men of Leek who lost their lives in the First World War. Two other notable publications are in existence which mention some of the casualties. The most recent of these is '*Over There*' by the late J.E. Blore and J.R. Sherratt published in 1991. This excellent book is a history of the Leek Battery which fought on the Western Front. Nine of the twenty-five men from the battery who died in the war are recorded on the Monument plaques. (The remainder presumably did not live in the town of Leek itself and are recorded on other war memorials). The other book, published in 1915, is entitled: '*Leek and District Sailors and Soldiers Roll of Honour*' and records the local men serving and killed during 1914 and 1915. This was compiled by the Leek Sailors and Soldiers Comforts Society in November, 1915. With three more years of war to go, it is a great pity that the Society could not continue its excellent work and produce volumes for the three remaining years of the war. '*Roll of Honour*' completes the job started all those years ago, at least as far as is humanly possible, and puts real people behind as many as possible of the long list of names on our Monument. It is dedicated to all those men, women and children of our town who were affected, in whatever way, by the turmoil and tragedy of four dark years of war.

(Imperial War Museum)

'All quiet on the Western Front'

After war broke out in 1914, men flocked to the colours in droves, ready to 'do their bit' for King and Country and eager for a taste of the action before the war was won. Little did they realise that the war would drag on, seemingly forever, and that men would be repeatedly thrown into often futile attacks against an enemy determined to hold his ground. Soon, disillusionment with their leaders set in. Many thought that the war would never end. The number of men killed, wounded and missing or who died from disease during those four long years almost beggars belief. By the end of the war, some 9 million lay dead including 750,000 British soldiers, sailors and airmen. Over 400 were from the town of Leek. Many more from the moorlands villages also died...... but their story will, hopefully, be told in future publications. As the casualty lists grew longer and longer, blinds were drawn in hundreds of Leek homes. Some families lost two sons, one poor lady from Duke Street lost three. Almost every Leek family was affected by a serviceman's death in some way.

New words and strange sounding placenames became part of everyday language - 'Shellshock', 'Whizbangs', 'Blighty', 'Wipers' 'The Somme', 'Passchendaele'. These and others became shockingly familiar to those at the front and to the public at large. The First World War was the first industrial conflict which saw the use of such killing weapons as the machine gun, the tank and poison gas. It is said that the 'Flower of a Generation' was lost during those awful years. The world was never the same again.

This, then, is the story of the brave soldiers, sailors and airmen from Leek who died during the First World War. Most were young and fit and keen to have a crack at the Germans before the war ended. Most were volunteers, some joined up together with their friends. Many saw it as a great opportunity to get away from their tedious jobs in the dusty Leek mills, to see the world, taste some excitement and get properly fed and clothed for it in the bargain. Some mothers in the town had up to five, or even more, sons serving in the armed forces at the same time. Little did anyone realise as the great adventure started for these sons of our town, that roughly one in every eight would never come home again.

The Cross of Sacrifice stands guard over the graves of British and Commonwealth war dead in cemeteries all around the world.

Chapter 1

The Slippery Slope to War

"The lamps are going out all over Europe.
We shall not see them lit again in our lifetime"

(Sir Edward Grey, British Foreign Minister, on the eve of war.)

The causes of the First World War were many and complex and it is not intended to go into detail about them here. A few short paragraphs should suffice to set the scene and put into context the circumstances which allowed the various powers to slide into a war in 1914 that would develop on a gigantic scale, causing the deaths of millions.

One hundred years ago, Britain was the greatest nation on earth, ruling a quarter of the world and boasting a navy twice the size of any other fleet. Her industry - coal, iron, ship-building, engineering and textiles made the country strong. Imperial power and industrial strength, however, also meant poverty and hardship for many people and the townsfolk of Leek were no exception. Many of the young men who would fight in the coming war came from large families living in small terraced houses in poor, cramped conditions. Most worked in the large textile mills of the town, toiling in unhealthy conditions for long hours and small wages. Unskilled workers were at the bottom end of the scale. Little wonder that so many volunteered for the armed forces at the outbreak of war. They were driven not only by patri-otism but by the prospect of regular meals and pay, decent clothing and the chance of some excitement with their friends; a welcome change in an otherwise humdrum life. True, re-forms were being pushed through by the Liberal Government which would see improve-ments in the lives of the working classes and remove the "shadow of the workhouse from the houses of the poor", as David Lloyd George said, but all these reforms would take time.

Many other events occurred during the pre-war years which led to changes in our society.

The Suffragettes fought a determined campaign for the right of women to vote and Home Rule was being demanded in Ireland. There was a wide expansion in the growth of trade unions and the Transport Strike of 1912 threatened starvation of the inhabitants of London. The National Health Insurance Act of 1911 had, along with the Old Age Pensions Act, gone a long way to relieve the plight of the poor. Perhaps it was not surprising that the problems brewing in Europe which would lead Britain into war seemed less significant at the time with all these things happening at home.

How then, did our proud nation slide so quickly into war in 1914? Much of it was to do with the rivalry which had grown between the major European Powers of Britain, France, Austria-Hungary, Germany and also Russia. Trade rivalry, particularly between Britain and Germany, was a cause of jealousy as was the building of the Berlin to Baghdad railway which the British public thought to be some sinister German plot to threaten the British-owned oilfields in Persia (now Iran). There then followed a more serious problem - known as the 'Naval Arms Race'. Germany began building battleships - seventeen between 1906 and 1914. Britain, traditionally 'ruling the waves,' saw this as a major threat and built twenty nine in the same period.

Another important cause of tension existed between Germany and France. This concerned the border provinces of Alsace and Lorraine, both rich in coal and iron. In 1870 Germany was not a united country, more a collection of small states, the most powerful being Prussia. In that year, Prussia attacked and defeated France. Part of the peace treaty demanded that France hand over the two provinces. The French wanted those territories back. Many miles away, a separate quarrel had built up between Russia, Turkey and Austria-Hungary over the many races, particularly in the Balkans, who were ruled over by the Turks and Austrians. Russia supported the Slav minorities and demanded better conditions for them.

From this mixture of quarrelling nations came two armed camps - Germany and Austria-Hungary (both countries had formed an alliance in 1879), France, Russia and Britain. France and Russia signed a treaty in 1894 promising to help the other in the event of war; Britain had also signed a treaty with Japan. Improvements were made to the small British Army including the creation of the Territorials, made up of civilian volunteers, as a reserve. Each side expected a war and each side expected to win. All that was really needed now was an 'excuse' to start the fighting although Britain, in the main, wanting to avoid war, trembled on the brink up to the last moment.

Further problems between the two sides occurred when the German ruler, Kaiser Wilhelm11, visited French-held Morocco, in North Africa, and spoke against French rule. A few years later, the French were further angered by the appearance of a German warship in a Moroccan port. But perhaps what really led these nations on the slippery slope to war was a crisis in Bosnia where the then Turkish rulers handed over power to Austria. The Bosnians deeply hated the Austrians and the crisis and strength of feeling in this remote corner of the world would provide the spark that would lead the armed nations, including Britain, into a catastrophic war.

Prior to 1914, a number of Austrian officials had been assassinated in Bosnia by terrorists known as the 'Black Hand Gang', who were fighting to free their homeland. Despite the troubles, the Austrian Archduke, Franz Ferdinand, planned a visit to the Bosnian capital, Sarajevo, and insisted on a royal procession through the streets. The forthcoming visit was well-publicised and the terrorists spied their chance. There was no shortage of eager volunteers. They quickly recruited and trained six local teenagers.

On the sunny morning of Sunday, 28th June, 1914, as the Archduke and his wife toured the Sarajevo streets in the royal procession, the young conspirators were ready, armed and waiting. But, as the procession passed, two of them lost their nerve and did nothing. A third threw a bomb which injured several people in the car following the Archduke's. Shortly afterwards, the Archduke insisted on being taken to the hospital to see the injured, but by a different route that would avoid the crowds. His driver, however, took a wrong turning and was forced to stop and reverse the car. By pure chance, one of the would-be assassins was standing outside a cafe at this very spot. He was amazed to see the car and could hardly believe his luck. 19 year old Gavrilo Princip, a student and the son of a postman, jumped onto the running board and fired the fatal shots which plunged the opposing nations into war. As the lifeblood ebbed away from the Archduke and his wife, Sophie, so did the chance of peace. The wrong turn by the driver of the royal car proved to be the most disastrous in history. Within five weeks the world was at war.

(Imperial War Museum)
Archduke Franz Ferdinand with his wife in Sarajevo hours before they were shot dead

Suspecting that neighbouring Serbia was involved in the assassination plot, Austria sent an ultimatum to that country and when the demands were not all met, attacked Serbia on 29th July. Russia sent its armies to the Austrian and German borders in support of Serbia, and on 1st August, Germany declared war on Russia. Germany moved troops to the French and Belgian borders and declared war on France on 3rd August. Britain warned Germany not to attack neutral Belgium but they did just that on 4th August. Britain, bound by a treaty (signed 75 years earlier) to protect Belgium if she was attacked, declared war on Germany. Two days later, British troops were sailing to France. Like all other towns, Leek prepared itself for war. The Leek Times of 8th August reported that members of the Navy Reserve and Army Reservists had been called up and the Territorials (the 'Saturday afternoon soldiers,' as they were often irreverently called), were ordered to report to their headquarters. One police constable from Upper Hulme and six post office workers from Leek had already left to join the forces. Members of the local artillery unit, the Leek Battery, took over West Street School and busied themselves in readiness for the expected orders to leave for France.

Horses were 'conscripted' and even the watercart belonging to the Leek Urban District Council, the Leek Times sombrely reported, was commandeered for the war effort! It was said by most people at the time that the war would be over by Christmas - not in the opinion, it seems, of the manager of Brindley Baileys clothes shop in Derby Street. He was advertising: *"Remnants at half-price. Mourning clothing a speciality"* !

(J. E. Blore)

Men of the Leek Battery with one of their guns on the outbreak of war

Chapter 2

The First Leek Casualties

How noble the aim, how different the reality

Following a plan drawn up in 1905 by Count von Schlieffen, the then Chief of the German General Staff, the Germans marched through Belgium and into northern France with the intention of encircling Paris and forcing the French to surrender within six weeks. That would allow time for troops to be transferred back to the Russian frontier to face the threat there. Several things happened, however, to disrupt the plan and slow the Germans down. The Belgians were not such an easy walk-over as expected and the invaders were seriously delayed by the unexpected resistance. The Russians reached the eastern frontier far quicker than anticipated and the small but highly-trained British Expeditionary Force (BEF) had arrived on Belgian soil.

27 year old **Private Edward Merriman**, a former footballer with Leek Alexandra, was a regular soldier with the 2nd Battalion, Royal Irish Regiment. He was single, one of five children and lived with one of his brothers and sister-in-law at 14, Ashbourne Road, near to the Coffee Tavern. His parents came to live in Leek from their native Ireland when their children were small, making their home in Talbot passage. As Ted Merriman and his comrades arrived at the Belgian mining town of Mons on the night of 22nd August 1914, they were halted by their officers. Rumours were rife about German troops advancing in large numbers and there was talk about the BEF being cut off. There had been minor skirmishes between British and German troops that day, when the first British shots of the war were fired, and a large attack was expected the next day. Little did Ted Merriman know that this night would be his last and that he would be the first of over 400 Leek men to die for his country.

(Author's Collection)
Ted Merriman - the first to die in battle

On the morning of 23rd August, the two sides collided in what became known as the Battle of Mons. At first, the BEF held its own against superior German forces but was soon forced to retreat to keep in line with French forces on either side which were falling back towards Paris. But the Germans had had a shock. The German Kaiser had called the BEF a *"contemptible little army"* (hence the phrase: 'Old Contemptibles'), but not reckoned with its rate of fire and accuracy with the rifle. German soldiers at Mons thought they were actually facing machine gun fire. At the end of the day's battle at least 5,000 of the enemy were killed, wounded or missing. The cost to the BEF was also high, some 1,600 casualties. Amongst those killed was Private Merriman. His body was never found after the war and he is commemorated on the La Ferte-Sous-Jouarre Memorial on the banks of the River Marne, 50 miles east of Paris. He has a number of relatives still living in Leek. One of these is a niece who was born just three days after Ted was killed. Another is Keith Harrison, a Moorlands

(R. Lovatt)

George Graham with his wife

Councillor, Chairman of the Staffordshire Moorlands District Council in 2002 and town Mayor in 2003. He is a great-nephew of Ted Merriman's, as was his brother, the late Geoff Harrison.

The next major battle with the Germans took place at Le Cateau, France, on 26th August, as the BEF retreated. The British decided to make a stand here but despite their brave defiance, were forced to continue the retreat. During the fighting, which resulted in nearly 8,000 soldiers of the BEF becoming casualties (including some 2,000 taken prisoner), the second Leek soldier fell in action. **Corporal George Henry Graham**, like Ted Merriman, was in the 2nd Battalion, Royal Irish Regiment. He came from 43, Parker Street and was killed whilst his unit defended the orderly retreat of other units of the BEF from the battle-field. George was also a regular soldier and, whilst serving in Guernsey, Channel Islands, before the war, met the lady who was to become his wife. She was expecting his child when he was killed. Corporal Graham is buried in the Bethencourt Communal Cemetery near Le Cateau.

The third Leek man to die during this first month of the war was **Warrant Officer John Edward Walke**r. He was 36 and died at Shorncliffe Hospital in Kent on 29th August. He was serving in the Royal Garrison Artillery but attached to the Royal Corps of Schoolmasters. It is thought that Warrant Officer Walker died of illness. He was a married man and lived at 19 Shoobridge Street, Leek. His grave is in Dover Cemetery.

(Authors Collection)
John Walker

As the BEF and French forces continued their retreat towards Paris the Germans gave chase. The Schlieffen Plan, however, was now in ruins. The French capital would never be reached in time. In a decisive battle, the Allied armies stood and fought on the banks of the River Marne in early September. The Germans, exhausted by weeks of fighting, retreated to the River Aisne and made a stand there. The troops of the opposing forces dug the first trenches on 16th September, little knowing that most of them would be spending the next four years in 'holes' in the ground. **Private James Drury** from 7 Pickwood Road, Leek, was one of these men. Serving with the 2nd Battalion, South Staffordshire Regiment, he had landed in France on 12th August, a week after war broke out and marched many miles on the retreat from Mons towards Paris. As Jim Drury and his friends manned their new trenches, the Germans made determined attacks on the British lines. There were casualties on both sides and Private Drury was one of them. He died of his wounds on 20th September, 1914 and is buried at Braine Communal Cemetery where there are some 80 British graves from the First World War.

The 1914 Star, also known as the Mons Star.
Awarded to men who fought from August to
November in the France and Flanders Campaign.

Roll of Honour

Chapter 3

The Race to the Sea and The First Battle of Ypres.

*"I am proud to belong to Leek and being a soldier. I can assure you
I have seen some awful sights out here both fighting
and in destroying the homes of the French".*

(Private Arthur Tatton, in a letter home. Killed in action on the Somme, July, 1916.)

During the next few weeks, both sides attempted out-flanking movements to trap their opponents. Then, realising the danger of being cut off from the French ports on the English Channel, the BEF made a hasty march north towards the coast. They arrived in the nick of time but met the Germans at the Belgian town of Ypres (known as 'Wipers' to the troops). From mid-October, German forces made ferocious frontal attacks on the British lines, determined to take the town from the BEF. They were mown down in their thousands. Despite losing so many of their best troops, the Germans continued the offensive for five weeks until 22nd November when the winter weather discouraged further movement. The Allies had won the race to the sea and Ypres was saved. Both sides dug in for the winter and the opposing lines of trenches now stretched from the Channel coast to the Swiss border.

Although the offensive at Ypres cost the Germans dear, the sadly depleted BEF also paid a high price - some 70,000 casualties. Whilst the desperate fighting for the town of Ypres was at its height, three more Leek soldiers died, the first one of his wounds in hospital at Southampton after being evacuated from the Western Front. 27 year old **Private William Robson Trafford** of 14 Garden Street, lost his fight for life on 5th November 1914, whilst serving with the 1st Battalion, Kings Shropshire Light Infantry. He was brought back to Leek and was the first soldier from the Great War to be buried in the town's cemetery. His grave, and the graves of most of the other servicemen buried in Leek Cemetery, can be easily recognised by the distinctive Commonwealth War Graves Commission headstones. Two days later, on 7th Novem-

(Authors Collection)
William Trafford

ber, **Private John Machin**, aged 22, died of severe wounds sustained at Ypres. He had lived at one time in St Edward Street and was serving with the 1st Battalion, South Staffordshire Regiment. This battalion, originally 1,100 strong, suffered so heavily in the November fighting at Ypres that only 78 men remained. All the rest were killed, wounded or missing. John Machin was buried but his grave lost, as happened in so many cases. He is commemorated on the Menin Gate Memorial to the Missing at Ypres. The memorial lists the names of over 54,000 British and Commonwealth soldiers who died in the Ypres Salient and have no known grave. At 8 o'clock every evening, the Belgian Fire Brigade play the Last Post at the Menin Gate in honour of those who died. This moving ceremony has taken place every evening since 1929, only being disrupted between 1940 and 1944, when Belgium was occupied by the Germans.

(Authors Collection)

John Machin - died of wounds

On the same day that William Trafford died, 5th November, 1914, **Private John Goodwin** from 34, Pickwood Road, (off Derby Street) was killed in Flanders whilst serving with the 1st Battalion, Cameronians (Scottish Rifles). Known as Jack, this young soldier was no older than 18, and one of many under-age volunteers who would die in a foreign land far away from family, friends and home. (We shall see more examples of Leek soldiers who lied about their age to join up and paid with their lives later in this book). Jack's family recall the reason why this young lad left Leek at such a young age and volunteered for a Scottish infantry regiment before war broke out. The Goodwins were poor people, like so many others of that generation. Nevertheless, they were proud, honest, God-fearing people, well-respected by their friends and neighbours. They were horrified, therefore, when Jack came home one day with a pair of new boots, stolen, it is said, from a Leek shop. The lad desperately need new footwear for work but the family could afford none. Fearful of the consequences, should Jack

(T. Booth)

Jack Goodwin

24

be caught and punished, (3 months imprisonment would have been a likely sentence in those days) it was decided that he should run away and join the army. Quite why he went as far as Scotland to enlist is not known. Perhaps he thought it prudent to put plenty of miles between his home town and his new life? It is ironic that Jack Goodwin never did pay for his boots but he did pay for his mistake in the long run, with his life. His parents never got over the tragedy of his death at such a young age.

Before he was killed, young Jack Goodwin must have wondered what the world was coming to as it descended into war and what fate would have in store for him as his battalion was ordered to France. Scotland was the furthest he had ever travelled, and that was more than most Leek lads of his age had ever achieved. To Jack, it was probably all an adventure to start with, but, as each day passed, reality would gradually bring him down to earth as he experienced and witnessed the horrors of modern warfare. The War Diary of the 1st Cameronians gives an interesting insight into the daily life of a regular army infantry battalion (over 1,000 men) as it marched off to fight in this new war.

The first stage of Jack Goodwin's jouney, from which he and many of his pals would never return, starts at Glasgow on 13th August, nine days since war was declared. At 10.15pm, with memories of fond farewells and tearful partings from loved ones, the soldiers settled down in the four trains that would take them on the long jouney to Southampton. The next day, the men stretched their cramped legs before boarding the troopship, SS Caledonia, and sailed for Le Havre, arriving on 15th August. There is little doubt that this was the first time that any of them had seen the English Channel, let alone set foot on French soil.

To cheers and greetings from the locals, the men of the battalion marched five miles to a rest camp to recover from the long journey, sort out their kit and get used to being in a foreign land. Two days later, they were back at Le Havre and on a train bound for Busigny where, after a long, tiring journey, the battalion was given an enthusiastic reception followed by speeches of welcome and presentations of bouquets to each of the officers. When, the Scotsmen must have wondered, would the real war begin? Over the next few days, the troops were busy unloading trains carrying equipment, rations, munitions and all the paraphernalia needed by a battalion of men on a war footing. Eventually, their journey east to the Front continued and, by Saturday, 22nd August, Jack Goodwin and the rest of the battalion were at Valenciennes, 30 miles west of Mons, and poised for the expected German attack the next day. Confusion then reigned as the battalion was ordered to Mons on the 23rd and early the following morning, ordered to retire at once as the German onslaught (during which Ted Merriman was killed) made the position impossible. Jack Goodwin and his friends marched south-west, where, footsore and weary, they paused at Le Cateau. On the day that George Graham was killed there, 26th August, the Cameronians moved off once again, with little food in their stomachs and enemy bullets flying dangerously close.

As described in Chapter 2, the BEF retreated as far as the River Marne and then, in October, 1914, fought their way to the Belgian town of Ypres. The 1st Cameronians moved to trenches at La Boutillerie, northern France, a few miles west of Lille and close to the Belgian border. The beleagured town of Ypres was some 16 miles north. The Scotsmen had already lost over fifty of their soldiers killed, and many more wounded since they arrived in France. Young Jack Goodwin was killed, probably by shellfire, on 5th November. His long journey from Leek was finally over.

Private Jack Goodwin's body was never found and he is commemorated on the Ploegsteert Memorial near Ypres.

Whilst the battles around Ypres raged and the tortured earth around the salient began to resemble the surface of the moon, another conflict was about to take place half-way across the world which would claim the life of a young Leek seaman. Since the outbreak of war, ships of the Royal Navy had been scouring the seas in search of a German commerce-raiding force, which included the ar-

(Authors Collection)

H.M.S. Good Hope

moured cruisers Scharnhorst and Gneisenau, and were intent on harassing merchant shipping on the west coast of South America. The Navy's South American Squadron, patrolling the waters off Chile from its base in the Falkland Islands, consisted of two old cruisers, HMS Good Hope and HMS Monmouth, accompanied by two other ships. On the evening of Sunday, 1st November, 1914, the two opposing naval squadrons encountered each other. Superior in speed, gunnery range and numbers, the German commander, Admiral Graf von Spee, was able to position his ships favourably and fire at the British ships now silhouetted against the rising moon. The Good Hope and the Monmouth were reduced to blazing wrecks within minutes. Both sank with all hands. The German ships escaped without damage.

(M. Bowyer)

George Tomkinson

One of the sailors who died in HMS Good Hope was 26 year old **Able Seaman George Tomkinson**, a married man from 10, Stockwell Street. He was a Navy Reservist and had served on other ships, including HMS Suffolk, before the war. George Tomkinson, who was born and raised at 14, Moorhouse Street, died along with some 900 of the crew and is commemorated on the Portsmouth Naval Memorial.

The British defeat was avenged a month later when a powerful Royal Navy force caught the German raiders off the Falkland Islands and destroyed them. Admiral Spee went down with his ship. It is ironic, perhaps, that 25 years later the pocket battleship named after this famous officer was scuttled and sunk during the Second World War off South America at the mouth of the River Plate following a running battle with British cruisers.

Meanwhile, back on the Western Front, the troops settled down for the long winter and, unbeknown to them, four more years of war. At about this time, a man named William Lumsden, a driver for Porter and Co. Furnishers, Bath Street, Leek, who had been 'commandeered along with the firm's charabanc', as the Leek Times reported, wrote from France: *"The Germans have absolutely failed to move us and, before much longer, I am sure they will give in as they must know they are beaten now. I fully expect the war will be over by the end of the year".*

But, by late December, 1914, soldiers on both sides solemnly contemplated the fact that the war was not over and had not been 'won by Christmas' as so many had predicted. Instead, they were living in muddy holes in the ground, homesick and bitterly cold. No-one was predicting now when the fighting would end.

At Christmas, some humanity was shown and the tribulations of the soldiers shared when a spontaneous but unofficial truce began in some parts of the line. Both British and German soldiers climbed out of their trenches and greeted one another, some even exchanging chocolate and cigarettes. Carols were sung and, for one day at least, no shots were fired. Men from the 1st Battalion, North Staffordshire Regiment were some of those involved in this unique event. One company commander, according to the Battalion History, was settling down to his supper in a dug-out when the Company Sergeant Major looked in and announced: *"What am I to do sir? The Germans are sitting on their parapets lighting candles and singing hymns !"*

When news of the truce reached higher authority, orders were quickly issued to make sure that such a thing would never happen again. And it didn't.

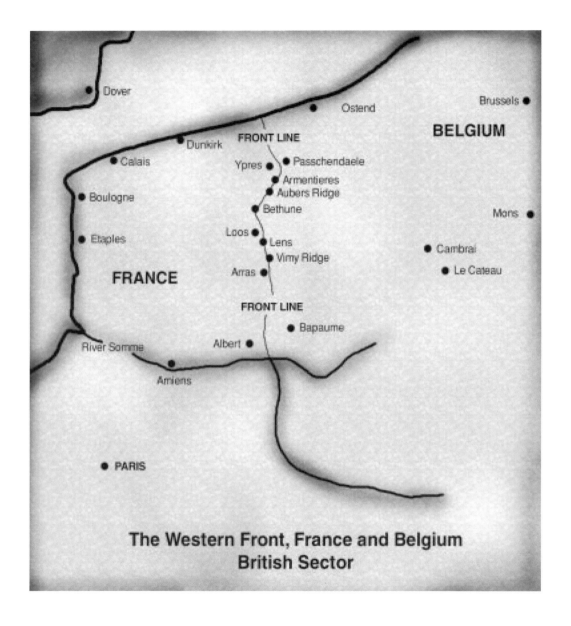

The Western Front, France and Belgium
British Sector

Chapter Four

The Call for Volunteers and the Early Battles of 1915.

Recruiting Sergeant: "How old are yer, son?" "Sixteen, Sergeant".
"Then gerrof 'ome and come back tomorrer when yer nineteen"

The casualty rates of the battered British Expeditionary Force were so high after the earlier battles of the war that replacements were urgently needed. In addition, many more army divisions were needed to fight if Britain was to remain a major combatant in this conflict. Two days after the outbreak of war in August, Lord Kitchener, a famous army general, was asked by the government to organise the recruiting campaign. Before long, posters appeared all over the country, urging men to enlist in the 'New Army' and Lord Kitchener hoped for 100,000 volunteers in 6 months. He had underestimated the sense of enthusiasm and patriotism that was sweeping the country. Men rushed to volunteer in droves. 500,000 volunteered in August alone followed by a monthly average of 180,000. Recruiting offices could not cope with the eager crowds of men. In Leek, Sergeant Major Cooley and Colour Sergeant Boughey were appointed to deal with recruiting and, before long, steady streams of volunteers were being sworn-in and taking the 'King's Shilling'.

(Author's Collection)
Kitchener's famous image still lives on today.

Many young men joined up on impulse or because their friends did. Some even lied about their ages, so enthusiastic were they to get a slice of the action, to do their duty and have a 'crack at the Hun' before the war ended. In some towns, men were encouraged to form 'Pals' Battalions'. This was particularly so in the industrial north where battalions such as the Accrington Pals, the Durham Pals and the Grimsby Chums were formed. These units could train, live and fight together but, in the end, they would die together. Hundreds of Leek men volunteered for the North Staffords and other regiments. Some Leek lads also joined some of the Pals Battalions from the northern towns and cities. Of the seven Leek soldiers killed on the opening day of the Battle of the Somme in 1916, two were members of Pals Battalions - the Sheffield Pals and the Manchester Pals respectively.

As is widely known, Leek had its own Royal Field Artillery unit, then known as the 3rd (Leek) Battery. Many local men served in the battery as Territorials and were mobilised on the outbreak of war. The officers and men of this unit fought with distinction on the Western Front throughout the war.

(Imperial War Museum)

Young men flocked in their thousands to the recruiting offices.

Now that the opposing lines of trenches in France and Belgium were well established, army generals on both sides had to decide on how to break though the fortified enemy lines, sweep into open countryside and finish the war. It was obvious that frontal assaults on a well dug-in enemy would result in massive casualties to the attacking troops. This had already been demonstrated in the October and November German offensive at Ypres. One of the main problems for the Germans was that they were fighting major campaigns on two fronts, the Western Front and the Russian Front. They were, however, fairly well equipped for trench warfare in France and Flanders and, although short of shells, possessed heavy guns, mortars and hand-grenades. They had also chosen the best places, usually the high ground, in which to dig their trenches. This often meant that any attack had to be made uphill, a clear disadvantage in many ways. The hapless soldiers of the BEF now held some 21 miles of line in northern France and Belgium. (The French held the line south of the BEF). The British line ran through the low-lying Flanders countryside where the trenches were often flooded. Apart from the misery caused to individual soldiers, many men suffered from frostbite or 'trench foot', a condition brought on by constant immersion in water. British equipment was in short supply; the troops often having to improvise with home-made weapons, grenades made from jam tins and mortars from drain pipes and old shell cases. Shells, or the lack of them, were a constant problem. Some field guns in 1915 were limited to firing no more than 4 rounds per day! Although steps were being taken in Britain to improve shell production, this took time. The shell shortage was to become a national scandal in May, 1915, after the Battle of Aubers Ridge, a British offensive in which hundreds of soldiers were killed, including three young Leek men. (See Chapter 6).

Despite the views held by the Generals commanding the Allied armies (some were trained as cavalrymen and still believed that horses, finely-honed swords and a glorious charge through a gap in the enemy defences could still win the day), the war from 1915 onwards followed more or less the same pattern. The Allies were always on the offensive, the

(Imperial War Museum)

Rain and mud added to the soldiers' discomfort
on the Western Front.

Germans had to be thrown off Belgian and French soil at all costs. Trenches were only to be temporary affairs, there was no need to build them to last. On the other hand, the Germans were content to remain on the defensive. They were, after all, fighting a war on two major fronts and were, on the Western Front, occupying their enemy's territory. There was all the more reason for them to dig deeper and stronger trenches and the effect of this would become tragically clear in July, 1916, on the Somme.

During the winter of 1914/15 the French mounted a number of costly offensives in their area of responsibility. The British were not in a position to help until the Spring so they and the Germans on the other side of No Man's Land contented themselves with sitting out the Flanders winter. Nevertheless, shell-fire, the sudden burst of a machine gun, the crack of a sniper's rifle and the dreadful conditions in the trenches all contributed to a steady casualty rate on both sides. On 24th January, **Lieutenant Charles Heritage Price** became the first Leek man to die in 1915. He was serving with Princess Patricia's Canadian Light Infantry (Eastern Ontario) Regiment. His origins in Leek are uncertain but it is believed that he lived at a farm on Abbey Green Road, near to the Abbey Inn. It is probable that he was one of the many local young men who emigrated to Canada before the war to start a new life there. Lieutenant Price joined the Canadian forces in September, 1914, went to France in December and was killed only five weeks later. He was the first Leek officer of the war to die and now lies buried at Voormezeele Enclosure No: 3 Cemetery, near Ypres.

Back home in Leek, local people tried to take their minds off the war and the constant worry about their young men at the front. One way, for those who could afford it, was to take advantage of a week-end trip in Magniers Motor Coach. A trip to Bakewell Races cost 4/- (20p), an afternoon run to Buxton 2/6d or a circular run to Congleton, Sandbach and Holmes Chapel, 3/6d.

Some of the 420 names on the Monument

Chapter 5

The Battle of Neuve Chapelle and the Gas Attack at Ypres

*"The Germans are trying to shift us out by using those shells
that burst and throw deadly fumes about"*

(Private Percy Malkin, aged 19, East Surrey Regiment. Killed in Action, 8th May, 1915.)

With the Spring of 1915 came the first of a series of British offensives on the Western Front. Neuve Chapelle was a German-held village and the purpose behind its capture was to secure the heights of Aubers Ridge and threaten road and rail communications in the town of Lille. The operation, commanded by General Sir Douglas Haig (at that time a Corps Commander), commenced at 7.30 on the morning of 10th March with a heavy bombardment of enemy positions. The Germans were stunned with the sudden ferocity of the shellfire. With speed and grim determination, the assaulting British infantrymen overran their front trenches and captured the village. At the moment of success, however, things started to go wrong and the BEF began to experience the problems which were to beset future offensives during the rest of the war. Orders did not get through, field telephones broke down, officers hesitated, reserve troops did not arrive in time and the Germans brought up reinforcements to put paid to any further British advance. Aubers Ridge was not taken and the BEF dug into their new positions on 12th March. Both sides had suffered around 13,000 casualties. The offensive demonstrated two important

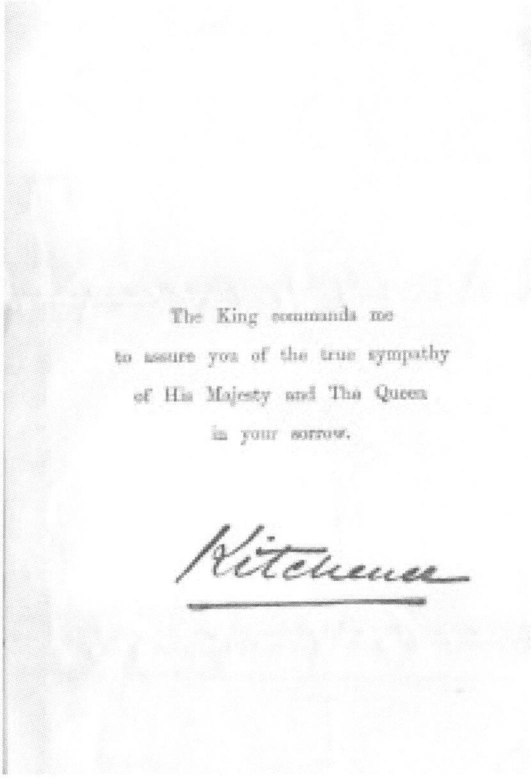

*The King commands me
to assure you of the true sympathy
of His Majesty and The Queen
in your sorrow.*

Kitchener

*Before his death in 1916, Lord Kitchener
signed the letter of condolence to bereaved
families*

(I Steele)

The Graham brothers. Arthur is the one in uniform

(P. Kirk)

lessons. Firstly, it was possible to breach enemy lines with careful planning and co-ordination. Secondly, the BEF had taught the Germans (and the French) that the 'contemptible little army' was a force to be reckoned with.

It was during this battle that the second Leek soldier to die in 1915 was mortally wounded. **Private Arthur Graham** of the 1st Battalion, Worcestershire Regiment, one of eleven children from No: 1, Mill Street, died of his wounds on 12th March. He is buried at Estaires Communal Cemetery in Northern France, seven miles west of Armentieres. He was only 19. Arthur's brother, Antony, was also to became another casualty of the war, three years later. He was killed in action seven months before the end of hostilities. Their cousin, Corporal George Henry Graham, was killed early in the war. (See Chapter 2).

The wet, cold and dangerous conditions of the trenches were, in the main, met with the stoical good humour of the British Tommy. When writing letters home, most of the soldiers put on a 'brave face', probably not wanting to worry their loved ones too much with problems they could do nothing about. They were also proud to be serving their King and Country and were happy to say so. **Lance Corporal Charles Henry Doody** from Kniveden Lane, Leek, was such a man. Serving with the Kings Own (Royal Lancaster) Regiment at the front, he

Charles Doody
(Authors Collection)

wrote to his mother: *"You must be proud of having three sons serving our King and I think you are doing your share by keeping a good heart. We are up to our necks in mud and water and though wet through we are happy as kings when we have fags to puff at and something to eat".*

Lance Corporal Doody was to become another Leek serviceman to sacrifice his life. He died from wounds on 19th March, 1915 and is buried at the Strand Military Cemetery, near Ypres. Meanwhile, what of the loyal men of the Leek Battery? Back in August, crowds had turned out to cheer the long column of horses, men and guns, led by Major W.F. Challinor, as it made its way along Frith Street, West Street and Derby Street before heading out on the Ashbourne Road enroute to Burton-on-Trent. There, the battery met up with other units and made its way to Luton where it joined the 46th (North Midland) Division. We shall meet this divison again later, at the Battle of Loos and on the Somme.

The Leek Battery, training completed, sailed to France in February, 1915 and was stationed in the Ypres Salient, facing the Messines Ridge, by early April. On Wednesday the 7th of that month the battery fired its first shot and, by coincidence, lost its first man whose name is recorded on the Monument. **Gunner William Sydney Howard** died in hospital at St Omer after an illness. He was 26 and came from 47, Picton Street. He is buried at Longueness Souvenir Cemetery, St Omer.

Staying with the Leek Battery for a moment, we should acknowledge the contribution to the war of the faithful horses which pulled guns and equipment over miles and miles of

(Authors Collection)
William Sidney Howard

mud on the Western Front. Thousands died on all the battlefronts during a conflict which was of no concern to these peaceful animals. One of the Leek Battery horses commandeered for the war was a fine specimen named 'Sigley' after its owners, S.Sigley and Sons, the Funeral Directors. The soldier responsible for Sigley was Driver Leo Wheatley, the lead driver of the team of six horses which pulled the gun carriage. As we shall see later, Driver Wheatley's brother, Private Bernard Wheatley, was killed at Passchendaele in 1917, but Leo and Sigley both survived the war and, at the end of hostilities, the horse was returned to its owners and resumed its former role of pulling hearses! Driver Wheatley told an amusing story of his experiences with Sigley. The horse, British-born and bred, was used to walking on the left of the road whilst the other five horses in the team, all reared in France, were naturally used to walking on the right. His patience taxed to the limit, Leo Wheatley cajoled, persuaded and

The Leek Battery passing under Lowe Hill bridge on the Ashbourne Road.

(J. E. Blore)

pleaded with the stubborn Sigley for the best part of twelve months before full team co-operation was achieved!

Barely two weeks after the Leek Battery fired its first shot in Flanders, the Germans unleashed a new horror on the Western Front, not many miles from where the Leek men were stationed. At around 5 o'clock on the afternoon of 22nd April, 1915, French troops holding the trench-lines near Ypres were subjected to a short, fierce artillery bombardment. Then, without warning, the unfortunate soldiers saw a greenish-yellow cloud drifting towards them. As it descended, men began to cough violently and gasp for breath. Frenchmen fled in panic from this new terror leaving a gap of nearly five miles in their lines. Fortunately, the Germans had used the gas largely as an experiment and did not have sufficient reserves to follow up the breakthrough in the allied line. This had been the first use of poison gas in a war which seemed to have no limit to the horrors it could heap upon mankind and was the start of what became known as the Second Battle of Ypres. Canadian and British troops established a temporary defensive line that night. Two days later, the Germans again attacked with gas. This time, Canadian troops holding the line where the cloud descended, used towels or handkerchiefs soaked in water or urine as makeshift gasmasks.

Between 23rd and 26 April 1915, British troops counter-attacked the new German lines in a series of costly assaults but were unable to recover the lost ground. Fighting continued until the end of May, the Germans used gas in their attacks on four more occasions, but still the BEF held on grimly to the battered town of Ypres. It was on 26th April that two Leek soldiers serving with the 3rd Battalion, Royal Fusiliers, were killed. The first, **Private Geoffrey Oldfield Goldstraw** was only 18. He had worked at Brough, Nicholson and Hall and lived with his parents at 58, Ball Haye Road. Records suggest that he enlisted at the age of 17. During the earlier part of the war, a soldier had to be 19 before he could be sent on active service, although some, as is well-known, slipped through the net. In his case, (he was born on 8th November, 1896), it is clear that Private Goldstraw was only 18 when he was killed. Whether he lied about his age or whether someone turned a blind eye is not known.

(Authors Collection)
Geoffrey Goldstraw

What is known is that this lad was not the only under-age soldier from Leek to be killed, as we shall see later.

The second soldier to die at Ypres that day was **Private Moses Sillito** from Mill Street. He had two brothers, one of whom won the Distinguished Conduct Medal for bravery during the war. Privates Goldstraw and Sillito are both commemorated on the Menin Gate Memorial to the Missing at Ypres. Neither has a known grave.

(C. Poyser)
William Poyser

The following day, 27th April, another Leek soldier died at Ypres from wounds to the head. **Private James William Poyser** of 78, Westwood Road was 24 and serving with the 2nd Battalion, East Surrey Regiment. The eldest of eight children, James went to West Street

School and later worked at Wardle and Davenports. His parents first heard the news of his wounds from the parents of another Leek soldier serving with James, Private Percy Malkin. In a letter home Percy had described the violent and frightening situation at Ypres: "............*I am alive and well and very lucky to be so. We have been in the thick of it and come through it successfully. My other Leek mates are all wounded and (James) William Poyser, I believe, got a very serious wound in the head. The Germans are trying to shift us out by using those shells that burst and throw deadly fumes about.*"

This early experience of the horrors of gas would become all too common as the war ground on.

Although Private Poyser was buried his grave was lost and he is also commemorated on the Menin Gate Memorial, Ypres. His father, John Thomas Poyser, never got over the death of his eldest son. He had worked at Wardle and Davenport's mill in the town since leaving school and it was he who had helped to get a job there for young James before the war. After his son was killed, John Poyser carried on working at the mill and eventually retired after 50 years service. He was presented with a clock to mark the occasion and this is now a cherished possession of his grandson, Private Poyser's nephew, in his Sneyd Green home.

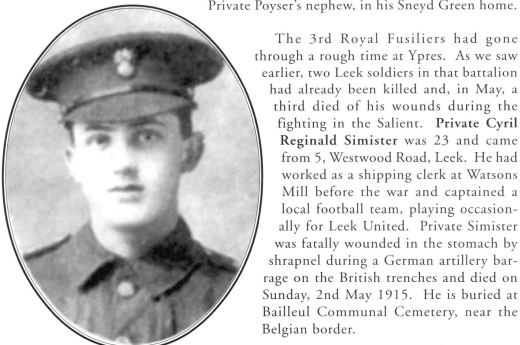

(Authors Collection)
Cyril Simister - killed by shrapnel

The 3rd Royal Fusiliers had gone through a rough time at Ypres. As we saw earlier, two Leek soldiers in that battalion had already been killed and, in May, a third died of his wounds during the fighting in the Salient. **Private Cyril Reginald Simister** was 23 and came from 5, Westwood Road, Leek. He had worked as a shipping clerk at Watsons Mill before the war and captained a local football team, playing occasionally for Leek United. Private Simister was fatally wounded in the stomach by shrapnel during a German artillery barrage on the British trenches and died on Sunday, 2nd May 1915. He is buried at Bailleul Communal Cemetery, near the Belgian border.

Six days after Cyril Simister died, the Ypres Salient claimed the life of **Private Percy Malkin** who, only days earlier, had written to his parents about his friend,

James William Poyser. Percy was only 19 and had volunteered for the army, like so many of the other Leek lads who died, in answer to Kitchener's call in the heady days of September, 1914. As the blinds were drawn at 11, Barngate Street, Percy's parents, Eli and Harriet Malkin, joined the growing list of Leek families whose lives would be changed forever.

(G. Robinson)
Percy Malkin

The words of the war poet, Rupert Brooke. He epitomized the romantic and idealistic view of warfare held by many during the early part of the war. He died of blood poisoning en-route to Gallipoli in 1915.

Chapter 6

The Battle of Aubers Ridge

"We have had four days in the trenches, but I am pleased to say all was very quiet".

(Private Fred Bloore, Royal Sussex Regiment, in a letter home,
two weeks before he was killed in action at Aubers Ridge, May, 1915.)

As the poppies in the shell-torn earth of the Ypres salient swayed in the early summer breeze, the attacks, counter-attacks and never-ending shellbursts continued. The fighting there did not die down until 27th May 1915. Both sides were exhausted and the Germans had failed in their attempt to achieve the hoped-for breakthrough. Meanwhile, the British First Army, commanded by General Douglas Haig, and the French Tenth Army launched a joint offensive some 30 miles south of Ypres. The French assaulted the prominent Vimy Ridge. They charged bravely uphill into devastating German machine gun fire losing 100,000 men, but never reached the top. (The ridge was taken by Canadian troops two years later when the skeletons and tattered uniforms of thousands of French soldiers were discovered lying out on the battlefield.)

The British part of the offensive was to take Aubers Ridge, originally the objective of the Battle of Neuve Chapelle in March. It turned out to be little short of a fiasco. The assaulting battalions went into the attack on 9th May, 1915. By now, German defences had been considerably strengthened and the artillery support for the British troops was woefully inadequate. Waves of heavily laden troops were sent over the top in attack after attack against positions heavily defended by machine guns. Soldiers were cut down as they moved forward, mostly before reaching the German wire. In the few cases where the attackers got into the enemy trenches and drove the Germans out, determined counter-attacks that evening put an end to any hopes of success. Haig called the battle off after losing almost 11,000 men killed and wounded in a few hours.

Six months earlier, in November, 1914, four young friends from Leek had made their way to Stoke railway station, intent on catching a train to Scotland. The friends, Fred Bloore, Jack Smethurst, Jack Winckle and Joseph 'Sammy' Hulme, all talked excitedly about their volunteering together for the Seaforth Highlanders, a Scottish regiment with a proud history. The journey to the far north, however, was thwarted when the friends received a message ordering their return. To their disappointment, the Highland regiment was refusing to accept any more volunteers who were not of Scottish descent. Undeterred, Sammy Hulme persuaded the other three to travel south with him to Sussex, where he was a professional footballer, and volunteer their services to the Royal Sussex Regiment. This they did and the four enlisted together, receiving consecutive army service numbers. Six months later, three of the friends lay dead at Aubers Ridge where the 2nd Battalion, Royal Sussex Regiment, suffered heavily, losing a total of 562 officers and men, 103 of whom were killed.

From the surviving letters of Fred Bloore and Sammy Hulme, it is clear that the four young Leek men were virtually inseparable. The letters, preserved by the sister of Fred Bloore, lay undiscovered for some 86 years. They provide a fascinating insight into the experiences of the friends before their lives were cut short so suddenly. Had the friends survived, they would surely have long remembered the first Christmas of the war when they were still in their training barracks at Dover, *""The dinner was very nicely served and the sergeants waited on us. We had goose and pork and beef. Then pudding and apples and nuts and fags afterwards. This afternoon we had a stroll to the sea which is not far off"*. (Private Fred Bloore).

24 year old **Private Fred Bloore** started the last day of his young life at 3.30am on 9th May when he and his mates were issued with tea and rum. He probably wondered if the fiery spirit would have the approval of his father, the landlord of the Queens Arms pub, back home in Queen Street. (Now the Blue Mugge). The rum was given to soldiers going into battle to warm them up in more ways than one. Fred heard the sudden crash of the British artillery opening up at 5am, the sound of whistles blowing, the urgent voices of officers shouting encouragement as he climbed from the forward trench and, finally, as he stumbled across No Man's Land, the 'tak tak tak' of the German machine guns. The Battle of Aubers Ridge had begun. Private (later Corporal) 'Sammy' Hulme takes up the story:

(Authors Collection)
Fred Bloore

"They went over the parapet like one man and when the order came and they reached about 100 yards when the Germans opened rapid fire on them and shelled them with shrapnel overhead and on the ground. They dug themselves in and the fellow in my section was next to Fred. He got one through the arm and Fred in the leg. They still remained out there waiting in pain until night time so as they could crawl back to safety............Just as they reached farther to a place of safety a big shell came over and killed poor

Fred". The letter also reveals that Fred Bloore wanted to wait for his missing friend (also killed), Jack Winckle, before trying to save himself. The writer, Sammy Hulme, was himself killed in action in 1916 on the Somme. (See Chapter 18).

(Authors Collection)
Jack Smethurst

The second of the friends, 20 year old **Private John Vernon Smethurst** from Parker Street, ('Jack' to his friends), had the same experience as Fred Bloore, losing his life in the gallant attack at Aubers Ridge. He was the 'kid' of the family being the youngest of five. Before enlisting he worked at Stannards mill and was a keen footballer. Jack's body was never found, neither was Fred Bloore's. It is probable that both were buried but the graves subsequently lost. Both soldiers are commemorated on the nearby Le Touret Memorial.

Private Jack Gibson Winckle was the third of the friends to die at Aubers Ridge. Aged 23, he died of his wounds on 11th May,

two days after the battle. Jack had lived at 33, James Street, and worked at the Churnet Valley Foundry. His grave is at the Chocques Military Cemetery in northern France near the site of a casualty clearing station where the wounded from the battles in this area were taken. He is the only one of the friends to have a marked grave. Nevertheless, somewhere under the fertile fields of France, the inseparable four remain united in death as they did in life.

The day before Jack Winckle died, another Leek soldier was killed in action, not

Jack Winckle
(Authors Collection)

William Higginbotham

far from Aubers Ridge. **Private William Higginbotham**, 1st Battalion, Royal Fusiliers, lived at 24, Regent Street, and was employed as a boiler attendant at the Spun Silk Company before enlisting in November, 1914. He left a widow and two young children. Two years later, his brother was also killed. Private Higginbotham is buried at La Chapelle d' Armentieres Cemetery, France.

The awful casualty lists, partly due to the shortage of shells available for Haig's artillery bombardment, did not go unnoticed at home. Hostility towards the then Liberal Government grew and the failures at Aubers Ridge largely contributed to the Prime Minister, Herbert Asquith, forming a coalition government and appointing Lloyd George as Minister of Munitions.

Before May was through, another Leek serviceman died, this time through illness. **Private Samuel Hampson** of the Army Service Corps died in hospital near Bristol on the 18th from what was then known as 'spotted fever'. At one time, he had been a wagoner and it is thought that his role in the army involved the provision and care of horses destined for the Western Front. Private Hampson was married and lived at 30, Nunn Street, working at Trafford and Whites mill before the war. He is buried at Bristol.

Samuel Hampson

Left: Retired Territorial Army officer from Leek, Brian Podmore, places a wreath in memory of Fred Bloore and Jack Smethurst at the Le Touret Memorial, France, November 11th, 2002. Their names are carved on the stone walls along with over 13,000 others who fell in this area before 25th September, 1915, and who have no known grave.

Below: Royal Sussex Regiment soldiers, pictured before being drafted to France. Private Fred Bloore is seated far right, front row and Private Jack Winckle is second from the left, front row. Jack Smethurst and Sammy Hulme are also thought to be in the picture but cannot be identified with certainty.

(J.Holden)

Chapter 7

The Dardanelles and Gallipoli

"How long, O Lord, how long, before the flood
Of crimson-welling carnage shall abate

(Robert Palmer, War Poet. Killed in action, 1916)

By early 1915, the Russians had suffered severe losses on the Eastern Front and desperately needed help from their allies. There were problems in getting supplies through to Russia, the sea routes being very long and frozen over for much of the year. The only real solution was to force a passage through Turkey to the Black Sea and on to the Russian ports. To do this, Allied shipping would have to pass through a narrow channel known as the Dardanelles into the Sea of Marmara and then through another narrow passage, the Bosphorus, before entering the Black Sea. Both channels were defended by Turkish guns in a series of coastal forts.

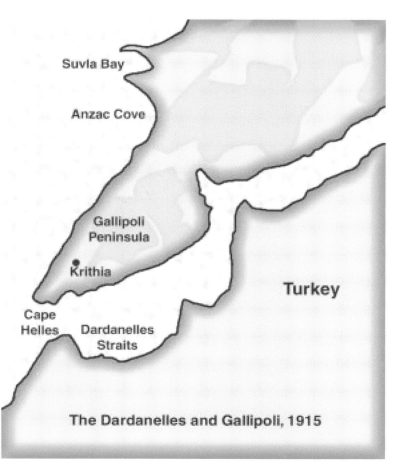

The Dardanelles and Gallipoli, 1915

The sorely-tried British Army could not spare large numbers of men for a land operation because of the commitments on the Western Front but, at the same time, there seemed to be no end to the deadlock of the trenches. Some thought that a second front might be a good idea. The then First Lord of the Admiralty, Winston Churchill, keen to see the Royal Navy more involved in the war, proposed an attack on the Turkish forts using the heavy guns of battleships. During February and March, 1915, British and French war-

Imperial War Museum

British troops attack Turkish positions on Gallipolli.

ships sailed to the narrow Dardanelles channel and fired on the forts. Some forts were destroyed but the Turks fought back. Allied ships were damaged and destroyed by shellfire and others by underwater mines and the action was called off. The operation had been a failure and Winston Churchill was sacked from his high-profile job.

Also destined to be a failure was the next plan; to send ground troops in to take the Gallipoli peninsular and capture the forts. On the morning of 25th April 1915, British troops landed on five different beaches at Cape Helles. Australian and New Zealand troops landed further along the Gallipoli coast. Their landing point became known as 'Anzac Cove'. Although there was some opposition to the landings, the Turks were initially thrown into disarray. The opportunity to press on overland whilst they had the upper hand, however, was lost as offic-

Commonwealth War Graves Commission

The Helles Memorial to the Missing

ers on the ground waited for instructions. The overall commander, General Sir Ian Hamilton, was at his headquarters on a battleship well offshore. His planning of the landings had been slipshod. The beaches were unsuitable, the troops having to climb steep cliffs where the Turks were quickly gathering reinforcements to fire down on and repel the invaders. Although British and Anzac forces captured some of the peninsular, this was only a few miles in length. As on the Western Front, trenches were dug and the situation soon became the familiar stalemate.

Life for the soldiers at Gallipoli became a struggle for survival. In the summer heat, the dust and flies were dreadful. Water was scarce and had to be carried by mules. Dysentery and skin sores were rife amongst the troops. In later months, thousands died from the cold. The Turks fought bravely to force the invaders from their land and saw this as a 'Holy War'. They often charged at the allied lines only to be mown down by machine guns. In the heat, the stench of rotting bodies became so unbearable that both sides held truces to enable the dead to be buried. During the nine months allied soldiers were at Gallipoli, over 200,000 died, almost three-quarters of them from disease or exposure. One soldier, Herbert Ball from 6, Albert Street, Leek, served with the Royal Fusiliers at Gallipoli. He fell victim to dysentery, a debilitating illness which affected thousands of men. In his diary he wrote: " .....nothing only sand and flies, half of the Brigade down with dysentery, look more like old men and cripples instead of soldiers. They are finding them dead every morning up at the latrines............the doctor sent 60 of us into the hospital..." Corporal Ball was eventually invalided back to Britain where he spent months in hospital before being declared fit for active duty again. He survived the war.

The first of eleven Leek soldiers to die in the hell that was Gallipoli was **Private James Hall** of the 1/6th Manchester Regiment. He was a former pupil of West Street School and had lived in Gaunt Street before moving to Manchester with his parents. He found employment there as an electrician and served with the Territorial Army before war broke out. Private Hall is recorded as dying on Saturday, 5th June, 1915. The previous day, British forces, including the Manchesters, had attacked Turkish positions around the village of Krithia on the Gallipoli peninsular. Although taking heavy casualties, the Manchesters captured the first and second-line Turkish trenches but were eventually forced to withdraw as sufficient reserves to hold the position could not be brought up. During the fighting on this hot summer day, Private Hall, under heavy fire, went to the aid of his captain and his sergeant who had become casualties, bandaging their wounds. At the end of the day's fighting, 21 year old Private James Hall was reported as 'missing'. He was never seen again and is commemorated on the Helles Memorial to the Missing. His sergeant later wrote: "........if ever a man deserved the D.C.M. it was Jimmy, who bandaged up both the captain's and my wounds at great risk to himself............"

The Helles Memorial stands on the tip of the Gallipoli Peninsula and can be seen by ships passing through the Dardanelles. Amongst the 21,000 names recorded there, nine belong to Leek soldiers.

William Baskerville

The next Leek casualty at Gallipoli was recently-married **Private William Baskerville,** the son of Mr A Baskerville the jeweller, then in the Market Place. William was serving with the 2nd Battalion, Royal Fusiliers, when he was shot in the head and severely wounded on 24th June, 1915. He died the next day, aged 23. A former pupil of West Street School, William Baskerville had worked at Porter and Co; Furnishers, Bath Street. He is buried at Twelve Tree Copse Cemetery, Gallipoli.

Clearly, the stalemate on Gallipoli could not be allowed to drag on. Plans were made for a new landing, this time north of Anzac Cove, at Suvla Bay. The objective was to capture the high ground of the peninsula, effectively the backbone of Gallipoli. During the first week of August, 1915, thousands of British and Anzac troops landed at Suvla Bay. But yet again, they were kept waiting around. Some swam in the sea, others sunbathed and made tea which gave the Turks time to bring up reinforcements. When the soldiers did get going they were severely hampered by the rough terrain and many became exhausted as they struggled to negotiate the peaks, gullies and ravines which made up this hostile landscape. Over the following few days, seven Leek soldiers lost their lives in the fighting for the ridges.

At home in Leek, mothers, wives and sweethearts waited anxiously for news from their loved ones fighting in France and Flanders and now in this strange sounding place, Gallipoli, which hardly anyone had even heard of before. Mrs Emma Tomkinson of 22, Duke Street, was just such a person. She was mother to eight children, five boys and three girls. Four of the boys, William, Thomas, Sam and Harry were all in the army and serving abroad, William was at Gallipoli. Now in her fifties, Emma had previously been married to Samuel Smith, a wheelwright, who was the father of William, Thomas and Sam. After he died, Emma met and married a man with the romantic name of Hamlet Tomkinson. With him, she had two more sons, Harry and Josiah and three daughters. Harry would go on to survive the war without a scratch; Josiah was an invalid and needed constant care at home. Emma Tomkinson had had enough to cope with in her

22 Duke Street, today.

life, rearing eight children in a small terraced house, losing her first husband and constantly caring for an invalid son. Now she had the added burden of worrying about her soldier sons away fighting at the front. What she could not have known, however, was that her family would soon lose not one son, or even two, but three in the war. Before August was through both William Smith and Thomas Smith had been killed and only ten months later, Sam Smith was dead. This poor lady herself died in December, 1915, aged only 55.

(V. Pegg)

William Smith

The first of the brothers was killed on 8th August, 1915, two days after landing at Suvla Bay. **Private William Smith** had, before enlisting, worked for the Leek building firm of Thomas Grace, but now, he was one of the men of the 8th Battalion, Welsh Fusiliers who, as dawn broke, were climbing a steep hill to reach and attack the Turkish positions. Unfortunately, they were caught out in the open as they toiled up the hill and Turkish gunfire caused many casualties. Amongst the dead was Private Smith. He is commemorated on the Helles Memorial.

The 7th Battalion, North Staffordshire Regiment, one of the battalions raised locally for the war, contained quite a number of Leek men. They had sailed for Gallipoli in June,

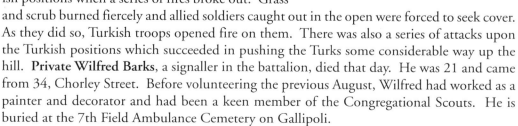

1915, 1128 strong, arriving at Cape Helles at the end of the Gallipoli Peninsula on 11th July and, almost immediately, received their first baptism of fire. Seven Leek soldiers from the battalion died in as many months during that campaign. The first fell on 9th August. This day, the weather was hot and the hills of Gallipoli were dry and dusty. British ships had been shelling the Turkish positions when a series of fires broke out. Grass and scrub burned fiercely and allied soldiers caught out in the open were forced to seek cover. As they did so, Turkish troops opened fire on them. There was also a series of attacks upon the Turkish positions which succeeded in pushing the Turks some considerable way up the hill. **Private Wilfred Barks**, a signaller in the battalion, died that day. He was 21 and came from 34, Chorley Street. Before volunteering the previous August, Wilfred had worked as a painter and decorator and had been a keen member of the Congregational Scouts. He is buried at the 7th Field Ambulance Cemetery on Gallipoli.

On 10th August the Turks launched a savage counter-attack on the allied troops who were then desperately clinging on to the gains thy had made in the Gallipoli hills. Every inch of ground was fought over bitterly with hand grenades and bayonets and the Staffords held their line. Two more Leek men from the 7th North Staffords died fighting during this desperate struggle. **Private Andrew Eaton**, a married man from 1, Kiln Lane and **Private Patrick Quinn** from 21, Bath Street were killed in action. Neither of their bodies were recovered and they are commemorated on the Helles Memorial. The next few days saw British soldiers being forced back down the hills, some in disarray, others in an orderly withdrawal, and two more Leek soldier's lives claimed on 14th August.

Before the war, **Lance Corporal James John Brennan** had worked as a gardener at Highfield Hall on the Macclesfield Road, the home of Sir Arthur Nicholson. Neither James nor his employer could possibly have foreseen what the coming war and its aftermath would bring. Sir Arthur's son, Basil, was killed at Ypres in July 1915 and James Brennan was killed only three weeks later.

(E. Ash)

Highfield Hall

Sir Arthur himself would finance the building of the town's massive war memorial ten years later and the names of his lost son and his gardener would be inscribed on the brass plaques along with all the others.

Although a native of Scotland, James Brennan had lived in Leek for two years, lodging at the home of Mr and Mrs Heath at Pool End, close to Highfield Hall. Like so many other local men he volunteered for the North Staffordshire Regiment. Posted to the 7th Battalion along with Wilfred Barks, Andrew Eaton and Patrick Quinn, he quickly proved his worth and was promoted to Lance Corporal. His death at the age of 21 on 14th August was a blow to the regiment. He too is commemorated on the Helles Memorial.

Another Leek name on the Memorial is that of **Corporal Frederick Wood**, described by his wife as a *"fine, big fellow"*. He was also killed at Gallipoli on 14th August whilst serving with the Royal Garrison Artillery. His father lived in Junction Road. Fred was an expert swimmer and a member of St Edwards Church choir in his younger days. Later, he worked at W.H. Eatons, the printers, in D e r b y Street, before moving to Blackpool.

Fred Wood

The campaign at Gallipoli was already doomed to failure but still the casualties mounted. On 23rd September, 1915, **Private William Farnell** , 2nd Battalion, Royal Fusiliers, died there. His connection with Leek is uncertain and his parents were living at Market Drayton after the war. On 21st October, another young soldier from the 7th North Staffords lost his life. **Private Henry Edward Trafford** died from dysentery whilst a patient on a hospital ship. He was buried at sea off the North African coast. Aged 20, Private Trafford had lived at 46, Picton Street and worked as a clerk at Wardle and Davenports mill. Privates Farnell and Trafford are both commemorated on the Helles Memorial.

As the winter set in, a decision was announced that must have been the best news the long-suffering troops on Gallipoli had heard for months; to evacuate everyone off this god-forsaken place before even more lives were lost.

In December, all troops from Suvla Bay and Anzac Cove stole away under the noses of the Turks to board waiting ships and, amazingly, without anyone being killed or injured, save for one happy soldier who drank too much rum and fell over! Plans were then made to evacuate the remaining forces from Helles at the tip of the peninsular three weeks later.

William Farnell

On 7th January, 1916, the day before the final evacuation of all allied troops at Gallipoli, Turkish soldiers bombarded the British lines with heavy artillery and then attacked in force. They were repelled by rifle fire, particularly from that gallant band of local men, the 7th North Staffords. The regiment and the town of Leek lost one more brave man on that day. **Quartermaster Sergeant William Rider**, a regular soldier, was 39 and had served his country for over 20 years. He originated from 35, John Street, but was living with his wife near to the Regimental Barracks at Lichfield. He, too, is commemorated on the Helles Memorial. The battalion commander, Lieutenant-Colonel F.H. Walker was also killed along with another 43 soldiers and 106 were wounded. The following day, men of the allied armies, sailing towards the blue Mediterranean looked back at the shores and peaks of Gallipoli and reflected on what the past eight months had achieved. All of them knew the answer - "nothing".

But Gallipoli had not quite finished its hold on the 7th North Staffords even after they left. On 10th January, 1916, 31 year old **Private John Biddulph** ,who was evacuated having been wounded on Gallipoli, probably at the same time that Q.M.S. Rider was killed, died in a military hospital in Alexandria, North Africa. He had lived in Belle View and operated a fish and fruit business in Mill Street. He is buried close to the hospital where he spent his last hours.

(Imperial War Museum)
Allied stores burning on Gallipoli following the evacuation.

Chapter 8

Return to the Western Front

"The urgent need for all able-bodied men to be trained as soldiers to help to keep our forces in the field at maximum strength is realised".

(Leek Post report on local recruiting, July, 1915)

We left the Western Front in May, 1915, after the Second Battle of Ypres and the debacle at Aubers Ridge. We now return to that area where the landscape was beginning to resemble the surface of the moon.

By June, 1915, there had been another British offensive south of the Aubers Ridge battlefield at a place called Festubert. Rapid initial progress was made but the British troops soon became bogged down, having pushed the Germans back little more than half a mile. Meanwhile, whilst plans were being made for another major offensive in the region of the mining town of Loos in the autumn, casualties continued steadily in the mud of Flanders. Over the next three months, another eight Leek men, including Basil Nicholson, lost their lives.

Private Joseph Rushton of the 1st Battalion, Bedfordshire Regiment, was 39 when he was killed in the Ypres salient on 2nd June, 1915. He came from Silk Street but his wife Susan, and their young child, later moved to 22, Wood Street. He has no known grave and is commemorated on the Menin Gate Memorial. A small wooden cross is still left in his memory on the Monument each Remembrance Sunday.

(Authors Collection)
Joseph Rushton

Private William Henry Carter also left a widow and one young child when he was killed on 27th June. Formerly a dyer at Watsons mill, Private Carter came from 22 Shirburn Road and had originally joined the North Staffords. Before he was killed, however, he had been transferred to the Duke of Wellington's (West Riding) Regiment. He was 32. Private Carter is buried at Voormezeele Enclosure No: 3 Cemetery outside Ypres. Three days later on the last day of June, Rifleman David James Green, aged 32, from 32 Well Street, Leek, was also killed near Ypres. He was serving with the 7th Battalion, Kings Royal Rifle Corps. His grave is at Bedford House Cemetery near Ypres.

(Authors Collection)
William Carter

(Authors Collection)
Bill Hilton

In July, Bombardier William Taylor Hilton of the Royal Field Artillery was severely wounded on the morning of the 16th. He died later that day. Bill, as he was known, was only 20 and came from 6, Livingstone Street. Before enlisting, he had worked for Mr M Knowles the butcher, (now Andrew Bould's) in Derby Street. In a letter to his parents, William and Elizabeth Hilton, Bill's commanding officer, Major R.B. Forwood wrote: "....*He was a splendid young fellow, most popular with the men and an excellent N.C.O. I deeply deplore his loss and beg that you will accept my very sincere sympathy....*" Bombardier Hilton is buried at Poperinghe New Military Cemetery near Ypres.

Mr. and Mrs. Hilton visiting their son's grave after the war.

On the same day, miles away at the large British base camp of Etaples in France, a stretcher-bearer with the 1/5th Battalion, North Staffords, also died of wounds. Aged 34 and a married man with three children, **Private Simeon Sims** came from 7, Shirley Street and had been employed as a signalman at Leek Railway Station before the war. He was wounded in the leg by gunshot and admitted to the 18 General Hospital at Etaples. Simeon wrote to his wife: *"I have got wounded and am in hospital with a broken leg. There is no need to worry, I seem to be going on alright. Will write when I get stronger"*. But he did not get stronger. Complications set in, necessitating the amputation of his leg from which he

did not recover. Private Sims is buried at Etaples Military Cemetery. It is believed that he had been recommended for the Distinguished Conduct Medal for bravery, although no award was actually made.

July, 1915 was also the month that saw the event which prompted the building of the Monument in Leek ten years later - the death of Basil Nicholson.

Simeon Sims

Lieutenant Basil Lee Nicholson, aged 24, the youngest son of Sir Arthur and Lady Nicholson of Highfield Hall was one of the officers serving with the Leek Battery, (official title the 3rd Battery, 2nd North Midland (Stafford) Brigade, Royal Field Artillery). He was killed on 24th July, 1915, shot through the head by a sniper. Basil had travelled with the Battery to France and Belgium in February that year but just before he was killed he had returned home to Leek on leave. On 20th July, Basil's brother, Captain Falkner Nicholson, was wounded in the shoulder by an exploding enemy shell. On his return from leave it seems that Basil, incensed by what had happened and uttering threats of retribution, made his way to the front line artillery obser-

Basil Nicholson's grave in a Belgian churchyard

vation post and ordered all four guns of the Leek Battery to fire on the Germans. As he looked over to observe the results of the falling shells, a sniper killed him outright with one shot.

Lieutenant Nicholson was buried in the nearby churchyard at Dranoutre. Like many other young men who died in the war, Basil Nicholson was robbed of a promising future. He was connected, of course, with his father's business and was the manager of the Bridge End Dye Works. Had he lived, he would undoubtedly have been a prosperous and extremely wealthy man. As it was, he left over £17, 000 in his will.

In August, 1915, whilst the preparations for the autumn offensive at Loos forged ahead, two more Leek soldiers lost their lives. The first, **Gunner Albert Goodfellow**, was killed

Basil Nicholson

Chapter 9

The Battle of Loos

"Come on, 'B' Company"

(The rallying cry and last words of Captain Reginald Tavernor Johnson,
1/5th North Staffords, killed in action leading his men in battle, October, 1915.)

(Imperial War Museum)

Left to right: General Sir Douglas Haig, General Joseph Joffre, French C. in C., David Lloyd George, the Minister responsible for munitions and later Prime Minister.

The last British offensive of 1915 was at the small mining town of Loos, now a suburb of Lens, and opened on 25th September. This was the biggest British effort to date and the commanders planned to take this area and, hopefully, press on to the town of Lille. Here, the first use was made of battalions of Kitchener's New Army. It was also the first time the British used poison gas, 150 tons of it, although this was, in the main, a failure. The wind shifted and blew the gas back towards the attacking troops. Amongst the British troops were thousands of kilted Scotsmen. They fought so valiantly that the Germans called them 'the ladies from hell', a nickname which the Highlanders kept for a long time.

The initial attack drove a salient some way into the German lines. But it was the usual story - reserves were not organised properly and determined German counter-attacks soon drove the British back to where they had started. It was another disaster.

This was one battle that General Haig and the then Commander-in-Chief, Sir John French, did not want. The ground was flat, provided little cover and was dominated by slag heaps which gave every advantage to

63

German machine gunners. Furthermore, the British Army was still short of shells. The attack went ahead, however, at the insistence of the French who simultaneously attacked either side of the British. It was almost suicidal. Troops attacked fortifications protected by belts of barbed wire which had not been cut by the bombardment preceding the assault. They were hampered by flannel gas masks, crude affairs at that stage of the war which made it difficult to see.

Killed on the first day of the attack, 25th September, was **Private Thomas Mellor** of the 1st Battalion, South Staffordshire Regiment. He was 23, lived at 10, Cornhill and had worked at Wall Grange Brick and Tile Company at Longsdon. His body was never recovered and he is commemorated on the Loos Memorial along with 20,000 others who fell in that area during the war.

On the same day but further north, towards Ypres, the British made attacks on the enemy lines in support of the Loos offensive. Another Leek soldier was killed there. **Private Stephen Salt** was with the 1st Battalion, North Staffords, which was

(Author's collection)
Stephen Salt - shot through the heart

harassing German lines with rifles, smoke bombs and artillery in the vicinity of Poperinghe. Returning fire caused twenty seven casualties amongst the Staffords, including Stephen Salt who was shot through the arm and heart. He was a married man with four children and lived at 34, Mill Street. Private Salt is buried at La Brique Military Cemetery near Ypres.

The next Leek soldier to die at Loos was **Guardsman Harry Gordon White** of the 4th Battalion, Grenadier Guards. He died on 27th September after a ferocious German counter-attack. He was 30 and came from 6, Alsop Street. The Guards Division was heavily engaged in the fighting amongst the pitheads and slagheaps and lost a lot of men. Harry White is also commemo-

(Author's collection)
Harry White

rated on the Loos Memorial. The next day, the fighting at Loos had ended with some 60,000 British killed, wounded and missing, but the casualties continued.

On 29th September, 22 year old **Lance Corporal Colin Dunn** of the 3rd Battalion, Royal Fusiliers died, believed from the effects of gas. He had lived at 40, Shoobridge Street and worked in the Goods Depot at Leek railway station. In his spare time, Colin Dunn had been a member of the Leek Lodge of an organisation with the fascinating title: 'The Independent Order of Good Templars'. After his death, a colleague wrote to Colin's mother "...........*we were in the trenches and had to retire but Colin would not come out. Colin stayed to look for Lieutenant Clark........*" There are numerous examples of ordinary soldiers risking their lives, and indeed losing them, in going to the rescue of junior officers. This is but one of them. Lance Corporal Dunn has no known grave and he too is commemorated on the Loos Memorial.

(Author's collection)
Colin Dunn - gassed

North of the town of Loos was a German strongpoint known as the Hohenzollern Redoubt. A fortified hillock, the redoubt jutted out from the German lines. It was captured briefly during the opening assaults at Loos on 25th September but German counter-attacks had forced the British out. Plans were made to capture it again, this time using the Territorial battalions of the 46th (North Midland) Division which included men of the North and South Staffords.

On the afternoon of 13th October, 1915, the Staffordshire men were in the forward trenches opposite the Hohenzollern Redoubt. One of the soldiers of the 1/5th Battalion, North Staffords, was young **Private Harry Allen Tudor** from Hugo Street, a clerk at the Leek branch of Parr's Bank. Earlier, he had been issued with three day's rations and 220 rounds of ammunition and the added weight did little to ease his discomfort. The sooner this was over and done with,

(Author's collection)
Harry Tudor

the better. Harry knew that before the attack the engineers would release a deadly cloud of chlorine gas which, hopefully, would soften up the enemy resistance. As he waited in the crowded trench for the signal to attack he listened to the 'crump' of British shells crashing into German positions and kept well out of sight. Then, at two o'clock, the whistles blew. Harry Tudor climbed up the trench ladder with the others and they were over the top at last. He got through the gap in the barbed wire and then heard orders to lie down in No Man's Land. Five minutes later, the orders came to advance and as Harry and his mates scrambled to their feet the cry went up: *"Potters For Ever"*. Then suddenly, a hail of machine gun and rifle fire swept through the advancing soldiers. Men fell, some wounded, some dead. Harry Tudor was one of those mortally wounded. He died later that day. He was only 21.

The officer commanding 'B' Company of the 1/5th North Staffords, **Captain Reginald Tavernor Johnson**, also died in the assault upon the Hohenzollern Redoubt. Aged 36, he was raised at Westwood Hall (now Westwood High School). A Cambridge graduate and veteran of the Boer War, Captain Johnson was a director of Messrs Johnsons Brothers, the pottery manufacturers in Stoke-on-Trent. He was seen standing on the parapet of the trench as the whistles blew, waving his cane and shouting: *"Come on B Company"* and encouraging his men as they struggled up and over the top. A few moments later he too was mortally wounded. Captain Johnson was never seen again and is commemorated on the Loos Memorial. Private Harry Allen Tudor lies buried in Vermelles British Cemetery, five miles from the battlefield which claimed his life.

(H. Birch)

Captain Reginald Johnson - never seen again

The attempts to take the Hohenzollern Redoubt had largely failed save for the capture of a small part of the fortified system. Out of the 700 officers and men of the 1/5th Battalion, North Staffords who went into the line the night before the attack, little more than 200 came out of it unscathed.

Extreme courage is not only confined to fighting men during wartime. The day before the attack on the Hohenzollern Redoubt, Nurse Edith Cavell, the 50 year old Matron of a British Red Cross hospital in Brussels was executed by a German firing squad for helping Allied soldiers to escape across the Dutch frontier.

One of the battalions involved at Loos was the 9th Royal Fusiliers. The next Leek soldier to die in that area was **Private Herbert Yates,** who lived at 2, Smithfield Cottages, off the Ashbourne Road. He was one of the youngest members of that proud battalion which lost so many eager young men during the war. Herbert Yates died of wounds to the head in a casualty clearing station on 19th October, 1915. Aged only 18, he had worked as a braid tenter at Wardle and Davenports mill. He is buried at Lapugnoy Military Cemetery, some 12 miles from the Loos battlefield.

After the failures at Loos, Sir John French, the British Commander-in-Chief, was removed from his post and Douglas Haig took his place.

(N. Hunt)

Herbert Yates

(Imperial War Museum)

Hohenzollern Redoubt under attack

The War Memorial at Ball Haye Green. The memorial is unusual in that the names of those who served but survived the war are recorded on the plaques, in addition to those who died. The names of the fallen can be seen on the left hand plaque. These names are repeated on the Nicholson War Memorial

Chapter 10

Another Winter of War

"I have a rendezvous with death
on some scarred slope of battered hill.......
I shall not fail that rendezvous"

(Alan Seeger, War Poet. Killed in action, 1916.)

Back at home in Leek, after 14 months of war, the reality of what the ordinary soldier was asked to do was brought home to the townspeople when the military funerals of two servicemen were held on the same afternoon. **Private Thomas Booth**, the son of the well-known leather merchant, Mr T.H. Booth, whose shop was then in St Edward Street, had emigrated to Canada before the war. Anxious to help his mother country, Tom volunteered to join a Canadian Infantry Regiment and, in the summer of 1915, found himself in Belgium. On 2nd September, whilst serving at the front, Tom was shot through the hip by a sniper. He was treated at a base hospital but eventually taken back to England and transferred to a hospital in Leicester. In those days, of course, antibiotics were unknown and gunshot and shrapnel wounds often caused serious infections. Tom Booth's condition began to deteriorate and he died on 30th September, a month after he was wounded.

(Author's Collection)
Tom Booth

The following day, **Private George Flanagan**, a father of nine, also died. He was serving with the 2/6th Battalion, South Staffords and had been ill with pneumonia. George was a widower and, despite his age, 54, enlisted when he heard Kitchener's call for volunteers. It is thought that he had spent some time in France but this is not certain. He gave one of his sons, Jim, quite a surprise when he enlisted. Jim was a serving soldier who had been sent to George's home at 2, Horton Street, Leek, on sick leave. When he arrived and found that his father had joined the colours he was told: *"If you can do it Jim, then so can I"*. Private George

(C. M. Lomas)

A section of soldiers of the South Staffords. George Flanagan is on the front row second from the left

Flanagan died on 1st October, 1915, and his funeral, along with Tom Booth's, attracted crowds of local people who lined the streets outside the church. Both soldiers were buried in Leek Cemetery.

As the troops on the Western Front prepared to face another long winter in the deadlocked trenches many reflected on the cost of the fighting so far. Victory was no closer. The search for a break-through had failed. Would the war last for another long year, or would it never end? Some soldiers even began to question why they were there and the cold, lousy conditions did little to help their morale. Before 1915 was over, seven more Leek soldiers died, six of them on the Western Front.

Private John James Greatbatch worked as a gardener on the Westwood Hall Estate for the Johnson family, who, as we saw earlier, lost their son, Captain Reginald Tavernor Johnson at Loos. Only four days after his death, Private Greatbatch was also killed. Aged 21, he was

(Author's Collection)

Westwood Hall - now Westwood High School.

a signaller with the 5th Battalion, Oxford and Buckinghamshire Light Infantry, and died when a mine or shell exploded in the Ypres salient on 17th October. It is thought that he was using a field telephone at the time. John had lived at 23, Sandon Road, (now Cheddleton Road) and was an active member of All Saints Church. His body was never found or identified and he is commemorated on the Menin Gate Memorial, Ypres. In his demise were echoes of the deaths of Lieutenant Basil Nicholson and his gardener, Private John Brennan, both of whom also died within a short space of time.

Another soldier who died on 17th October was 24 year old **Private William Prosser**, serving with the 1/5th Battalion, North Staffords. His parents were living in Burslem after the war and their son's connection to Leek is uncertain. Private Prosser is buried at Lillers Communal Cemetery, northern France. This town is several miles behind the old British front line and was used for billeting soldiers during the war and as a hospital centre. It is probable therefore, that Private William Prosser died there of wounds received in the fighting for the Hohenzollern Redoubt four days earlier.

On 4th November, **Private Percy Victor Murray**, 12th Battalion, Royal Fusiliers, was shot dead near Ypres. He was 25, married with a young child and lived at 3 Court, 4, West Street. Private Murray had worked at the Upper Hulme Dyeworks below the Roaches. He is buried at Spoilbank Cemetery, Zillebeke, Ypres. Two days later, 24 year old **Sergeant Edgar Arrowsmith**, serving with 'D' Company, 8th Battalion, North Staffords, was killed in action. He is buried in a military cemetery at Festubert in northern France. This little village is about four miles from Neuve Chapelle and Aubers Ridge and was the scene of a British offensive in May, 1915. It remained in British hands throughout the war and was later adopted by the town of Southport.

(Author's Collection)
John Broome

Not far from Southport is where the next Leek serviceman met his death. **Gunner John Broome** was attached to the Royal Marine Artillery serving in the armed merchant cruiser, HMS Virginian, which was then at Liverpool Docks. He was accidentally drowned there on 8th November. Aged 34, he came from Fountain Street and joined the Royal Navy in 1898. John had served in a number of warships until he was discharged to the Reserve in 1910. He then worked as a postman in Leek before being recalled to the navy in August, 1914. After his body was recovered from the water, it was brought back to the town and is buried in Leek Cemetery.

The last two Leek soldiers to die in 1915 marked yet another blow for the hard-pressed 1st Battalion, North Staffords, then serving in the Ypres salient. **Private John Cartlidge** from 2 Court, 2, Kiln Lane was killed on 8th November. He was 23 and formerly a printer at Wardle and Davenports. His friend, **Private William Lowe**, had also worked there and lived nearby at 136, Mill Street. He died of wounds on the same day, aged 19. Both are commemorated on the Menin Gate Memorial, Ypres.

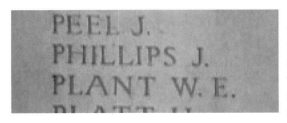

It is said that if the British and French offensives and, indeed the Gallipoli campaign, had succeeded in 1915, then the war could have ended and millions of lives would have been saved. Instead, the conflict was destined to drag on to a murderous finish three years later.

Above: The names of two of the Leek soldiers as they appear on the panels of the Menin Gate Memorial to the Missing at Ypres. In all, the names of fifteen Leek men appear on the panels.

(Photographs: K.Perrin)

Chapter 11

1916 -A Year of Slaughter.

"They were shelling and bombing us night and day, it was pure slaughter. I am very pleased to say that I am in the land of the living.........."

(Private Robert Wilson, 10th Scottish Rifles, in a letter to his sister eight weeks before he was killed whilst attending to wounded men, January, 1916).

(M. Derry)
Bob Wilson - killed whilst rescuing wounded men.

As the cold winter of 1915 held its grip on the battlefields of the Western Front, plans were being made for the next Allied offensives. The emphasis for 1916 would be simultaneous attacks on the Western Front, the Eastern Front and the Italian Front. On the Western Front the assault would take place in the summer and be a joint British and French operation. The British would use the New Army divisions raised by Kitchener. This was going to be the 'Big Push' which would end the war. At the end of 1916, the 'Big Push' would become known by another name, a name which still today conjures up a dramatic picture of the horror, hopelessness and misery of trench warfare:- 'The Somme'.

We shall return to the Somme battlefield later. In the meantime, many other things were happening in the first half of 1916, including the Allied withdrawal from Gallipoli in January, continued fighting in Mesopotamia (now Iraq) and a dramatic sea battle in May between the Royal Navy and Germany's High Seas Fleet. But first, we look at the Leek men who died as a result of fighting or trench-holding on the Western Front during the early months of 1916.

"I was so upset when I heard the news about poor William Lowe..........I could not help but cry for he was my best pal and, God bless him, for he was a nice lad and knew his manners..........". So wrote **Private Robert Wilson** of the 10th Battalion, Cameronians, (Scottish Rifles) in a letter home to his sister in December, 1915. As we saw in Chapter 10, Private William Lowe was the last Leek soldier to die in 1915. Little did Bob Wilson realise, as he wrote these words, that he himself would be the first to be killed in 1916.

Young Bob Wilson was a good son to his mother. The family lived at 18, Ashbourne Road and Bob joined the All Saints Church Lads Brigade. An only son, he worked as a knitter at Trafford and Whites mill but, not long after war broke out, answered his country's call, enlisting in a Scottish regiment in November, 1914. The family had Scottish blood in their veins. He could never have foreseen what war was really like until his battalion was thrown into the hell that was the Battle of Loos in September, 1915. Fortunately, Bob came through that unscathed. The 22 year old was a bugler in 'A' Company and his duties included tending to the wounded. In another letter he wrote: *"..............I have been up in the trenches again for 12 days and it was terrible. They are knee deep with mud and water and the firing line was a damned hot shop, I can tell you. We lost a lot of men and another officer but the trenches were very low and were only about 24 yards from the enemy. They were shelling and bombing us night and day, it was pure slaughter. I am very pleased to say that I am in the land of the living.........."*

Bob's last letter to his worried mother arrived at her home on 27th January, 1916. That same day, he was killed by a shell-burst along with another stretcher-bearer whilst attending wounded men in a trench in the Loos/Lens area. He was buried close by and a small wooden cross placed on the grave. As so often happened, the grave and marker were subsequently lost and Private Robert Wilson is now commemorated on the Loos Memorial to the Missing.

Three Leek men died during February 1916. On the 12th, **Sergeant John William Lear** of the 3rd Battalion, South Lancashire Regiment, died of wounds at a hospital in England. He was 34 and is buried in Leek Cemetery, close to his former home at 31, Sandon Road (now Cheddleton Road). On the 18th, **Private Harry Hammersley** from 73, Grosvenor Street was killed by a hand-grenade in the Loos area whilst serving with the 9th Battalion, Royal Fusiliers. He had worked in the knitting department at Brough, Nicholson and Hall and was 23. He is also commemorated on the Loos Memorial.

The third soldier to die that month is perhaps better remembered for the part his son played in the history of Leek. **Private Ernest Bostock**, the father of the boxer, Tiny Bostock, was serving with the 1st North Staffords in the Hooge area of the Ypres salient. The trenches were more or less in full view of the Germans and, at that time of the year, thigh-deep in mud. Private Bostock was killed on 21st February, along with several others, during a four-

hour bombardment of the Staffords' positions, when there was a direct hit on their dug-out. He is buried in a small cemetery outside Ypres with the curious-sounding name: Divisional Cemetery, Dickebusche Road. Ernest Bostock lived at 48 Duke Street and was 31 when he was killed. Two of his nephews, Ron and Fred Bostock, were killed on active service during the Second World War. Tiny Bostock visited his father's grave in 1937 (below) whilst on a tour of the continent during his boxing days.

(Photographs H. Bostock)

Above: The Menin Road, Ypres. The soldiers who fought in the Ypres Salient would never forget the horrors of this place.

Below: Horses struggling to pull an ammunition limber through the mud. Scenes like this were commonplace on the Western Front.

Chapter 12

Mesopotamia

"From little towns in a far land we came
to save our honour and a world aflame.
By little towns in a far land we sleep
and trust that world we won for you to keep"

(Rudyard Kipling)

It is time now to look farther afield at other Leek soldiers who died in 1916. Mesopotamia, now Iraq, was part of the Turkish Empire at that time. Britain owned vital oil wells in the Persian Gulf and was fearful of a Turkish attack upon them. British and Indian troops landed in Mesopotamia in late 1914 and eventually established a cordon of security around the oilfields. Gradually, throughout the war, British forces moving northwards across the scorching deserts, extended their control of Mesopotamia as they fought the stubbornly resisting Turks. But in late 1915, British troops were cut off and besieged by the Turks at the town of Kut-el-Amara. Thousands of soldiers died of thirst and disease in the months that followed and then, on 29th April, 1916, the British surrendered.

The 7th North Staffords had arrived in Mesopotamia in January, 1916, after the mauling at Gallipoli and was one of the battalions eventually sent to Kut to attack the Turkish forces besieging the British forces there. Several assaults on the enemy positions were made by the Staffords in April and casualties were heavy. On

(Commonwealth War Graves Commission)
Basra Memorial, Iraq.

77

Wednesday, 5th April, **Private William O'Shaughnessey** was killed. He was married with a child, worked as a braid tenter at Wardle and Davenports and lived at 71, Shirburn Road, Leek. His body was lost and he is commemorated on the Basra Memorial, Iraq. Between 20th and 23rd April, fighting was continuous and bombing parties of the Staffords were wresting sections of trench from the Turks. Casualties were heavy and two Leek more soldiers were amongst those killed.

Private James Sharratt from 50, Ashbourne Road was 23 and, before the war, had worked in a shop near to where he lived. He was killed on 20th April, 1916. **Private James Edward Keates** from 1, Step Row, was 28 and the first of sixty-three members of the Leek Congregational Church to join up. He was killed on 22nd April. Each year, at the Remembrance Sunday parade in Leek, a small wooden cross is left in his memory on the steps of the Monument. Neither have a known grave and are also commemorated on the Basra Memorial.

Five weeks later, on 29th May, **Private Joseph Godwin,** also of the 7th North Staffords, died, believed by drowning, whilst the battalion was at rest away from the lines. The troops were camped near to the River Tigris and swimming in the river was a welcome respite from the intense heat. Private Godwin was married and lived at 1, Nelson Street. His grave is at Amara War Cemetery, Iraq. The town of Amara is on the banks of the Tigris and became a large hospital centre for the British during the war.

Back on the Western Front, as preparations for the 'Big Push' forged ahead, the casualties continued and still more Leek men fell in action. On 27th April, **Private John Joseph Hulme,** known to his friends as 'Joe', was killed by a shell explosion. He was serving with the 1st North Staffords and came from 16, Angle Street. He was buried in the same cemetery as Basil Nicholson, Dranoutre Military Cemetery, near Ypres. Joe Hulme was a bricklayer at Bayley and Morris Builders, Leek. Three days later on 30th April, 25 year old **Private Frank Sigley**, 10th Battalion, Royal Welsh Fusiliers, was killed by a gas attack during a German assault on the British lines in the Ypres Salient. He came from 33, Osborne Street and is buried at Lindenhoek Chalet Military Cemetery in Belgium.

On 9th May, **Guardsman Edward Robinson** of the 1st Battalion, Grenadier Guards was shot by a sniper in the Ypres salient and is now buried at Ypres Reservoir Cemetery. His brother, Thomas, was killed in action in 1918. Less than two weeks later, on 21st May, **Private Arthur Sproson** of the 2nd Battalion, Lincolnshire Regiment, was mortally wounded by a shell, apparently whilst he was standing talking to the cook in the trenches. He came from 37, Frith Street and had worked as a binding weaver at Antony Ward and Co. Private Sproson, aged 31 when he was killed, was buried at Warloy-Baillon Communal Cemetery, 8 miles west of Albert, the Somme town that was to feature very prominently in the fighting of the next few months.

Meanwhile, back at home in Leek, business people in the town centre were receiving the unwelcome attention of the local police. Thirty five of them were hauled up in front of the magistrates for breaching the black-out regulations! Gilbert Cope, the chemist in Fountain Street, was one man who was fined ten shillings (50p), another was Ernest Simpson, the tobacconist, in Derby Street.

(Commonwealth War Graves Commission)
Lindenhoek Chalet Military Cemetery in Belgium

Chapter 13

The Battle of Jutland

" There seems to be something wrong with our bloody ships today ".

(Vice-Admiral Sir David Beatty,
Commander of the British Battlecruiser Fleet at Jutland, 1916.)

Earlier in this book, we saw how one Leek sailor went down with his ship at the Battle of Coronel in November, 1914. It is time to return to the Royal Navy and look at events during 1916 in which three more Leek sailors were lost at sea.

As noted in Chapter 1, Britain and Germany had been busily building capital warships before the war and these remained a major threat to both sides during the years that followed. There were few battles between the two fleets as neither country wanted to risk serious loss or damage to their battleships and battlecruisers. There had been clashes, and ships sunk, at the

(Imperial War Museum)
British warships in line astern.

Heligoland Bight and Dogger Bank in 1914 and 1915, but the two mighty fleets were yet to meet in full strength. The British battleships were stationed at Scapa Flow in the Orkney Islands and the battlecruisers at Rosyth. The German High Seas Fleet spent most of its time at Wilhelmshaven. Effectively, the Royal Navy enforced a blockade of German ports throughout the war and this was one of the major causes of Germany's eventual defeat.

On Wednesday, 31st May, 1916, the two fleets did finally meet in strength. This was off the coast of Jutland (Denmark), in the North Sea. The action which followed became known as 'The Battle of Jutland' and has been surrounded in controversy, ever since, over

81

who actually won. The German warships, including 27 battleships and battlecruisers protected by dozens of smaller destroyers and cruisers, ventured out into the North Sea intending to shell the English port of Hartlepool and entice out British battlecruisers. Although this plan was abandoned for a less ambitious sweep of the Danish coast, the British Grand Fleet with around 150 ships was soon out in force and battle was joined. At the end of the day, the German High Seas Fleet retired to its home port, having lost one battleship and one battlecruiser sunk along with nine smaller ships. Some 2,500 sailors were killed. The British Grand Fleet lost three battlecruisers and eleven smaller ships and about 6,000 men. Although the Germans can be said to have won a tactical victory in terms of the losses inflicted on the British, their fleet never really ventured out of port again for the rest of the war. Two of the thousands of sailors who died came from Leek.

Able Seaman **Arthur Billing** was on the 567 foot long battle-cruiser H.M.S. Invincible. This ship was hit by shells from the German battlecruiser 'Derfflinger' at about 6.30pm. Sparks reached the gun magazines and Invincible exploded, breaking in half. Six survivors were rescued by a destroyer but over a thousand officers and men, including Arthur

(Imperial War Museum)

HMS Invincible sinking

Billing, went down with the ship. He came from Broads Bridge Cottages, Abbey Green Road, and had seen action at the Falkland Islands in late 1914, when his ship avenged the deaths of George Tomkinson and the others who died at Coronel on 1st November.

(Imperial War Museum)

HMS Barham

The second Leek sailor to lose his life at Jutland was only 17. **Boy (1st Class) Ralph Johnson** from St Edward Street was on board the 27,000 ton battleship, H.M.S. Barham, which, although not sunk, received two hits from heavy calibre shells during the course of the battle. The ship sustained damage and casualties, including young Ralph Johnson. He is commemorated on the Plymouth Naval Memorial. Able Seaman Billing is commemorated on the Naval Memorial at Portsmouth.

Only days after Jutland, another young Leek sailor went down with his ship when it sank off the Orkneys. It is a coincidence that the only two boy sailors from Leek to be killed in the war died within days of each other and an even more remarkable one that the ship in which the second one died was carrying an illustrious passenger who also drowned - Lord Kitchener.

Boy (1st Class) Thomas Bloor of 17, Garden Street, was a crew member for 12 months on the heavy cruiser, H.M.S. Hampshire, which was detailed to take Kitchener and his staff to Russia for an Allied conference. Kitchener's influence had waned,

(Author's collection)
Thomas Bloor

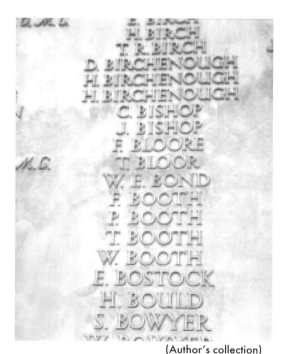

(Author's collection)
Thomas Bloor's name on the
Portsmouth Naval Memorial

particularly since the failed Gallipoli campaign, and his dogmatic and contradictory manner did not win him many friends in the British Government. Nevertheless, his face was known to millions and he had been responsible for raising the volunteer armies which, three weeks after his death, received their baptism of fire on the Somme.

Young Tom Bloor felt safe in the 10,850 ton cruiser, now at the naval base of Scapa Flow in the Orkneys. Her captain, Herbert Savill, was experienced and his ship had been specially chosen for this mission. Unfortunately, by Monday, 5th June, 1916, the day of the sailing, the weather had deteriorated and it was raining heavily with a strong north-easterly gale. Nevertheless, Lord Kitchener boarded the

Hampshire at 4.30pm, anxious to be on his way. An hour later, the ship was forcing its way through the heaving seas, and a 50 knot gale, past the island of Hoy. Unable to keep up, two destroyers which had escorted the Hampshire out of Scapa Flow, returned to the shelter of the base. At 7.30pm, HMS Hampshire was passing the cliffs of Birsay, about a mile out to sea, when she struck a mine. Local people saw dark smoke and heard a loud explosion. Flames shot up from the forward gun turret, the ship slowed, changed course and then sank.

Some 200 men got away on life-rafts but these overturned when they reached the shore, killing most of the occupants. Only 12 of the 655 men in the Hampshire survived the disaster. Neither Kitchener or Tom Bloor were ever found.

Tom, a former pupil at West Street School, was only 18. He loved the navy but missed his family dearly. On returning to the Hampshire after a spell of leave at home some months before his death, he wrote to a friend: *"I felt alright coming but when I got aboard I felt very badly homesick"*. He is commemorated on the Portsmouth Naval Memorial.

(Author's collection)

HMS Hampshire

Chapter 14

Build up to the 'Big Push'

"They sent us 200 whiz-bangs over yesterday morning before breakfast............."

(Private Harold Plant, 16th Sherwood Foresters, in a letter home three months before he fell in action.)

By June, 1916, the build-up of men and resources for the forthcoming offensive on the Somme was well under way. Before the battle started, several more Leek men lost their lives, mainly on the Western Front. We will look at these in a moment, but let us briefly return to Leek where the town was mourning the death of a popular and respected man who had done much to encourage young local men to enlist during the early stages of the war. **Sergeant David Pickford**, attached to the Royal Field Artillery, died on 2nd June after a long illness. He was 61 and had volunteered his services despite being retired from the army for a good number of years. Sergeant Pickford lived at 11, Court 2, Overton Bank, Leek. He is buried in Leek Cemetery and was the oldest serviceman in our story to die. By coincidence, another sergeant named David Pickford, who died of wounds four months later, is also buried in Leek Cemetery (see Chapter 18).

On the Western Front on 7th June, **Private Robert Johnson**, 1st Battalion, North Staffords, was the next man to die of his wounds. He was 36 and came from 2, Step Row. An army reservist who worked at Liverpool Docks before the war, he is buried at Bailleul Communal Cemetery Extension, Northern France. This cemetery is some 10 miles south-west of Ypres and is the final resting place of nearly 4,500 men from the war. On 17th June, **Private Henry James Messham**, serving with a Canadian Machine Gun Company, also died of wounds. He had lived in the Market Place at one time and is now buried at Boulogne, France.

Rifleman Herbert Spencer Bert Trafford was the next Leek victim of the war. He was serving with the 21st Battalion, Kings Royal Rifle Corps, in the Ypres salient. Shortly before daylight on the morning of 24th June, Bert was looking over the parapet of his trench towards the enemy lines for any sign of activity. This was the dawn 'stand-to' when a sudden attack by the Germans was a possibility. A sniper, his rifle trained for such an opportunity, took aim and fired. Bert Trafford was shot through the head and died instantly. He was only 19.

(B. Hall)

Bert Trafford - shot through the head

Bert's battalion had only crossed to Flanders in May, 1916, taking front-line duties at Ploegsteert (known as 'Plugstreet' to the troops) south of Ypres. He was one of the earlier casualties of the battalion but there would be many more in the months that followed. The 21st took appalling casualties during the Battle of the Somme. Bert Trafford lived at Spencer House, Newcastle Road, and was one of six children. One of his nephews was Mr Spencer Trafford, the well-known Consultant Surgeon at the North Staffordshire Royal Infirmary. Another was Aircraftman Jack Trafford who was killed in a flying accident during the Second World War. His great-niece and her husband own Greystones Restaurant in Stockwell Street, next to the library.

Rifleman Bert Trafford is buried at Berks Cemetery Extension at Ploegsteert, not far from where he was killed. The day on which he died, 24th June, 1916, marked the start, much further south, of the great offensive on the Somme. This was the day when the guns opened up with their ear-shattering roar designed to kill all the Germans in their defensive positions and lead to the long hoped-for breakthrough. The bombardment was planned to go on for five days and the infantry to attack on the 29th. In the event, the assault was postponed until 1st July, due to bad weather. The artillery boasted twice as many guns as used in the Battle of Loos and six times as many shells. During this week-long

8" Howitzers of the Royal Garrison Artillery firing on German positions
(Imperial War Musuem)

bombardment, more shells were fired from British guns than were fired in the first twelve months of the war.

The 24th June also saw another Leek man killed. **Private Harold Shenton** of 20, Alma Street and an employee of Wardle and Davenports, was serving with the 1/5th Battalion, North Staffords, which was a Territorial unit. The battalion was at Fonquevillers (Funky Villas to the troops), a small village opposite Gommecourt, and had come under machine-gun and shell-fire. Harold Shenton's grave was lost and he is commemorated on the Thiepval Memorial to the Missing. The next day and some miles further north, **Private Edward Wheeldon**, of the Machine Gun Corps, was killed by a shell whilst on sentry duty in the Loos/Lens area. He was 31, a bricklayer by trade and came from 64 Southbank Street. He is buried at Bois-de-Noulette British Cemetery near Lens.

As the build-up of troops continued in readiness for the infantry assault on the Somme, so the bombardment continued. Shell after shell struck enemy positions destroying earthworks and blowing in trench-sides. The German artillery replied with their own guns and the waiting British infantry took casualties from the exploding shells. One of these was **Corporal Robert Ford** of the 1/5th Battalion, South Staffordshire Regiment. This Territorial battalion, like the 1/5th North Staffords in which Private Harold Shenton was killed, was part of the 46th (North Midland) Division. The Divisional Commander was Major-General Montagu Stuart-Wortley and his battalions comprised men from Leicester, Lincolnshire, Nottinghamshire and Derbyshire as well as the Staffordshire men. As we shall see later, this Division did not fare well on the opening day of the Somme battle on 1st July but covered itself in glory in the breaching of the Hindenburg Line in the autumn of 1918.

25 year old Corporal Ford was killed by an enemy shell which struck a dug-out near the village of Gommecourt on 26th June. He lived at Wharf House, Leek, and worked in the North Staffordshire Railway manager's office at Stoke. His grave is at Gommecourt Wood New Cemetery, Foncquevillers. The cemetery faces no man's land where the 46th (North Midland) Division attacked on 1st July, as we shall see in the next chapter. The tiny village of Foncquevillers was the forward base of the division and is a pretty place to visit today.

Three days later and thousands of miles away, the third Smith brother from 22, Duke Street died

(V. Pegg)

Sam Smith, the last of three brothers to die.

87

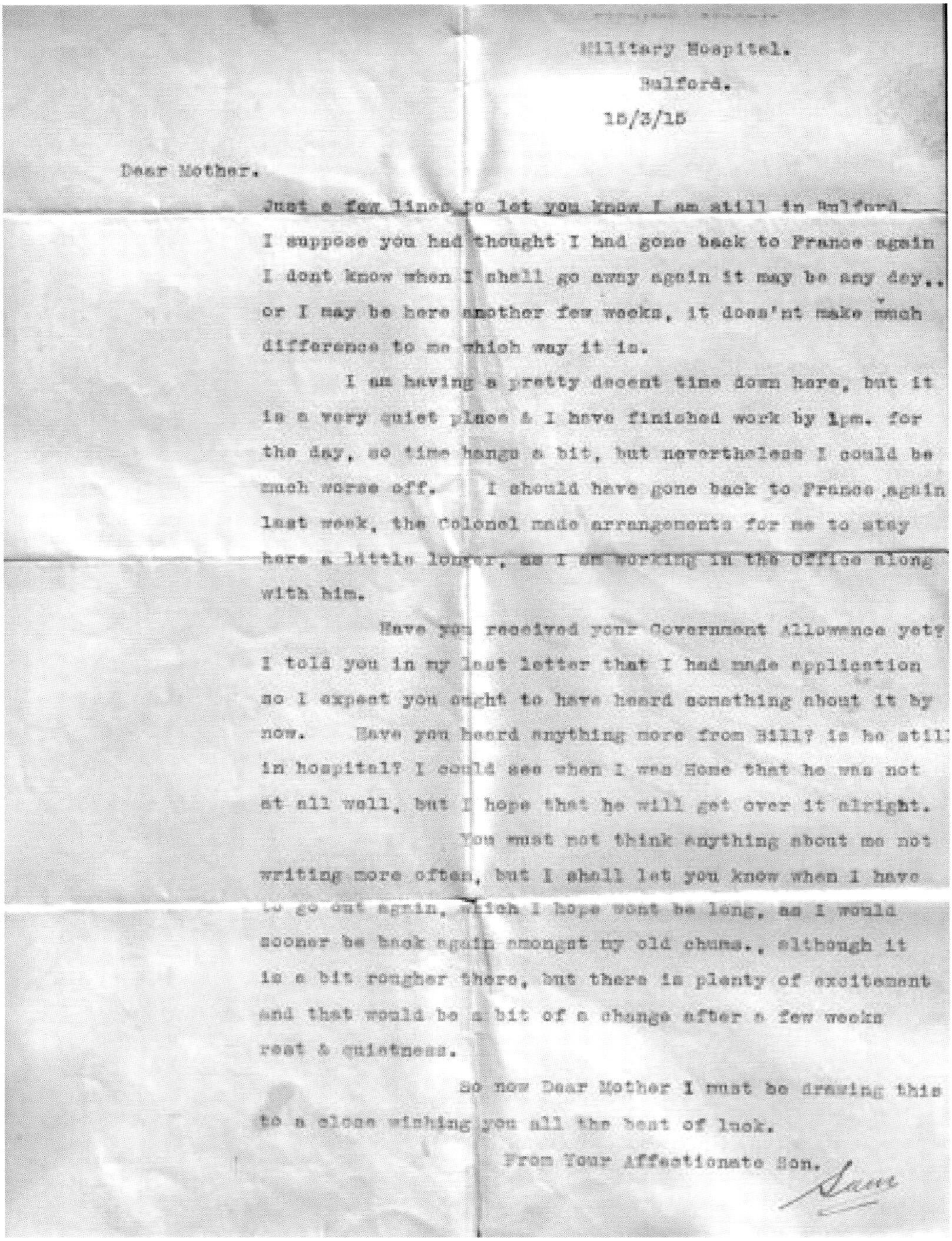

Military Hospital.
Bulford.
15/3/15

Dear Mother.

Just a few lines to let you know I am still in Bulford. I suppose you had thought I had gone back to France again I dont know when I shall go away again it may be any day.. or I may be here another few weeks, it does'nt make much difference to me which way it is.

I am having a pretty decent time down here, but it is a very quiet place & I have finished work by 1pm. for the day, so time hangs a bit, but nevertheless I could be much worse off. I should have gone back to France again last week, the Colonel made arrangements for me to stay here a little longer, as I am working in the Office along with him.

Have you received your Government Allowance yet? I told you in my last letter that I had made application so I expect you ought to have heard something about it by now. Have you heard anything more from Bill? is he still in hospital? I could see when I was Home that he was not at all well, but I hope that he will get over it alright.

You must not think anything about me not writing more often, but I shall let you know when I have to go out again, which I hope wont be long, as I would sooner be back again amongst my old chums., although it is a bit rougher there, but there is plenty of excitement and that would be a bit of a change after a few weeks rest & quietness.

So now Dear Mother I must be drawing this to a close wishing you all the best of luck.

From Your Affectionate Son.
Sam

(V. Pegg)

The letter typed by Sam Smith in 1915

88

on 29th June. **Private Samuel Smith** was attached to the Royal Army Medical Corps at a military hospital in India. Sam had survived the Gallipoli campaign, unlike his brother William (see Chapter 7), but succumbed to the extremes of temperature, dying from heat-stroke at a hospital in Bombay. Letters which Sam sent to his mother before she died in the winter of 1915 have survived. One of these (opposite page) was actually typed by Sam Smith when he was stationed at a military hospital in England. For a mother to receive a typed letter from her soldier son 87 years ago must have been a rare occurrence indeed! The Royal Army Medical Corps armband worn by Sam has also survived and is now in the possession of his niece. Private Sam Smith is commemorated on the Kirkee 1914-1918 Memorial in India.

(Imperial War Museum)

The Royal Army Medical Corps worked long and hard to save the lives of so many men during the war. Here, a wounded soldier undergoes surgery for his wounds at a casualty clearing station.

The Somme (British Sector)
July - November 1916

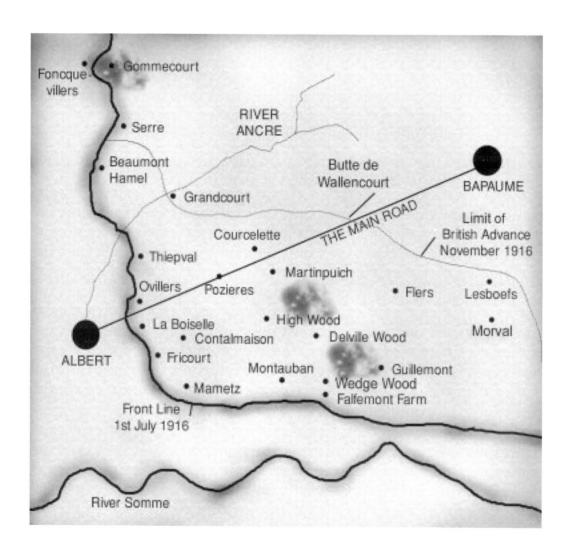

Chapter 15

The Battle of the Somme

"You will meet nothing but dead and wounded Germans.........."

(A senior officer of the 11th Sherwood Foresters to his men on the eve of the battle.)

At 7.30 on the sunny morning of Saturday 1st July, 1916, the British guns suddenly ceased their firing for a few seconds whilst the artillerymen adjusted the sights for the next targets behind the German front line. The waiting troops were amazed to see birds hovering and swooping over the trenches. Their song could be heard clearly; it all seemed so unreal. Then suddenly, as the barrage crashed on to the next line of enemy positions, the whistles blew and the infantrymen climbed up the ladders, spurred on by their officers. But then, reality returned. The Battle of the Somme had begun.

To Leek men like Harold Billing and Tommy Taylor, both of whom would be killed that day, the Somme region held a certain attraction. Unlike the drab, industrial sector of Lens and Loos and the flat, wet and squalid areas of Flanders, the Somme was a land which pleased the eye. Gentle fields stretched into the distance, small streams sparkled, green woods and farmhouses dotted the landscape. This was a place far removed from busy towns, cities and highways. Up to now, the Somme front had been a relatively quiet backwater and much of it was untouched by the ravages of war. Crops still grew in the fields and wild flowers adorned the roadsides.

The 'Big Push' on the Somme was originally planned as a joint British and French affair. The British would attack north of the River Somme, astride the Albert to Bapaume

(Imperial War Museum)
British soldiers going 'over the top' on 1st July 1916

road, with thirteen divisions. (A division comprised some 12,000 infantry with artillery, cavalry and other necessary support). The French would attack south of the river on a slightly longer front. But, in February 1916, the Germans suddenly attacked the French fortress city of Verdun. Their intention here was to 'bleed the French white'. That battle of attrition ground on until the end of the year, costing the French and the Germans over 300,000 casualties on both sides. Verdun changed the focus of the French and the Somme offensive was to become a largely British affair, the French putting only a few Divisions into the attack. The British attacked on an 18 mile front, towards the fortified villages of Serre in the north and Montauban in the south. In between lay some of the other villages which were first-day objectives for the assaulting troops: Beaumont Hamel, Thiepval, La Boisselle, Fricourt and Mametz. A diversionary attack at Gommecourt, north of Serre, was designed to draw the attention of the Germans away from the main assault further south. The 46th (North Midland) Division containing many Staffordshire men, attacked at Gommecourt along with a London division. The Leek Battery supported this attack.

(Imperial War Museum)

Men of the Tyneside Irish Brigade advancing towards the German lines on 1st July.
Very few returned.

As soon as the heavily-burdened soldiers climbed over the parapet they formed up in orderly waves as if on a parade ground. There was no shouting or rushing. There was no need, or at least that is what they had been told. The Germans would all be dead from the seven-day bombardment, not even a rat would be left alive, some officer had said. Many of the troops had been told that they could smoke their pipes and shoulder their rifles as they walked across. They were also told that the German wire would have been cut by the constant shelling. It was just a matter of walking over and occupying the enemy front-line trenches.

But then, the unimaginable happened. German machine gunners, nerves shredded from the British barrage but otherwise largely unhurt, climbed from their deep dugouts and opened fire. They could hardly miss. Men were cut down in their hundreds but still others

As this terrible day ended, so did the once popular idea of Pals Battalions. The casualty lists in local newspapers, mainly in the industrial northern towns of England were too long and more than the public could bear. Kitchener's citizen army of enthusiastic volunteers had been decimated. It was said that they were 'two years in the making and two hours in the destroying'. As darkness descended on the 18 mile front, the cries of the wounded still lying out in No Man's Land unnerved and upset those soldiers lucky enough to have made it back to their trenches. The day's total casualties had been some 20,000 killed and 40,000 wounded, mainly in the first hour. This was the blackest day for the British Army to date and only a fraction of the objectives for that first day had been achieved. In their sector, the French had done better.

(A. Prime)

George Prime.

There had been mistakes and misinformation in the planning and preparation. For example, in most places the German barbed wire had not been cut during the bombardment as the wrong type of shells had been used. In addition, many of the shells failed to explode, thus diluting the effect of the barrage. The Germans had also constructed deep, strong dug-outs in their trenches which enabled them to withstand the seven day bombardment. They had also perfected the technique of carrying their heavy machine guns to the surface within a couple of minutes. Thus, when the bombardment stopped all they had to do was get the machine guns up into what was left of their trenches before the British soldiers got there. And, in most cases along the line, this is what they did. They were helped considerably, of course, by the fact that the British had been told not to run, but to merely walk across at a leisurely pace. Although the German machine guns accounted for thousands of dead and wounded men that day, the accurate artillery barrage laid down in No Man's Land, which the British had to cross, claimed more lives; some 60%.

Despite the events and appalling casualties of the opening day, the Commander-in-Chief, Field Marshal Sir Douglas Haig persuaded the government and his generals that the battle should go on. The Battle of the Somme raged for over four months until it ground to a halt in the November mud. By then, it had claimed the lives of some 125,000 British soldiers. More than twice that number were wounded or captured. A mere seven miles of enemy held territory had been gained. Before the fighting on the Somme ended in November, dozens more Leek soldiers lay dead.

Before we leave that tragic 1st July, 1916, we move back north, some 70 miles, to the Ypres salient near Kemmel (a few miles from where Lieutenant Basil Nicholson was shot) where a young army officer from Leek was killed that day. Although this area was not involved in the Somme offensive, shelling by both sides continued to claim casualties. **Lieutenant Arthur William Dale** came from 19, Spring Gardens and was attached to the 7th Battalion, Northumberland Fusiliers. Aged 20, he was the officer commanding a line of trench which was receiving attention from the German artillery. By the standards of the day, this was regarded as more of a 'nuisance' than anything worse and retaliatory fire by our artillery was generally the answer. At 5.15pm, one of the German guns started firing again and Lieutenant Dale was struck in the thigh by a large splinter. He died a short while later. He is buried at La Laiterie Military Cemetery, near Ypres and there is a large memorial to him in Leek Cemetery. Lieutenant Dale had been studying at Sheffield University to be a teacher and joined the Officer Training Corps from there. He had only been at the front for seven weeks when he was killed.

(Aurthor)

Arthur Dale's memorial in Leek Cemetery.

At home in Leek, people were unaware of the terrible events of that first day of July. It would be a week before the heavy casualty lists began to appear in newpapers around the country. In the meantime, families in and around Mill Street that Saturday morning were getting ready for the Jumble Sale at the Mission Church, no doubt trying to decide in advance if it would be worth the twopence entry fee. In the town, shoppers passing Copes Chemist in Fountain Street paused at the notice urging them to: *"SEND YOUR SOLDIER: Trench Powder 3d, Flash Lamps 1/6d, Trench Oxo Outfits 1/- "* A glance at Skinners shop window would reveal a wide range of hand-crafted garden tools and wire-netting for sale and, further along Derby Street, the Maypole store was offering: *" Maypole Margarine at 7d per pound - Summertime Saving".*

Chapter 16

July on the Somme

".......Germans shell us heavy, dug-out smashed in...........
three killed, two wounded. Many horses killed......"

(From the diary notes of Private Sidney Simpson M.M. Died of wounds, July 1918.)

This chapter will look briefly at the events of the remainder of July, 1916 and the fourteen Leek men who died on the Somme in that period.

Sunday, 2nd July dawned bright and clear. Further attacks, on a very much smaller scale than the previous day, resulted in the capture of Fricourt and part of La Boiselle. Some small gains were also made in the days following, including the clearing of La Boiselle. But it was on Friday, 7th July, that the next three Leek soldiers were killed, two of them in the assault upon the fortified village of Ovillers.

Preserved trenches at Beaumont Hamel on the Somme.
(Author)

At 8 o'clock that morning, the 9th Battalion, Loyal North Lancashires and a battalion of Cheshires advanced on the German front line at Ovillers which was protected by rising ground giving an excellent field of fire for the defenders. Many of the attackers were shot down by machine-gun fire and the attack was halted. One of the dead from the Lancashire battalion was Leek born **Private Thomas Meakin**. No details are known about him but his body was recovered and he is buried at Pozieres British Cemetery about a mile from where he fell.

Whilst this attack was in progress, three more battalions of infantry advanced on the German lines from another direction. These came under fire from enemy artillery and took heavy casualties. Nevertheless, they continued and captured the first and second German front lines of trench. One of these battalions was the 8th Royal Fusiliers and one of its soldiers killed was **Private Enoch Gibson**, aged 38 from 1, Strangman Street, Leek, a silk twister in civilian life. Enoch was no stranger to the perils of the battlefield, having been gassed the previous year necessitating eight months recuperation. He also had a son who served in the First World War, with a Scottish Regiment. Private Enoch Gibson is commemorated on the Thiepval Memorial.

The third Leek soldier to be killed that day was **Lance Corporal William Francis Wheeldon** of the 12th Battalion, Manchester Regiment. He had lived in John Street but moved to Manchester some years before the war where he worked for the London and North-Western Railway Company. Lance Corporal Wheeldon, a cousin of Lieutenant A.W. Dale who, as we saw, was killed at Ypres a week earlier, died when the Manchesters attacked enemy positions near the village of Contalmaison but were cut down by machine guns firing from nearby Mametz Wood. He too is commemorated on the Thiepval Memorial.

Author's Collection

The shattered remains of Delville Wood

On Sunday 9th July, **Private James Thomas Slater**, 13th Battalion, Royal Fusiliers, became the next Leek soldier to be killed on the Somme. Aged 31 and a dyer at Joshua Wardles, Leekbrook, he had lived at 90, Portland Street with his wife, Emma Jane, and their three children. His brother-in-law, Rifleman D.J. Green, had fallen at Ypres a year earlier. (See Chapter 8). Private Slater is commemorated on the Thiepval Memorial.

Mr Ernest Green and his wife, Annie, of 1, High Street, Leek, were proud of their two young sons, Charles and Norman. Charles was married with three young children and employed as an assistant master at Britannia Street School before moving out to Rhodesia, South Africa, to make a new life there. When war broke out, he was commissioned into a south midlands regiment and came back to Europe to fight for his native country. Norman Green had enlisted as a trooper in a cavalry regiment in England as soon as war broke out but quickly gained recognition and was commissioned into the 7th North Staffords as a 2nd Lieutenant. Sadly, Mr and Mrs Green's high hopes for their two boys turned to grief when the brothers were killed within six months of each other. **Lieutenant Charles Ernest Green** was attached to the 7th Battalion, Kings Shropshire Light Infantry. On 14th July, this unit was deployed in the attack upon German positions in front of Delville Wood. Again, the barbed wire had not been cut and casualties were heavy. Lieutenant Green is recorded as dying on the 15th, no doubt from wounds. His body was lost or never identified and he is commemorated on the Thiepval Memorial. His brother, Norman, died in Mesopotamia in January, 1917. (See Chapter 18).

On the same day that Charles Green died, another Leek man was killed. **Sapper Harry Tomkinson,** serving with the Royal Engineers, was 36 and lived at 10, Weston Street. He is buried at a small cemetery a few miles from Albert, Mericourt-l'Abbe Communal Cemetery Extension, with 400 other soldiers.

The next pair of Leek soldiers in our story were killed on the Somme front the following day, Sunday, 16th July. These two lads were friends who served together in the 13th Battalion, Royal Fusiliers. And they died together, killed by the same shell.

Lance Corporal Henry Ashworth lived at 32, Parker Street and worked as a painter and decorator at Edwin Phillips & Son, Stockwell Street. **Private John Clarke** came from 19, Gaunt Street and also worked as a painter and decorator. He was only 19. It seems that Harry and Jack, as they were known, were buried together at the time but only Harry Ashworth could be identified, either then, or later by the Graves Registration Units. He is now buried at Pozieres British Cemetery on the Somme. Jack Clarke has no known grave and is commemorated on the Thiepval Memorial. There are, however, as in most Commonwealth War Cemeteries, hundreds of unidentified servicemen buried at Pozieres. Their headstones are marked: "A Soldier of the Great War - Known Unto God". Jack Clarke may still be close to the friend with whom he served, fought and died.

There is an added twist to the story of Jack Clarke. Some years ago, a lady digging her garden at a house on Ladderedge, Leek, found a brass plaque with Jack Clarke's name on it. Identical plaques were sent to the families of all servicemen and women who were lost in the war. They are some four inches in diameter and have the words: "He Died For Freedom and Honour", along with the name of the deceased person, inscribed upon it. Many of these still

survive today and are treasured by the descendants of
those who gave their lives. In the case of the plaque
found at Ladderedge, it seems likely that a member of Jack Clarke's family lived there at some
time and either lost or buried the plaque in the
garden.

The bronze plaque, along with a scroll, was
designed by a man named Preston, a Liverpud-
lian, in a competition for the design which attracted
800 entries. For his troubles, Mr Preston won a
prize of £250.

The Somme battlefield was dotted with a number of
woods which the Germans occupied and the British needed to clear in order to press on to their
objectives. Long, bitter struggles took place for the woods which, in the course of the fighting,
were mainly reduced to shattered tree-stumps and little else. Their names, High Wood, Mametz
Wood, Trones Wood, Bernafay Wood and the infamous Delville Wood, were to live on forever as
reminders of the costly struggles to capture them. These woods are still there but, in some of
them, the majestic trunks and foliage belie the dangers of unexploded munitions still to be found
within their boundaries.

Four days after the deaths of Harry Ashworth and Jack Clarke, another two Leek soldiers,
again serving in the same battalion, were killed. **Private Arthur Tatton** and **Private John Dickenson**
were in the 2nd Battalion, Royal Welsh Fusiliers which was to be involved in an attack on High
Wood on 20th July. Already reduced to some 400 strong by earlier casualties, the battalion was
heavily shelled whilst still some distance from High Wood losing around 100 killed and wounded.
The poet, Robert Graves, was amongst the wounded, Arthur Tatton and John Dickenson were
amongst the dead. Arthur lived at 89 Mill Street and had been in the army for four years. His
brother, Rupert, also a soldier, died after the war, in 1919. John Dickenson came from 3, Moorhouse
Street and worked at Wardle and Davenports before enlisting in April, 1915. He was only 18
when he was killed and is buried at Caterpillar Valley Cemetery on the Somme. Arthur Tatton
has no known grave and is commemorated on the Thiepval Memorial.

Private Harry Perkin Johnson of the 8th Battalion, North Staffords, was the next Leek
casualty. He was killed on 22nd July,1916. The battalion had marched to the front line at
Bazentin-le-Petit after a period of training, refitting and drafting in reinforcements to replace
men lost in earlier actions. On the way to the line, the troops had to make their way through a
valley which was previously in German hands and well-known to their gunners. A barrage
opened up on the men and around thirty were lost. Harry Johnson lived at 7, Prince Street (now
demolished), had worked at Brough, Nicholson and Hall and was a drummer in the North
Staffords Regimental Band. A former Boy Scout, Harry was only 18 when he was killed. His
body was lost and he is listed on the Thiepval Memorial.

The band of the 8th Battalion, North Staffordshire Regiment.
Private Harry Johnson was a drummer in this band.

(Author)

The former West Street School

The staff and pupils at West Street School had cause to be proud of their contribution to the war effort. In the year 1916 alone, the infants had brought into the school pennies and halfpennies amounting to over seven pounds and four shillings, a not inconsiderable sum in those days. This money was donated to the local Roll of Honour Fund and the Leek Red Cross Hospital. Older girls at the school knitted 85 pairs of socks, 31 pairs of mittens, 6 mufflers and 40 scarves for soldiers at the front. A letter written by the knitter and placed inside the article no doubt brought wistful memories of home and a tear to the eye of more than one Leek soldier. Many of the former pupils were serving their country abroad, some had won decorations for bravery but, by the end of the war, at least 31 had lost their lives. One of these, a captain when he was killed, had served in the Boer War with the Cheshire Regiment and was commissioned into the Australian Infantry Force during the First World War.

Captain John Leadbeater of the 5th Battalion, Australian Infantry, originated from 26 Grove Street and was no stranger to tragedy. His wife died in India in a drowning accident whilst he was serving there. The battalion was part of the 1st Australian Division which was involved in the assault upon the German-held fortified village of Pozieres on the main Albert to Bapaume Road during the third week of July. Captain Leadbeater and the men of his company left their trench on the outskirts of Pozieres in the early hours of Tuesday, 25th July, 1916. Their mission was to attack and capture two lines of trenches known as 'OG 1' and 'OG 2'. Under the cover of darkness and protected by an artillery barrage on the German lines, the troops seized 'OG 1' and pressed on to the second line, 'OG 2'. They entered this but the Germans attacked them with grenades and rifle fire, forcing them to retire back to 'OG 1'. The Australians lost a lot of men during the assault on the German trenches. Captain Leadbeater was one of them, shot through the head. A week later, his battalion commander wrote to John's father, Mr Alan Leadbeater, at Grove Street: *"By his death I lost one of my best company commanders and I am only voicing the feelings of every man in his company when I say how sorry I am. He died with the call: "Come on, lads" on his lips, death being instantaneous - a bullet through the brain.............".*

(Commonwealth War Graves Commission)
Villers-Bretonneux Australian Memorial

104

Captain John Leadbeater has no known grave and is commemorated on the Villers-Bretonneux Australian Memorial near Amiens.

The last two Leek soldiers to be killed on the Somme in July, 1916, both died on the 27th in the fighting for the bitterly contested Delville Wood (called 'Devil's Wood' by the soldiers). Again, both men served together in the same battalion, the 1st Bedfords. 24 year old **Private William Plant** was last seen with a wound to his leg. He was married and lived at 3 Court, 6, West Street, working at Watson's mill before the war. **Private Ernest Prince** came from High Up Cottage, High Up Lane, off the Macclesfield road. (The cottage was only demolished in the Spring of 2003). He was 21. Both are commemorated on the Thiepval Memorial.

The Bedfords had advanced against enemy positions in Delville Wood where bitter fighting took place. It eventually took six weeks to clear the Germans from the wood. The shattered trees and tangled undergrowth witnessed some of the most vicious battles of the Somme campaign. Positions constantly changed hands and an inferno of shellfire fell on the troops of both sides. Delville Wood is now owned by South Africa and men from that country fought their first battle here. They went into action over 3,000 men strong and captured most of the wood between 14th and 20th July. When the South Africans emerged, only 778 answered the roll

(J. Neilson)

High Up Cottage

call. The South African National Memorial, an impressive museum and a visitor centre now stand within Delville Wood.

Chapter 17

August and September on the Somme

"The sights you saw were cruel. Men blown to pieces; it made you weep to see them."

(Leek-born Corporal Herbert Ball of the Royal Fusiliers. Wounded on the Somme but survived the war.)

August, 1916, saw the deaths of another nine Leek soldiers on the Somme battlefields. On the 4th, exactly two years to the day since Britain entered the war, **Sergeant Charles Salt** of the 1/5th Battalion, North Staffords, died. His connection to Leek cannot be determined but he lies buried at De Cusine Ravine British Cemetery, a few miles from Arras. On the 9th, a Wednesday, **Private Harry Sweetmore** of the 13th Battalion, Royal Fusiliers, was killed when a shell exploded in the vicinity of Mametz Wood. He was apparently buried in the north-west corner of the wood but his grave was lost. Harry, aged 22 and one of four children, had worked on the estate at Haregate and lived at Haregate Lodge. He is commemorated on the Thiepval Memorial.

Private Albert Trafford of the 1/5th North Staffords was, at the tender age of 19, already a seasoned soldier. His two older sisters, Lily and Nellie, back home at 4, Nelson Street, Ball Haye Green, and their father, Jabez and mother, Hannah, probably still thought of him as the baby of the family. He had survived the terrible shelling of the bat-

(H. Owen)
Harry Sweetmore - killed by shell

talion at Gommecourt on 1st July but died of wounds on Friday, 11th August. Two days before, men of the battalion were constructing forward trenches in a supposedly 'quiet' area north of Gommecourt when they were discovered by the Germans and machine-gunned. There were eighteen casualties and it is thought that Private Trafford was one of those wounded.

Albert Trafford had been employed as a knitter at Clemesha Brothers and Birch and was a former member of the All Saints Church Lads Brigade. His grave is at Warlincourt Halte British Cemetery, some six miles from Gommecourt.

Although most British military cemeteries abroad, for instance, Delville Wood Cemetery, are named after their locations, others have curious names which conjure up the imagination.. Thistle Dump Cemetery, Railway Hollow Cemetery and Caterpillar Valley Cemetery are examples of these. Named by the soldiers when the original burials took place during the war, these cemeteries reflect the area of the fighting at the time. Another one, Flatiron Copse Cemetery, Mametz, so named because of its proximity to a small piece of woodland shaped like a flat-iron, contains the bodies of three Leek men thought to have

(K. Dickens)

Albert Trafford

been killed by shellfire on Saturday, 12th August. (The Commonwealth War Graves Commission have recorded the date as 13th August; discrepancies like this are not uncommon). **Private James Turner**, **Private Ben Goldstraw** and **Private Arthur Astles** were serving with the 9th Battalion, North Staffords, then serving as a Pioneer battalion. (Pioneers had the task of supporting the divisional infantry with trench construction work and the like.)

(Commonwealth War Graves Commission)

Flatiron Copse Cemetery

The 9th North Staffords were in the vicinity of Mametz Wood which had finally been taken from the Germans after a long, bitter struggle. Seven soldiers of 'B' Company were killed by shellfire and, according to the battalion history, fourteen others were wounded.

James Turner, 24, came from 71, Shirburn Road, where he lived with his sister, and had worked at the nearby Brough, Nicholson and Hall's mill. Ben Goldstraw was 38 and had worked in a limestone quarry at Froghall. Arthur Astles, a father of four, worked for Thomas Grace, the builder, in Broad Street. He had lived at 34, Compton although his wife was living at 54, Picton Street, after the war. A fellow-soldier reported that Arthur Astles was attending a wounded comrade when he was killed. All three men lie buried in Flatiron Copse Cemetery which lies just to the east of Mametz Wood. Privates Turner and Astles are in adjacent graves. The cemetery was visited a few years ago by local Great War historian and travel consultant, Malcolm Sperring-Toy, who wrote an interesting article for the Leek Post and Times on the existence of the three graves.

Another name which would be added to the Thiepval Memorial on the Somme was that of **Private Arthur Nowland**, who, like a few others in this book, was aged 38 when he was killed. Arthur was serving with the 9th Battalion, East Surrey Regiment, in the vicinity of Trones Wood on Wednesday, 16th August. He had worked for Adams and Co; dyers, and lived at 57 Grove Street. His twin brother, Hezekiah, was killed almost exactly a year later. Two days later, on 18th August, 22 year old **Private Samuel Bowyer**, a native of Meerbrook, was killed whilst serving with the 6th Battalion, Duke of Cornwall's Light Infantry. Troops of this unit had attacked and cleared an enemy trench known as 'Edge Trench' but were counter-attacked by Germans with grenades and forced to withdraw. Private Bowyer is also commemorated on the Thiepval Memorial.

(M. Nowland)
Arthur Nowland

The last Leek man to die on the Somme that August was **Private Joseph Doxey** of the 1/6th North Staffords. His home was at 11, John Street and he was employed at Leek Gasworks. At one time he had worked as a groundsman at Beggars Lane Cricket Club. Private Doxey died on the 26th and is buried at De Cusine Ravine British Cemetery near Arras.

Before we look at the eleven Leek men who died on the Somme in September, 1916, let us briefly go farther afield - to Greece and Mesopotamia - where two more died around this time.

In October, 1915, British and French troops were despatched to Salonika in Greece to help with the threat from Bulgaria. On 12th August, **Private William Hammond** of the 2nd Battalion, Cheshire Regiment died of malaria at a hospital in Salonika and was buried in the cemetery there. He lived at No: 1 Court, 6, Mill Street and left a widow and two children. A former pupil of West Street School, Private Hammond had worked as a painter and decorator for Stevenson Brothers in the Market Place. Less than three weeks later, **Sergeant William Moss** died in Mesopotamia on 1st September. He was serving out there with the Army Veterinary Corps. An auctioneer by profession, Sergeant Moss was a married man and had lived in Abbots Lane. He is buried at Amara War Cemetery in what is now Iraq.

On Sunday, 3rd September, it was raining on the Somme. It was rain, combined with shell-torn earth and the movement of men, animals and vehicles that churned up the chalky ground into a morass of mud which could only get worse as the winter months approached. But for now, the British had more battles to fight, more ground to take. It was on this wet Sunday that two more Leek soldiers were killed in the fighting for the enemy-held strongpoints of Beaumont-Hamel and Guillemont, two small villages some ten miles apart.

Private Harold Plant was only 17 but keen to have a crack at the Germans before the war was over. He resigned from his job as a lithographer at David Morris and Co; London Street, Leek and enlisted in the 16th Battalion, Notts and Derby Regiment (Sherwood Foresters) in the Spring of 1915. By March 1916, from his training camp in Surrey, he was writing excitedly to his mother and father, Gertrude and Harry Plant of 51, Picton Street: *"....we are going to France tomorrow. Reveille goes at three in the morning.......we shall be all right with a rifle and 250 rounds of ammunition too. What do you think?"*

Like so many young men of his generation, Harold Plant soon began to experience the reality of the war on the Western Front as it actually was. He wrote of the camaraderie of soldiers thrown together in the trenches and how he had made good friends, of the pleasure in receiving food parcels from his family and of reading news of home in the Leek Post which his parents dutifully sent on. But he also wrote of the death and destruction he had seen: *"We came out of the trenches last night and we were all pleased to get out for it's the hottest shop we have ever been in..........We had a bit of bad luck. We lost 12 men, two killed and ten wounded. We have been in for four days and it is quite enough too."*

(G. Whiteman)
Harold Plant - enlisted under-age

There were other horrors for the young soldier: *"........I had a fright the other night in the dug-out. The Germans were shelling us in the dug-out and of course we returned to the first shelter...........There were five of us and a rat came and clung on to the chap's hand next to me and he slung it off. I had my coat collar up, it was raining and the rat dropped between my coat collar and my neck. I nearly had a fit. It was clawing to get out and its dirty nose rode against my face. It was awful. That is the biggest plague to the British Tommy in the trenches. There are millions of them. It's absolutely snide with them. Great big rats with thick tails.....they are bigger than cats..... We are more afraid of them than the Germans........"*

(G. Whiteman)

Harold Plant's niece lays a wreath at the Thiepval Memorial

But the horrors of war were not to last for Harold Plant. Within 6 months of landing in France he was dead. Shortly after 5 o'clock on the morning of 3rd September, the 39th Division attacked the German front line near Beamont Hamel. Private Plant and the men of 16th Sherwood Foresters were in a reserve role but deployed as carrying parties for the assaulting battalions. Some of the parties had to cross No Man's Land several times. Others were involved in forward supply to the trenches. Enemy fire was heavy. Casualties in the 16th Sherwood Foresters were 18 killed or missing and 82 wounded. Harold Plant was amongst those killed. He has no known grave and is commemorated on the Thiepval Memorial.

There are many stories, as we will see with other young soldiers in this book, of teenagers lying about their age to enlist. In the case of Harold Plant, there is documentary evidence to show that he was serving on the Western

(G. Whiteman)

Harold Plant's birth certificate

Front, with a fighting unit, whilst only 18. In fact, he was still only 18 when he was killed. As we saw earlier, the minimum age for a man to serve with a fighting unit at the front was 19, until the rule was relaxed in 1918. Harold Plant's birth certificate shows that he was born on November 5th, 1897. When he enlisted in early 1915, he was 17. By April, 1916, he was writing letters home from the front line trenches in France. He was then seven months short of his 19th birthday.

(G. Whiteman)

Harold Plant's death certifacte shows, wrongly, his age as 20 when he died.

The second Leek soldier to lose his life on 3rd September was **Private George Goodwin**, aged 29. He was born at 15, Prince Street but later lived at 131, Ball Haye Green. He was serving with the 1st Battalion, Bedfordshire Regiment. There had been heavy fighting for the village of Guillemont and its surrounding enemy-held trenches since July. A small copse outside the village, known to the troops as 'Wedge Wood', was captured by the 1st Bedfords whilst other battalions captured and cleared what was left of Guillemont village. George Goodwin was killed during the assault upon Wedge Wood. He is buried at Guillemont Road Cemetery just outside the village. Close to his grave is that of Lieutenant Raymond Asquith, the son of the then British Prime Minister.

George Goodwin
(I. Bailey)

(E. Ash)

John Hudson in his postman's uniform before the war.

The following day, Monday, 4th September, **Private John James Hudson**, also with the 1st Bedfords, was killed whilst attacking a fortified farm, Falfemont Farm, 700 yards south east of Wedge Wood. The Bedfords, starting from their newly-captured positions, bombed their way along the German trench linking the wood with the farm and captured part of the defensive positions there. John Hudson who was 24 and had a twin sister, Molly, was apparently killed when he was bayoneted by a German whilst fighting his way along the trench. A former postman in Leek, he was married with two children and had lived at 41, Stockwell Street. Private Hudson has no known grave and is commemorated on the Thiepval Memorial. Another Leek man serving with John Hudson in the 1st Bedfords was killed the next day. **Private Richard Wallis** from Pickwood Road was only 19. The troops had captured and occupied Falfemont Farm that day. Private Wallis is also commemorated on the Thiepval Memorial.

On Thursday, 14th September, 1916, a cold wind swept across the shattered battlefields of the Somme. That day, British troops stormed trenches near to Thiepval and captured a feature known as the 'Wonderwork'. Also on that day, **Private Tom Thornton** of the 5th Royal Fusiliers, died of his wounds at the age of 21. Tom lived at 11, Macclesfield Road and had attended West Street School before getting a job as a postman. He is buried at La Neuville British Cemetery at Corbie, behind the front lines.

Friday, 15th September 1916 was to see good progress made by the Allied forces on the Somme during the first day of the Battle of Flers-Courcelette. An advance of between one and two miles on a six mile front was made. The villages of Flers and Martinpuich were captured along with the bitterly-contested High Wood. This was the first day that the British used tanks, dramatically so at Flers when the new metal monsters and troops together captured the village and marched up the main street. Although they were initially unreliable, often breaking down or getting stuck in the mud, tanks were increasingly used throughout the rest of the war. The word 'tank' was originally given to this new machine as a cover-name to keep its development and delivery secret from the enemy. It was generally put about that they were 'water tanks bound for Mesopotamia'. The name, of course, stuck. Not so im-

(Imperial War Museum)

The early version of the tank appeared on the Somme in September 1916

pressed was Lord Kitchener who, on seeing one actually demonstrated in 1916 declared: *"A pretty mechanical toy, but the war will never be won by such machines".*

Killed that day were two Leek soldiers, one a former railway signalman and the other a textile worker. **Guardsman William Booth** was a member of the 2nd Battalion, Grenadier Guards. A father of four, he worked at Cheddleton Railway Station before the war and lived at 4, School Street, off West Street. The Guards left their positions in the village of Ginchy at 7.30 that morning to attack the German trenches south of Flers. They came under fire from an enemy trench known as 'Serpentine Trench' but gaining a foothold in it, bombed their way along, capturing the position. William Booth was killed during this attack. The second soldier, **Private Ernest Kirkham** was 23 and had worked at Brough, Nicholson and Hall. He was known locally as an accomplished violinist and lived at 8, Southbank Street. Private Kirkham's battalion, the 1/4th Northumberland Fusiliers, attacked and captured an enemy trench west of Flers but came under machine gun fire from nearby High Wood. Ordered to attack with grenades in the direction of High Wood, the battalion made some progress but was eventually forced back by shell-fire. Ernest Kirkham was amongst those killed. Both Guardsman Booth and Private Kirkham are commemorated on the Thiepval Memorial.

The following day, 16th September, **Private Reginald Bestwick** was killed during an unsuccessful attack by the 1/5th Durham Light Infan-

(C. Chell)

William Booth, pictured on the front row, second from the right

try on enemy positions known as 'Prue Trench', just to the right of Martinpuich village. Another former pupil of West Street School, Private Bestwick lived at 41 Picton Street and had worked at Premier Dyers on Buxton Road. He is also commemorated on the Thiepval Memorial.

The Memorial Tower to the Sherwood Foresters at Crich, Derbyshire.

The 2nd Battalion, Sherwood Foresters lost many men in the September fighting on the Somme. One young Leek officer, not long out of college, was wounded, probably on the 15th when men of his battalion advanced against uncut wire and machine guns just outside the village of Ginchy. **Lieutenant Frank Johnson Mellor** died of his wounds at a casualty clearing station near Albert on 19th September and was buried at Grove Town Cemetery. He had lived with his parents at 'Braeside', Spencer Avenue, Leek, and was educated at Denstone College, receiving his commission in April, 1915. Lieutenant Mellor, aged only 20, had served at the front for a mere four months before he died. Despite stories of some senior officers being unfamiliar with the conditions which their men had to endure and the dangers they faced, this was rarely the case with the more junior officers like Lieutenant Mellor. They were expected to lead their men into the attack from the front and, as a consequence, suffered a high casualty rate.

The last week of September, 1916, saw another major push on the Somme. This became known as the Battle of Morval and involved Allied attacks on the small German-held villages of Morval, Lesboeufs, Gueudecourt and Combles. The ruins of these once-quiet little places were captured but at great cost. The long fought-over strongpoint, Mouquet Farm, near Thiepval, was also finally captured on the 26th. Three more Leek soldiers fell during this offensive. **Private John Harold Robinson** of the 1st Battalion, The Buffs, (East Kent Regiment) was killed when shrapnel struck him in the head on Monday, 25th September. The Buffs were involved in the assault on the villages of Morval and Lesboeufs and took their objectives. Private Robinson, aged 31 and formerly a stage manager at the Grand

Theatre, Leek, lived with his wife and young child at 39, London Street. He is commemorated on the Thiepval Memorial.

(J. Bratt)

Reuben Crombie

   Private Reuben Crombie, 11th Battalion, Manchester Regiment, was 35 when he was killed in the fighting for Mouquet Farm on 26th September. This part of the Somme Offensive was known as the Battle of Thiepval Ridge. Private Crombie was married, worked at Joshua Wardles, Leekbrook, was a member of the Leek Temperance Band and lived with his wife at 13, Moorhouse Street. He was one of eleven children raised in a small house in New Street. A brother, Arthur, won the Military Medal during the war for saving the life of his officer. The youngest sister, Daisy, only died in June 2002, aged 100. Private Crombie is buried at Regina Trench Cemetery, Grandcourt, a mile outside the village of Courcelette.

   The last Leek victim of the Somme fighting that month was **Private John Giddings** of the 7th Bedfords. He was killed on the afternoon of Thursday, 28th September, in the assault upon an enemy strongpoint near Thiepval, the Schwaben Redoubt. Aged only 21, John Giddings had lived with his parents at 13 Court, 6, St Edward Street. His body was never found and he is commemorated on the Thiepval Memorial.

(G. Whiteman)

Above and left:
Two examples of the postcards sent to Leek by soldiers on the Western Front. Many of these were embroidered, very intricate and beautifully made.

Chapter 18

The Somme - The Autumn of 1916

".....the Army Council have been regretfully constrained to conclude that he is dead......".

(The War Office correspondence familiar to so many bereaved families.)

Sunday, 1st October, 1916, was a fine, sunny day with a pleasant temperature of 63 degrees Fahrenheight. But for **Private Sam Cheshire,** another former pupil at West Street School, it was to be his last. He was killed by a shell whilst the men of his battalion, the 10th Cheshires, were consolidating their positions and preparing to attack another German strongpoint close to Thiepval known as Stuff Redoubt. Private Cheshire was 29 and had lived at 23, North Avenue, working at Westwood Hall Farm before the war. He is buried close to Reuben Crombie in Regina Trench Cemetery, Grandcourt. His brother James died the following year whilst serving with the North Staffords in Mesopotamia. (See Chapter 20). Two days later on Tuesday 3rd October, **Corporal Joseph Arthur Hulme** from 9, Parker Street was killed whilst serving with the Royal

(B. Podmore)

'Sammy' Hulme

Sussex Regiment. He was one of four friends who joined up together and, as the reader will recall, three of them were killed at the Battle of Aubers Ridge. (See Chapter 6). 'Sammy', as he was known, was a well-known footballer and at one time had been the trainer for Leek Alexandra. He is pictured here in the strip of Brighton and Hove Albion in 1907. Corporal Hulme is commemorated on the Thiepval Memorial.

The third of the eight Leek soldiers to die on the Somme in October was **Private**

117

Frederick Rhead of the 9th Battalion, Royal Fusiliers. He was another ex-West Street School pupil and came from 19, Picton Street. On Saturday, 7th October, the Fusiliers advanced against enemy held Bayonet Trench, to the left of the village of Gueudecourt. Despite being machine-gunned before they even started the attack, the troops crossed No Mans Land and entered Bayonet Trench, but were forced out by the Germans. Amongst those killed was Private Rhead. He is commemorated on the Thiepval Memorial. On Monday, 16th October, **Guardsman Harry Smith** of the 4th Grenadier Guards, died of wounds in the 1st Canadian Hospital at the large base camp of Etaples, on the French coast. Harry was 30, had worked in Leek as a joiner and lived at 56, Southbank Street. He is buried at the large military cemetery at Etaples. The next day, Tuesday, 17th October 1916, a young Leek officer attached

to the Royal Flying Corps was killed when his 2-seater Nieuport aeroplane crashed, believed behind enemy lines on the Western Front. **Lieutenant Philip Challinor Ellis** was posted as missing from Number 1 Squadron whilst on a mission. He was the observer on the aeroplane and the pilot, Lieutenant C. C. Godwin, was also killed. Lieutenant Ellis was 23 and lived at Kniveden Hall, now a residential home for the elderly, on Mount Road, Leek. He and his pilot are buried in adjacent graves at Pont-du-Hem Military Cemetery, north of Lens. The day before he was killed, Lieutenant Ellis and his pilot were involved in a skirmish with German aeroplanes over the Front and at least one was seen to lose height out of control. On the day the two young airmen were killed, the squadron had attacked buildings used by the enemy with incendiaries and 20-pound bombs.

(D. Rhead)

Frederick Rhead

(I. Bailey)

Harry Smith

Above - A Nieuport - similar to the one in which Philip Ellis died.
(Author's Collection)

Left - Knivedon Hall, the former home of the Ellis Family
(Author's Collection)

An all too common factor in the Somme fighting was the frequency with which ground gained was lost to the enemy in a counter-attack. Sometimes, the same small stretch of mud would change hands several times and at incredibly high casualty rates. The Schwaben Redoubt, where Private John Giddings was killed in late September, was captured by the British on 14th October but on 21st October, German troops attacked and entered it again. They were driven out after fierce fighting. The 11th Royal Sussex was one of the battalions involved in the fighting in the area on that day and **Private Uriah Alcock** from 25, London Street was one of those killed. Private Alcock was 25 and had worked as a braid tenter at Brough, Nicholson and Hall. His body was never recovered and his is amongst the names on the Thiepval Memorial. A fellow employee at Broughs, **Private John Desborough** serving with the 7th Battalion, Loyal (North Lancs) Regiment, was killed on the 25th and is also commemorated on the Thiepval memorial. It is not known where he lived in Leek but Private Desborough was born in Nottingham. He originally joined the North Staffordshire Regiment, like so many other local men, but was transferred to another regiment later in the war.

Before leaving October, 1916, let us return to Leek where the town was mourning the loss of a brave soldier who died of his wounds in an Essex hospital after being evacuated from France. **Company Sergeant-Major David Pickford** was awarded the Distinguished Conduct Medal for consistent good work and devotion to duty during his war service with the 9th Battalion, Sherwood Foresters. He was wounded on the Somme and died on 23rd

October. David Pickford was 31, married with a young child and lived at 76, Sandon Road (now Cheddleton Road). Before the war he worked at Brough, Nicholson and Hall but, before that, had served for eight years in the regular army. C.S.M. David Pickford is buried in Leek Cemetery, not far from his former home. Two of his brothers-in-law, Private J. Turner (see Chapter 17) and Private W. O'Shaughnessey (Chapter 12) also died in the war.

By November, 1916, the Battle of the Somme was coming to a standstill. Despite all the weapons and manpower the two sides had thrown at one another, neither could beat nature. The weather would draw the battle to a close before the month was through.

(H. Spearing)

Harold Spearing

The first Leek soldier to die on the Somme in November was **Gunner Harold Spearing,** 59th Brigade, Royal Field Artillery. He was 22 and worked at an auctioneers in Stafford before enlisting in the army. Gunner Spearing, who was killed on the 8th, was born in the Market Place where his family ran a corn and cheese merchant's business at the corner of Church Street. His body was never recovered and he is commemorated on the Thiepval Memorial. A week later, on the 16th, a 24 year old soldier in the 6th Bedfords, **Private James Fogg** from 42, Brunswick Street, was walking back from the lines to a dressing station, nursing a wounded arm, when a shell exploded and he was killed. Such were the fortunes of war. Had his luck not run out, young Private Fogg would probably have been sent back to England for a few months for treatment and recuperation. Wounds of that nature were often called 'Blighty wounds' by the troops, (Blighty was their word for England) and, as the fighting dragged on, many disillusioned soldiers prayed for such a wound which would, for a few weeks at least, allow them some respite from the harrowing dangers and conditions at the front. Private Fogg, the son of a coal merchant, had worked for James Heath and Sons, a building firm in Shoobridge Street. He is also commemorated on the Thiepval Memorial. His brother, Thomas and a cousin, also named James, were killed on the Western Front in early 1917.

From early November, 1916, until the fighting ground to a halt through the weather, the mud and the sheer exhaustion of soldiers on all sides, the last attempts to push the line forward were made. During this period the villages of Beaumont Hamel and Beaucourt were captured. This stage was known as the Battle of the Ancre, named after the River Ancre, a tributary of the River Somme. On the 18th and 19th November, when the fighting on the Somme finally ceased, no less than five Leek soldiers were killed, four of them from the same battalion.

Saturday, 18th November saw the first snow of the year. By the time the final attack of the Somme campaign by British troops got under way at ten past six in the morning, the snow had turned first to sleet and then to rain. The 2nd Battalion, Kings Own Yorkshire Light Infantry, had the task, with other battalions of the 32nd Division, of attempting to take German trenches between the villages of Beaumont Hamel and Serre. Resistance was fierce and some of the Yorkshiremen were left fighting in No Mans Land until dusk fell. One of those killed was **Private Rowland Sigley** from 70, Portland Street. His body was never found and he is also commemorated on the Thiepval Memorial. Surviving letters from Roland Sigley's mother to the authorities clearly show the terrible anguish so many families suffered when a son was lost in this way and, because there was no recorded grave, posted merely as "Missing". Despite numerous letters to and from the Red Cross (this organisation helped trace missing servicemen) and the War Office, most of which said

(M. Sigley)

Roland Sigley

"....no further information on this soldier......", it was not until 29th December, 1917, over 12 months later, that the War Office finally wrote: *".........the Army Council have been regretfully constrained to conclude that he is dead.........."*.

But the Battle of the Somme did not end for the town of Leek with the death of Private Sigley. Four more local soldiers, all from the same battalion, lay dead that day amongst the last victims of a four and a half month struggle which claimed the lives of some 125,000 British and Commonwealth servicemen and wounded another 294,000. These dreadful figures are the main reason why the Somme is remembered along with Ypres, Passchendaele and Gallipoli as the killing grounds of a generation.

The 8th Battalion, North Staffordshire Regiment, was raised in 1915 as part of the 'New Army' and first went into the line near Loos, August, 1915, attached to the 19th (Western) Division. In the ten months before the Somme offensive opened, it had lost nearly 140 men killed and wounded. During the month of July, 1916, the battalion was heavily involved in the fighting on the Somme and sustained well over 400 casualties, around half its fighting strength. Some of the casualties were due to sickness caused by the bad weather conditions.

The low-lying country in the Ancre valley was now a muddy morass and the trenches were virtually waterways. One General later described the conditions as the worst he could remember in the war. Now, on 18th November, there was to be a last-ditch attempt by the British to seize more of the enemy positions. The task of the Staffordshire men was to capture the trenches overlooking a depression known as Battery Valley, clear them and link up with other units involved in the assault. The ground over which the troops were to advance had hardened with frost over the past two days and this would make conditions better for the troops. Unfortunately, however, a thaw set in on the morning of the 18th November turning the ground back into a quagmire and a snow blizzard made it impossible to see for more than a few yards. To make matters worse, the Staffords, due to alterations in planning at higher level, would have to attack over ground they had never seen or had the chance to reconnoitre.

Nevertheless, in these impossible conditions, the attack went ahead and at 6am, the soldiers went over the top towards their objectives. The 8th North Staffords fought their way into the German trench system and pressed on for a considerable distance. Unable to see

properly in the dark and driving snow, the men passed over the first trench without apparently realising it, reached the second line but then became cut off. Behind them, enemy troops rose from their dug-outs and opened fire. Many of the Staffords were killed or captured and less than a quarter of them managed to escape in small parties. These were seen making their way back along Battery Valley to the British lines later in the day. The four Leek men amongst the dead of the 8th North Staffords were **Lieutenant Hubert Llewelyn Gwynne, Private Sampson Hollinshead, Private John Atkinson** and **Regimental Sergeant-Major Arthur Wilson.**

Lieutenant Gwynne was 24, a Cambridge graduate and the son of Clement Gwynne, a solicitor at Challinors and Shaw in Derby Street. The family lived at 100

(R. Wilson)
Arthur Wilson - highly respected N.C.O.

Westwood Road. Private Hollinshead was married and lived at No: 21 Court, 5, Derby Street. Unfortunately, nothing is known about Private Atkinson but the opposite is true of R.S.M. Wilson who has a grandson living in Northamptonshire and descendants living in Leek and Yorkshire. His case is interesting as he is the only Regimental Sergeant-Major from Leek to be killed in action and, being twice the age of the young 18 and 19 year olds under his command, he had already seen action in the Boer War.

Arthur Wilson was born in Ball Lane, Leek, in 1878 and his family later moved to 26, Duke Street. At the age of 21 he married a local girl, Clara Fisher, who lived at 4, Mill Street. The couple made their home further down the street at number 77. Between the wars, Arthur transferred to the Army Reserve, moved home to 33, Manor Road, Uttoxeter, and became a rural postman in that area. He was also the proud father of three children. When the clouds of war gathered again in 1914, he re-joined the North Staffordshire Regiment and was posted as R.S.M. to the newly-formed 8th

(R. Wilson)

Clara Wilson and her children, the youngest boy holds a picture of his father.

(R. Wilson)

Arthur Wilson's grave at Connaught Cemetery.

Battalion. His rank made him the most senior non-commissioned officer in the battalion. His age and experience was respected by all, and in particular by the junior officers who would rely on him for guidance and advice on many matters. Two points of interest highlight the humanity of Sergeant-Major Wilson and the responsibility he felt for those under his command. The Battalion history, written shortly after the war, records an incident when enemy shells fell on the battalion headquarters. *"Great damage was done to the farm buildings, several dug-outs were destroyed, including the C.O's, and there were many casualties. R.S.M. Wilson distinguished himself by the way in which he tended the wounded, for during the whole time the shelling was in progress he remained in the open with them, showing absolute disregard of the danger of his position".* The second incident concerned a would-be deserter from the 8th Battalion who left his position in the trenches. He was found by Arthur Wilson, given another rifle, a suitable admonishment and promptly returned to his post. Had he been reported, the soldier would have been court-martialled and could have been added to the list of 300 or more British soldiers who were shot at dawn for cowardice or desertion. (The story was related after the war by the deserter himself, a resident of Uttoxeter, to Arthur Wilson's son who also lived in that town). The National Memorial Arboretum at Alrewas, near Lichfield, contains an impressive 'Shot At Dawn' memorial to these soldiers and is well worth a visit.

It is believed that Regimental Sergeant-Major Arthur Wilson died after being shot in the jaw during the attack on the German trench system.

Lieutenant Gwynne and Private Hollinshead were never found and they are commemorated on the Thiepval Memorial. The remains of R.S.M. Wilson and Private Atkinson were recovered, possibly from their initial graves at Grandecourt, and buried at Connaught Cemetery, Thiepval, not far from the Thiepval Memorial. Also buried there is Lieutenant G.B. Bolton, the son of Thomas Bolton (of Froghall Copperworks fame), who was killed in the same attack.

The day after the four Leek men were killed, the Battle of the Somme was finally called to a halt. Snow from the previous day had thawed and the entire battlefield was a vast swamp. The energies of the men on both sides would now have to be directed towards surviving the elements until battle could be resumed afresh in 1917. A depth of about seven miles had been achieved by the Allies. Kitchener's New Army had more than proved its worth in battle, but at a terrible cost.

Before 1916 was through, three more Leek soldiers died, two from natural causes. **Sergeant Colin Cormack Robinson,** a father of three from Nab Hill , Leek, died from pneumonia in hospital in Perth, Scotland, on 2nd December. He was 46 and serving with the Black Watch. Sergeant Robinson was employed at Challinor and Shaw's, solicitors, before joining the army as a regular soldier. After some 12 years service, he trained as a solicitor himself and appeared on numerous occasions in Leek Police Court. At the outbreak of war in 1914, he re-joined the army and was involved in recruiting. Over in Ireland, **Sergeant Peter Walwyn** of the Royal Army Veterinary Corps died on 6th December in the Currah Military Hospital from appendicitis. He was married with a child and came from Fountain Street. Both sergeants are buried in the cemeteries attached to the hospitals where they died.

The last Leek soldier to die in 1916 was **Private Samuel Yates** from 50, Gladstone Street. Serving with the 1st Battalion, Rifle Brigade, in the Ypres salient, he was buried up to the neck by a shell-burst which killed five others. A second shell-burst inflicted more damage and when he was extricated, Private Yates was found to have multiple shrapnel wounds and had lost a leg. He was evacuated back to England for hospital treatment which lasted for some considerable time. Medical science was not as it is today and, of course, there were no antibiotics to counteract infection. In December, the young soldier's condition deteriorated and he died on the 23rd. He was only 19. Private Yates is buried in Leek Cemetery.

(J. Crosby)

Norman Green

We left Iraq in April/May 1916 at the time of the siege of Kut when three Leek soldiers of the 7th North Staffords died. Many Leek lads were in that battalion and five more lost their lives in further fighting around Kut during January and February, 1917. The first was **Corporal Thomas Wrench** from 141, Mill Street. He was killed on Friday 12th January when the battalion advanced several hundred yards into Turkish positions. There was a bright moon and the Staffords were spotted and shelled. 21 men were killed and many more wounded. Corporal Wrench was one of the dead. He was 20, had worked for Goodwin and Tattons and was a drummer in the All Saints Church Lads Brigade Band. His grave is at Amara War Cemetery, Iraq.

On 25th January, a cold, bright, sunny day, the battalion took part in a major assault against the Turkish positions capturing the first line using bayonets. The Turks replied with machine gun fire from well-concealed positions and then counter-attacked, almost re-taking their trench. The Staffords and other units charged the Turks and re-established the line but casualties were heavy. One of the five officers who were killed that day was **Lieutenant Norman Green** from Number 1, High Street, Leek. He was 24, a keen hockey player and the brother of Lieutenant Charles Ernest Green who, as we saw earlier, was killed on the Somme in July, 1916. (See Chapter 16). Norman Green had enlisted as a private soldier in another regiment on the outbreak of war but was commissioned in late 1915. He too is buried at Amara War Cemetery.

Buried at Amara close to Corporal Wrench and Lieutenant Green is **Private Arthur Noble.** He died of wounds, believed sustained in the attack described above, on Saturday, 27th January. It is thought that he was bayoneted in the back. Arthur Noble lived at 55, London Street and was at one time a silk dyer at Joshua Wardles, Leekbrook, but he was perhaps best remembered by his generation as a post driver before the war. This involved delivering mail from Leek to Stoke each morning, via Ladderedge, using horse and cart

(M. Sheldon)
Arthur Noble - bayoneted

transport. Private Noble is one of the few people recorded in this book who still has a living relative who can remember him. His niece, Mrs Marjorie Sheldon, now 93, remembers: *"I remember seeing Uncle Arthur in his uniform when I was a little girl. He was a fine, handsome man with jet-black curly hair. I used to help him polish his buttons and he even showed me how to clean his boots - with spit and polish! After he had been home on leave I remember waving him off from the top of Duke Street. I never saw him again".*

On 22nd February, 1917, General Sir Frederick Maude, commander of the British forces in Mesopotamia, pushing northward towards Baghdad, launched another major offensive on the Turks at Kut. After fierce fighting, the Turkish forces withdrew and by the 25th February, Kut was once again in British hands. But, that very day, two more Leek soldiers of the 7th North Staffords died, one killed in action and the other from disease. **Private Thomas Edward Lowe** was 24 when he was killed. The battalion had attacked the retreating Turks over flat, open desert, capturing the enemy trenches 'at the point of the bayonet'. A counter-attack followed and fierce hand-to-hand fighting took place. The Staffords were also shot at by machine-gunners. Despite all this, hundreds of Turks were captured and the rest driven off. As usual though, the cost was heavy.

(J. Glancey)
Tom Lowe (far right) and his family pose for the photograph outside their house in North Avenue.

Some 200 Staffordshire men were killed, wounded or missing. The dead, including Private Lowe, were buried at dawn the next morning but, most, and probably all, of the graves were subsequently lost.

Tom Lowe had lived at 19, North Avenue with his aunt and sisters. Raised at 144, Mill Street, he was a silk dyer at Hammersleys mill before enlisting in August, 1914 and had been an enthusiastic member of the Leek Athletic Football Team. Years later, his nephew, Tom Lucas, a seaman in the Royal Navy, was lost at sea during the Second World War when his ship was torpedoed by a U-boat. Private Lowe has no known grave and is commemorated on the Basra Memorial in Iraq.

Private William Fowler died on 25th February from malaria, aged 27. His grave was subsequently lost and he is also commemorated on the Basra Memorial. He lived in New Street at one time but after the war, his wife and three young children lived at 23 Waterloo Street. He was the fifteenth Leek soldier of the 7th North Staffords to die.

The Foxlowe in the Market Place was used as a convalescent home for soldiers during the war. These patients are dressed up for the 'Foxlowe Follies', a concert event at the home.

Chapter 19

1917. Renewed Hope, Renewed Slaughter

" ....he has died a gallant death in the performance of his duty."

(Lieutenant Colonel H.Child, Royal Field Artillery, in a letter to the mother of
Bombardier Harry Crabtree of the Leek Battery, killed in action 10th January, 1917.)

The New Year saw a change at the top of the Allied leadership on the Western Front.
The French commander-in-chief, General Joffre, was replaced by General Robert Nivelle.
General Haig remained as the British commander-in-chief but was under pressure to succeed
from the new Prime Minister, Lloyd George. The year was also dominated by the outbreak
of the Russian Revolution which allowed the release of German troops for service on other
fronts and by the entry of the United States into the war. The British offensives planned for
1917 were at Arras and Vimy Ridge, Ypres and, later, at
Cambrai. Meanwhile, the new French commander planned
a major offensive in the Champagne region in April. Despite Nivelle's promises that he held the formula for success, the offensive was another failure and, fed up with the
slaughter, thousands of French soldiers mutinied. Amazingly, the Germans never learned of this and the mutiny
was settled by shooting some of the ringleaders, imprison-
ing others, improving conditions and replacing General
Nivelle.

For the town of Leek, 1916 had been terrible enough
with over 80 servicemen lost. But 1917 would be even worse.
Perhaps the only really good news in the town during the
chilly weeks of January was the fact that Mr Charles Smith,
from Getcliffes Yard, celebrated his 100th birthday on the
18th!

The first Leek serviceman to be killed in 1917 was
Sapper James Fogg from 13, Portland Street. He was a
married man of 39, serving with the Royal Engineers in

(Author's Collection)
James Fogg

(Commonwealth War Graves Commission)
Bienvillers Military Cemetery. The resting place of Harold Bailey and Harry Crabtree
of the Leek Battery.

France and was the cook for his field unit. James was seriously wounded by a shell-burst whilst cooking a meal for his section on Friday, 5th January and died shortly afterwards. He is buried at Warlincourt Halte British Cemetery, 16 miles from Arras.

On Wednesday, 10th January, the Leek Battery suffered another misfortune when two of its men were killed. **Corporal Harold Bailey M.M.** and **Bombadier Harry Crabtree**, both signallers, were out near the village of Pommiers (4 miles north-west of Gommecourt), repairing field telephone wires when German shelling began. Both men failed to return and were reported missing. Their bodies were later recovered and buried at Bienvillers Military Cemetery, some two miles from where they were killed. Corporal Bailey, earlier awarded the Military Medal for his bravery, was 23 and had lived at Harpers Gate, Rudyard. Before the war he had worked at Wardle and Davenports. He was due to come home to Leek on leave just before he was killed. Harry's brother, Isaac, was killed in action three months later. Bombardier Crabtree was a married man from 63, Grosvenor Street. His wife received a letter from the Commanding Officer of the battery a few days later. *"......your husband has rendered excellent service to his battery and has always performed his duties in a gallant and fearless manner. His loss will be much felt......."*

Despite the fact that no major offensives were undertaken on the Western Front during the winter months, the casualties continued to mount on all sides, usually from shelling, sniping and night patrols. **Private Harry Edge**, 26, from 82, Buxton Road, was killed on 19th January 1917 whilst serving with the 27th Battalion, Northumberland Fusiliers. He was a left-hand batsman with Leek Cricket Club and worked at Brough, Nicholson and Hall. The battalion diary for 16th to 19th January indicates how 'normal' it had become for men in the front line to get killed or wounded: *"During this tour, enemy were fairly quiet except for occasional 'minnenwerfer' (shell) activity. Casualties sustained were 2 O.R. (other ranks) killed and 1 O.R. wounded".* Private Edge is buried at Ration Farm Military Cemetery, near Armentieres.

The end of the month saw another military funeral at Leek with the death of 43 year old **Sapper George William Heath** from Spencer Avenue. He was wounded whilst serving with the Royal Engineers on the Western Front, evacuated to England and died on 27th January. He left a wife and one child. Sapper Heath is buried in Leek Cemetery. Also buried at Leek is **Private Edward Chappells** of the 16th Sherwood Foresters. He was 21 and lived at 14, Langford Street. He was invalided home ill from the Western Front and treated in hospital but died at home on 3rd February after being discharged.

(Author's Collection)
Edward Chappells

Three days later on 6th February, **Private Ernest Richardson** of the 22nd Royal Fusiliers died from illness in France. He was a married man of 34, living at 6, North Avenue, Leek and had worked as a gardener for one of the local silk manufacturers. Private Richardson is buried at Bouzincourt Communal Cemetery, France.

On 11th February, **Private John William Mayers** of the 10th Battalion, Worcestershire Regiment, became the next casualty of the Western Front. He was 22, came from 21, Ball Haye Green, and is buried at Queens Cemetery, Puisieux, 12 miles north of Albert on the Somme. A week later, **Private Thomas Fogg**, the older brother of James Fogg who was killed in November, 1916 (see Chapter 18), became the next victim whilst serving with the 7th Battalion, South Lancs Regiment. He was wounded in the leg by gunshot and taken to a casualty clearing station where he died on 18th February. Thomas Fogg was 33, lived at 42 Brunswick Street and had worked as a silk weaver at Brough, Nicholson and Hall. He is buried at Puchevillers British Cemetery, some 13 miles west of Albert.

(M. Bowyer)
Thomas Fogg - died of gunshot wounds

February, 1917, also saw the death of a Leek-born man who had already received a Good Conduct Medal in recognition of 18 years service. **Colour Sergeant Albert Ernest Edge** was 44 and serving with the Royal Marine Light Infantry in command of an anti-aircraft unit at a naval base in Hampshire. He fell ill in December, 1916 and was taken to hospital. He was later transferred to a naval hospital near Great Yarmouth but died there on 12th February and was buried at nearby Caister-on-Sea. Colour Sergeant Edge was a former employee of Brough, Nicholson and Hall but had left the town to take up his career in the armed forces. Although his wife was living in Birmingham, his brother lived at 47 Fountain Street, Leek, and his parents still lived in the town.

(R. Duffett)

Albert Edge

By March 1917, the Allies were busy preparing for the new offensives around Arras and on the Aisne. Germany had begun unrestricted submarine warfare on the high seas and the United States of America were about to declare war. The Germans had pulled back from much of the old front lines on the Somme to the heavily-fortified Hindenburg Line. It was on Wednesday the 14th that two Leek soldiers of the 1/5th North Staffords were killed. The battalion was then in the region of Gommecourt on the Somme where it had suffered so badly on the 1st July. **Private Jack Travis** from 141, Compton was wounded in the head during an attack on German positions and died shortly afterwards. He is buried at Rossignol Wood Cemetery, Hebuterne. This is a pretty little cemetery containing less than 50 British graves. **Private Joseph Brookes** from 63, London Street was slightly wounded during the same action but carried on to the German wire where he was killed by a shellburst. He has no known grave and is commemorated on the Thiepval Memorial. Private Brookes was 29 and worked at Joshua Wardles, Leekbrook. A week later, on Thursday, 22nd March, **Gunner George Thomas Hill** of the Royal Garrison Artillery was

(Author's Collection)
The preserved trenches on Vimy Ridge.

killed. He was 26 and lived at 53 Wellington Street. Gunner Hill is buried at Habarcq Communal Cemetery Extension. Habarcq is a small village a few miles west of Arras.

The first major British offensive of 1917 commenced at dawn on Monday, 9th April in the Arras Sector of the Western Front. After a five-day bombardment, fourteen British Divisions attacked either side of Arras and the River Scarpe and the Canadians assaulted Vimy Ridge. Fighting continued until May and, although there were some successes, there was no strategic gain. The most notable success was the capture of Vimy Ridge by the Canadians on the first day of the offensive. The ridge rises over 60 metres and it then protected an area of German-held territory in which coal mines and factories were in full production for the German war effort. Previous attempts by the French to take the ridge had ended in disaster but a combination of meticulous planning, training and sheer bravery won the day. As always, there was a price to pay. Canadian losses at Vimy Ridge alone were over 10,000 including nearly 3,600 dead. One of these was **Private James Robinson** who originated from Prospect Cottage, Ashbourne Road, Leek. He had emigrated to Canada six years earlier to start a new life as a farmer. There, he enlisted in the 10th Battalion, Alberta Regiment, Canadian Infantry in 1916 and was 27 when he was killed. His body was lost and he is commemorated with 11,000 other Canadian soldiers who fell on the Western Front and who have no known grave.

Vimy Ridge Memorial
(B. Podmore)

The Canadian Memorial on Vimy Ridge is now a major tourist attraction, as are the preserved tunnels beneath the ridge and the trenches around the summit.

The next Leek soldier to die in the Arras offensive was also killed on the first day, 9th April. **Private William Ernest Oakes** was 29 and had been the chauffeur to Doctor J.C. McClew in Leek. He also owned a cycle and motor trade business in Buxton Road. He was serving with the 21st (Tyneside Scottish) Battalion, Northumberland Fusiliers. His body was never found and he is commemorated on the Arras Memorial.

Three days into the Battle of Arras, another Leek soldier fell. **Bombardier Harry Shute** was killed on Thursday, 12th April whilst serving with the Royal Field Artillery. He was 27, lived at 37 Grosvenor Street, and had worked as a lithographer for Brough Nicholson and Hall. He is buried at Nine Elms Military Cemetery, between Arras and Lens. On the same day, **Private James Henry Harry Street** of the 1st North Staffords died in England, believed from illness. He was married, aged 25, and lived at 117, Belle View. Private Street was buried at Chipping Barnett Churchyard in Hertfordshire.

We saw in Chapter 19 where Corporal Harry Bailey M.M. of the Leek Battery was killed in France. Three months later, on Sunday, 15th April, 1917, his older brother, **Private Isaac Bailey** was killed in the Arras Sector. He was 30, had worked as a gardener at Horton Lodge and was serving with the 4th Battalion, Bedfordshire Regiment. The family home was at Harpers

(Author's Collection)

Harpers Gate, Rudyard

Gate, Rudyard. Isaac Bailey is among the the 21 men commemorated on the Arras Memorial.

In mid-April, 1917, whilst the Battle of Arras was raging in France, British and Empire forces were locked in battle against the Turks in Palestine. On 19th April, the British attempted a frontal assault on Gaza but the advance became bogged down in complex Turkish defence systems. By nightfall, only a few small gains had been made at a cost of over 6,000 British casualties. One of those killed was 22 year old **Private Harry Birch** of 3, Portland Street, Leek. He was serving with the 1/4th Norfolk Regiment and is now buried at Gaza War Cemetery, Israel. It was around this time that the famous 'Lawrence of Arabia' was leading Arab tribesmen in 'hit and run' attacks against the Turks. Turkey had ruled over the Arab tribes in the Middle East for centuries and Lawrence, a British Army officer, won the trust of the Arabs and used their hatred of the Turks to organise them into an efficient fighting force on the British side.

Harry Birch's older brother, Edgar, was also killed fighting the Turks in the Middle East, towards the end of the war. (See Chapter 29).

Back in France and Flanders, the casualties continued. On 22nd April, **Private Harry Hulme** of the 11th Battalion, Royal Sussex Regiment was killed in the Ypres salient by an exploding shell whilst returning from duty at the front line. He lived at 148, Mill Street and worked at Brough, Nicholson and Hall. Only 19 when he died, Harry Hulme was buried at Vlamertinghe Military Cemetery, Ypres. His great-nephew is a serving soldier, a corporal, with the Queen's Royal Lancers.

(Author)

3 year old Harriet Webb, the great-great niece of Private Harry Hulme, killed in action in 1917, gazes at the wreaths on the monument, Remembrance Sunday 2001, and wonders why.

Further south in the Arras sector, **Private Arthur Smith** of 53, Park Road was killed on 23rd April. He was in the 1/5th Durham Light Infantry and had worked at Wardle and Davenports. Aged 26, Private Smith was never found after the war and he is commemorated on the Arras Memorial to the Missing. The next day, again in the Ypres salient, **Private Horace Mycock**, 27, of the 32nd Battalion, Royal Fusiliers, was killed. He had lived at Tittesworth Cottage and worked on the Haregate Estate. Private Mycock had been wounded in 1916 and treated at a Glasgow hospital before returning to the front. He is buried at Dickebusch New Military Cemetery, just outside Ypres.

May, 1917, was another bad month for the town of Leek with at least ten local soldiers losing their lives. Worse still, this monthly average, not seen since the fighting on the Somme the previous summer and autumn, was to continue for the next six months at least. There was continuous heavy fighting for two weeks around the village of Bullecourt, south-east of Arras, from the 3rd May. Bullecourt formed part of the Hindenburg Line, heavily fortified defensive positions to which the Germans had withdrawn in February, 1917. On that day, a Friday, two more Leek men were killed. **Private Harry Simpson**, 2/6th Battalion, West Yorkshire Regiment, was 24 and failed to return from an attack on enemy positions. He lived at 43, Shoobridge Street and ran a joinery business in Ashbourne Road. His brother, Sidney, was mortally wounded in 1918 and is buried in Leek Cemetery. (See Chapter 28). Harry's body was never found and he is commemorated on the Arras Memorial to the Missing.

(B. Simpson)

Harry Simpson

The second Leek soldier to die that day was **Private Frederick Astles**, a married man of 8, Westwood Grove. He was 35 and had worked in the Leek mills as a braid tenter and was serving with the 1st Battalion, Northumberland Fusiliers when he was killed. He is also commemorated on the Arras Memorial. This memorial, sited in the western part of the town of Arras, lists the names of nearly 35,000 servicemen from Britain, South Africa and New Zealand who died in the Arras sector between 1916 and 1918 and who have no known grave.

On 9th May, whilst the fighting on the Hindenburg Line around Bullecourt was still causing heavy casualties, two more Leek men were lost. **Private John Thomas Wardle** of the 2/6th North Staffords died of wounds after being shot in the arm and chest. He was 28 and lived with his wife and their two young children at 7, Ball Lane. A former employee of Wardle and Davenports, Private Wardle is buried at Hargicourt British Cemetery a few miles south of Cambrai. His son, George, now 91 and living in Manchester, remembers his father. *"When I was a little boy I remember my dad making me a wooden wheelbarrow for Christmas and I was thrilled with it. Later on, he was called up for the army and I went with my mother and sister to wave him off. He was in a queue of men which stretched all the way down Broad Street to the railway station. They were all conscripts and were boarding a train for their first training depot. I never saw my dad again, he was killed only ten weeks after being drafted to France. My mother was told that he was shot by a sniper in the trenches when he stood up to recover a rifle carelessly left*

(G. Wardle)

Workers at Wardle and Davenports.
John Wardle is on the back row 3rd from the left.

there by a sentry. That's how my dad was. He would help anybody, but it cost him his life. When they sent his effects back home, they also sent his shoulder badge which was broken in half by the bullet which killed him."

The damaged shoulder badge

Private Herbert Stannard, serving with the 44th Battalion, Manitoba Regiment of the Canadian Infantry also died that day. His parents lived at Roche View, Ashbourne Road, Leek, but Private Stannard, reported to be 45, had emigrated to Canada eleven years before the war. He is commemorated on the Canadian Memorial which stands on Vimy Ridge.

The next day, Thursday, 10th May, another former pupil of West Street School was killed in the Battle of Arras. **Private Edward Hartley Clowes**, 27, of the 4th Battalion, Royal Fusiliers, was married and worked in the counting house at Brough, Nicholson and Hall. He was raised at 20, Shirburn Road and had two brothers serving in the army. Private Clowes is commemorated on the Arras Memorial. On the same day, **Private William Bowyer**, aged 57, of 38, Ashbourne Road, died whilst serving in the United Kingdom with the Royal Defence Corps. He is buried in Leek Cemetery.

On Saturday, 12th May 1917, **Private Frank Pickford**, 25, of the 1st Battalion, East Lancashire Regiment, was the next Leek soldier to die in the Arras sector. He worked at Portland Street Mill and was married. His widow was living in Cheadle after the war. Private Pickford is also commemorated on the Arras Memorial. On the same day, but a few miles south of Arras in the Somme sector which had seen so much bloodshed the previous year, **Private Francis Moorcroft** from Cruso Street, was killed. He was shot through the chest whilst repairing barbed wire defences. Apparently, the same bullet also hit and killed the soldier next to him. Private Moorcroft, aged 35 and a former clerk with the Prudential, was serving with the 15th Battalion, Sherwood Foresters. His grave was subsequently lost and he is commemorated on the Thiepval Memorial.

Gunner William Harrod of 24, Chorley Street was the next Leek victim of the fighting around Arras. Serving with a heavy trench mortar battery of the Royal Field Artillery, he was 20 and had worked for Fallons, the fruit and vegetable merchants. Gunner Harrod died of wounds on 18th May 1917 and is buried at Duisans British Cemetery, six miles west of Arras. The following day, **Private Frederick William Keates** of the 1st Battalion, Royal Inniskilling Fusiliers, was killed. No further details are known of him and he is commemorated on the Arras Memorial.

The first of ten Leek servicemen to die on the Western Front in June, 1917, was **Lieutenant Charles Challinor Watson**, the son of a magistrate from Wood View, Leek. His family owned Watson's mill in Leek. Previously 'Mentioned in Dispatches' for good work, Lieutenant Watson was 28, married, and educated at Rugby and Cambridge. He was seriously wounded in the right side whilst serving with the Royal Field Artillery and died on Friday, 1st June. He is buried at Fosse No:10 Communal Cemetery Extension, Sains-en-Gohelle, a mining village near Lens.

Buried in the same cemetery is **Sergeant George Bestwick** of the Leek Battery. He was killed a week after Lieutenant Watson on Friday, 8th June, along with two of his men when their gun received a direct hit whilst the Battery was deployed in the Lens area. Sgt Bestwick was 35, a former member of Leek Cycling Club, lived at 47 Leonard Street and had worked before the war as a general smith at a workshop in the Market Place. He had only been married for two or three weeks when he was killed. His widow, Edith, lived at 16, Alsop Street after the war. She never remarried. In 1920, Mrs Bestwick made the trip from Leek to France to visit her husband's grave, quite a feat in those days. She went again in 1922. Her passport, stamped with the embarkation details at the time, still survives. Sergeant Bestwick was the great-great-uncle of Mrs Linda Brown, the present Clerk to the Leek Town Council.

(J. E. Blore)

George Bestwick

On the same day, 8th June, **Private Alfred Barnett**, 41, of the 11th Battalion, Suffolk Regiment, was killed in the Arras sector. He was married with five children, lived at 1, Nab Hill Cottages and worked for the Johnson family at Westwood Hall. He is commemorated on the Arras Memorial. Another casualty of that day was **Private William Constantine** of the 1/6th North Staffords. He died of wounds whilst a prisoner of war and is buried in a cemetery at Tournai, Belgium, some miles east of Lille. Private Constantine was 25, a silk weaver by trade, and lived with his sister at 25, Ball Haye Green. His family had already gone through the pain of believing him to have been killed when he was first reported missing in action. This was followed by the relief that he was a prisoner of the Germans but, sadly, that was only to be short-lived.

Chapter 20

Messines Ridge and the Battle of Lens

"No man who took part in the First World War ever completely shook off the experience. Individuals struggled to come to terms with what they had seen and heard. For some, the only solution was silence"

(Professor Keith Robbins, author of "The First World War", 1984.)

For some time, Douglas Haig had been determined to attack the Germans in Flanders, and, once again, the salient in front of the beleaguered town of Ypres would become the scene of bloody and costly fighting. The failure of the French offensives further south, and the mutiny of part of its army, meant that the French were unable to mount further offensives for the time being. This left Haig free to pursue his long-cherished aims. German submarines had been sinking an alarming number of British ships in 1917 and he wanted to capture the ports of Ostend and Zeebrugge which were bases for U-boats. He also believed that the Germans were badly weakened from earlier battles. Haig therefore planned to mount a series of offensives to force the enemy from the ridges around the Ypres salient, clear the Belgian coast and batter the Germans into submission.

On the Home Front in Britain, conditions were bad. Many civilians were suffering from hunger and malnutrition, particularly the poor. The numbers of farmworkers, and consequently production of food, had declined as the war dragged on, consuming men and horses normally employed in feeding the nation. The U-boats were doing their best to starve Britain into submission, sinking 371 merchant ships in one month during early 1917. With the nation relying on two-thirds of its food from overseas, the future looked very bleak. Many women were now working in munitions factories to feed the insatiable demand for shells at the Front. Around one thousand

(Imperial War Museum)
Many women worked in the munitions factories

died, mainly in explosions, performing this dangerous work. Although it seemed that Britain was a nation united, illegal strikes and social unrest threatened to bring the British war economy to a standstill. Amongst all this, the Government propaganda machine urged the nation on to strive for victory. What was not so well publicised were the results of a survey showing that some one in eight war widows, grief-stricken and weakened by hunger and deprivation, died within twelve months of losing their husbands.

A few miles south of Ypres is the Messines Ridge. From early in the war the ridge had been held by the Germans who enjoyed commanding views over the British trenches. British troops experienced in mining had dug some 20 tunnels under enemy positions on the ridge and packed them with explosives. At ten past three on the morning of Thursday, 7th June, 1917, these were blown up under the feet of the Germans killing around 10,000 of them. The effect was shattering and the noise so loud that it was heard in London. British and Empire troops rushed the ridge and had captured it by noon. Despite the success of the attack and the speed with which it was pursued, there were still some 17,000 British casualties. The inevitable German counter-attacks failed to recover the lost ground and the British were in full control of the Messines Ridge by 14th June. (Two mines failed to explode. One eventually did so during a thunderstorm in 1955, killing a few cattle, but the location of the second one remains unknown).

One soldier who died on the Messines front was 30 year old **Lance Corporal Fred Higginbotham** from 19, Fountain Street, Leek. He was serving with the 8th Northumberland Fusiliers and died on 19th June. The battalion had been in the line for eight days and, as the fighting there had by then died down, it is interesting to pause and look at the activities and casualty rates of soldiers on front-line duties in that area. The battalion history shows that most of the time was spent in consolidating, repairing and improving trench positions and barbed wire defences. Two small-scale attacks were made on enemy positions and night patrols were sent out. The Germans constantly bombarded the Fusiliers' trenches. During the eight-day period a total of 129 men from the battalion became casualties. This included one officer killed and five wounded, eleven other ranks killed and one hundred and twelve wounded. And this was a relatively quiet period! Lance Corporal Higginbotham was married and worked before the war for a firm of solicitors in Derby Street. His body was lost and he is commemorated on the Menin Gate Memorial at Ypres.

Private Harvey Shaw was the next Leek casualty of the Ypres salient. He came from Cornhill Street, worked at Wardle and Davenports and was serving with the 16th Battalion, Royal Welsh Fusiliers, when he was killed on Friday, 22nd June. He is buried at Bard Cottage Cemetery, Boezinge, near Ypres. Two days before his death, a former Leek choirmaster serving with the Royal Garrison Artillery was killed by shrapnel. **Corporal James Ernest Lillie-Mitchell** who owned a music shop in Derby Street is buried at the Cite Bonjeau Military Cemetery at Armentieres, a French town on the Belgian border. Aged 34 and married, Corporal Lillie-Mitchell had been a member of the Leek Amateur Dramatic Operatic Society, a scoutmaster with the Wesleyan Boy Scouts and a keen player at Abbey View Tennis Club.

The town of Lens in Northern France stands in a triangle between Bethune, Arras and Douai. Like nearby Loos, it is an industrialised area and in 1917, was home to pitheads and slagheaps with dull, terraced houses crowded together in narrow streets. The German front line in this sector ran through the streets and houses making it hard to attack and relatively easy to defend. Nevertheless, British intelligence sources had it that the German troops defending Lens were demoralised and some small successes by British forces, including the Staffordshire Division (46th North Midland) gave rise to the possibility of capturing the town. Plans were made for an assault by three brigades of infantry to take place on 1st July, 1917. Before that took place, however, several Leek men were killed in advances on the town.

On Thursday, 14th June, 'A' and 'C' Companies of the 1/5th North Staffords comprising 8 officers and 160 men raided enemy positions in Lens. One party was repulsed at the wire but a second wave, led by Captain Charles Masefield from Cheadle, got into the trenches, cleared dug-outs of Germans and were involved in some heavy fighting. When they withdrew from the raid, 50 Germans lay dead but the Staffords had lost some 16 dead and 37 wounded. One of those who died was **Private Joseph Ellis Warbrick,** aged 27, from 35, Nelson Street, Leek, an employee of Brough, Nicholson and Hall. He is recorded as dying on 15th June and is buried at Noeux-le-Mines Communal Cemetery, a few miles north-west of Lens. As this cemetery was used at the time by a casualty clearing station, it is likely that Private Warbrick died of wounds sustained on the raid of 14th June. Captain Masefield was awarded the Military Cross for his gallantry on the raid.

On 27th June, **Private William Thomas Smith** of the 1/5th North Staffords was killed in the Lens sector. He lived at 8, South Street, Leek, and was only 19. He has no known grave and is commemorated on the Arras Memorial. Three days later on 30th June, a Saturday, men of the 1/6th North Staffords and the 7th Sherwood Foresters again advanced on Lens but were checked by heavy shellfire. Whilst in the vicinity of the small mining town of Lievin, just to the west of Lens, six men of the 1/6th North Staffords were killed when a large shell, possibly 'friendly fire' from British artillery, fell amongst them. One of these was **Lance Corporal Charles Edwin Hill,** a former manager of the scarf department at Wardle and Davenports. He was 21, lived at 40, Picton Street and was the son of Benjamin Hill, a silk manufacturer and the owner of William Hill and Co; Burton Street. His nephew, Geoff Robinson, is the present chairman of the Leek

(A. Hambleton)
William Smith

141

branch of the Royal British Legion. Enquiries made by him some years ago revealed that the bodies of six soldiers of the North Staffords were buried in an annexe of the local cemetery at Lievin, close to where they were killed. None could be identified due to their injuries. Their graves bear the inscription "Known Unto God" as do all war graves where the casualty has not been identified. Research by Mr Robinson into his uncle's fate indicates that the 'Unknown' graves at Lievin are likely to be those of Lance Corporal Hill and his comrades, but this cannot be officially confirmed. Consequently, Lance Corporal Hill is commemorated on the Arras Memorial to the Missing. The story, however, is supported by a letter sent to Lance Corporal Hill's parents by a friend, Private Albert Hudson, a Leek soldier in the same battalion. In the letter, he wrote that Charles Hill had been killed accidentally by British artillery along with several other men. Albert Hudson only lived for three months after sending the sad news. He himself was killed in September, 1917, along with several other men, again by shell-fire.

(G. Robinson)

Charles Hill

Early on the morning of Sunday, 1st July, 1917, the troops of the 46th Division assembled for the attack on Lens. The 1/5th North Staffords were in the centre of the assault line and their objective was a suburb to the west of the town called Cite du Moulin. This area consisted of four streets leading to a square. Most of the houses on either side of the streets were damaged or in danger of collapsing. Just before dawn, the Staffords attacked under the protection of a 'creeping' barrage which was to lift to more distant targets every three minutes. At first, the attack went fairly well although some units were held up by machine-gun fire and severe hand-to-hand fighting. 'C' Company, led again by the redoubtable Captain Masefield, and 'D' Company were more successful, pushing forward down the streets to take their objective, an enemy trench. Then tragedy struck. The two companies were cut off by German counter-attacks and all efforts by the remaining units to rescue them failed. The remnants of the 46th Division were withdrawn having lost a total of over 1,000 officers and men.

Meanwhile, the soldiers of the two trapped companies fought on until their ammunition was exhausted and they were killed or captured. Amongst the dead were three Leek soldiers. **Private William Foster** was 21 and a former pupil at West Street School. He was an only son and had lived at 92, Mill Street. Before volunteering in March, 1915, Private Foster was employed at the Churnet Works.

Private George Lovatt of 38, John Street was one of three children and is thought to have been a joiner before joining the army. He was 23 and a single man.

Private Harold Barber was aged 26. He was married into a Leek family who lived at one time in Grove Street. His parents were living in Derby after the war and no further details are known about him. The bodies of the three soldiers were never found and they are commemorated on the Arras Memorial. Captain Masefield is also listed on the Cheadle War Memorial. He was badly wounded whilst defending the captured trench, taken prisoner and died the next day. He is buried at a cemetery between Arras and Lens. Major-General

(S. Breeze)
The grave of an unknown soldier. There are thousands of these headstones in British cemeteries around the world. Each 'unknown' is commemorated on one of the many memorials to the missing.

Thwaites, the commander of the 46th Division, in congratulating the troops involved in the battle, said: "*The magnificent manner in which the 5th North Staffords reached their objective is beyond all praise...............*"

Before the 1st July, 1917 was through, a fourth Leek soldier lost his life that day. **Private William Tomlinson** of the 1st Royal Fusiliers, died of wounds received a week earlier. He was 23, lived at 7, Kiln Lane and had worked as a braid tenter for Wardle and Davenports. Private

Tomlinson is buried at Lijssenthoek Military Cemetery, Poperinghe, near Ypres. On 3rd July, wounds to both legs claimed the life of a young soldier in the 1/7th Battalion, West Yorkshire Regiment. **Rifleman Victor Sales** of Ball Haye Green, a former textile knitter, was only 20. He is buried at Laventie Military Cemetery, France, not far from Neuve Chapelle.

On Thursday, 6th July, **Gunner Sidney Plant**, a married man of 32 and the father of two children, was killed in the Ypres salient whilst serving with the Royal Garrison Artillery. He was raised in Garden Street and had worked as the manager at the Cheadle branch of the Leek and Moorlands Co-op. Gunner Plant is buried at White House Cemetery, north-east of Ypres. Still further north of Ypres, on the Belgian coast near Nieuport, British troops of the 1st and 32nd Divisions were holding the line when the Germans began an intense bombardment on Tuesday, 10th July. There then followed an attack on Nieuport itself and many

of the defenders were cut off from escape and killed. One of the battalions involved in this desperate fighting was the 2nd King's Royal Rifle Corps and one of the soldiers who died that day was **Lieutenant Arthur Guy Boucher** of Sharpcliffe Hall, Ipstones. He was an only son and 19 years old when he died. His commanding officer wrote to the Times newspaper: *"..........never have I seen men take to an officer as they did to him........."*. Lieutenant Boucher had been in action all day against the Germans but was shot through the head during the final enemy assault during the evening. His body was subsequently lost and he is commemorated on the Nieuport Memorial to the Missing. His cousin, Lieutenant Basil Boucher, was killed after the war in a motor cycle accident (see Chapter 32).

(J. Crosby)
Arthur Boucher - shot through the head

On Monday, 23rd July, another Leek gunner died near Ypres of wounds to the leg and buttock. **Gunner Ernest Pickford** of 17, Livingstone Street, was 25 and had worked for Knowles Butchers in Derby Street. He is buried close to Private William Tomlinson in Lijssenthoek Military Cemetery at Poperinghe. On the same day, 27 year **Private James Cheshire** of the 7th North Staffords succumbed to the crippling diseases faced by soldiers in the Middle East. He died from heat stroke in a Baghdad hospital and is buried in Baghdad Cemetery. Private Cheshire had already spent ten weeks in hospital suffering from dysentery. He was another ex-pupil of West Street School, had been employed at the Churnet Works and lived at 23, North Avenue. His brother, Sam, was killed on the Somme in October, 1916. (See Chapter 18).

Back in France on 26th July, **Private William Scotton** of the 1st Battalion, The Kings (Liverpool) Regiment, died of wounds. At the time he died, Private Scotton was attached to a Tunnelling Company of the Royal Engineers. These men worked in dark and dangerous conditions digging tunnels under enemy positions, a common feature of the trench warfare on the Western Front. No other details are known of Private Scotton who is buried in the town cemetery at Bethune.

On Sunday, 29th July, 1917, the Leek Battery lost one of its most respected officers in France. **Lieutenant Charles Gilfrid Lewthwaite M.C.** was 33 and very popular with his men. The battery was then operating in the Loos-Lens area and came under enemy shell-fire. One of the gun pits was hit and set on fire. Lieutenant Lewthwaite attempted to put the fire out by removing his steel helmet for the purpose of carrying water in it to extinguish the flames. Suddenly, another shell exploded and the top of his exposed head was

(J. E. Blore)

Charles Lewthwaite

blown off. He died immediately. Lieutenant Lewthwaite was buried at Fosse No: 10 Communal Cemetery, not far from where he was killed. He had earlier won the Military Cross for conspicuous gallantry and devotion to duty. His citation, recorded in the Supplement to the London Gazette reads: *".....He showed great courage and promptness in extinguishing a fire which heavy hostile shell fire had caused to break out in and around his gun position. He also went out into the open under heavy fire and rescued a wounded infantryman. His work at all times has been remarkably good".*

Sergeant Percy Pickford was awarded the Military Medal for his part in this courageous action but was killed towards the end of the war (see Chapter 29).

Chapter 21

'Passchendaele'

"If I should die, think only this of me:
That there's some corner of a foreign field that is for ever England"

(The War Poet: Rupert Brooke, died from blood poisoning, 1915.)

Encouraged by the successes at Messines in June, 1917, Field Marshal Haig now turned his attention to his earlier plans to push out from the Ypres salient. Thus began, on 31st July, following a ten-day bombardment of enemy positions, what was officially known as the Third Battle of Ypres. It is often referred to as the Battle of Passchendaele, although the fighting for the village of Passchendaele and the ridge upon which it was perched, occurred in the later stages of the offensive, in October and November, 1917. Most of the British, Canadian, Australian and New Zealand troops involved were raw recruits and, as ever, anxious to do their bit for King and Country. But, like the tragedies on the Somme a year earlier, the battle became one of unspeakable horror, fear and death. It was called off when the village of Passchendaele was finally captured on 6th November. Five miles of enemy-held territory, which was of no strategic importance, had been gained. The long-sought after breakthrough had again slipped through Haig's fingers. The Third Battle of Ypres proved to be the last great battle of attrition and cost the Allies some 300,000 killed, wounded and missing in four months of fighting. At least 27 of the dead were Leek men.

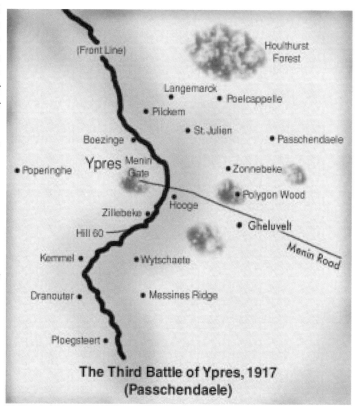

The Third Battle of Ypres, 1917
(Passchendaele)

At 3.50am on the opening day of the offensive, Tuesday, 31st July, 1917, thousands of men went over the top towards their first objectives. By the end of the day, gains of between half a mile and two miles were made and some objectives, including the Pilckem Ridge, seized. **Private Frank Cox** of the 16th Sherwood Foresters, (Notts and Derby Regiment), was one of two Leek soldiers to be killed that day. He lived at 25, Wellington Street. The other was **Private Ernest Lees** of the 20th Battalion, Durham Light Infantry. His home was at 4, North Street and he was a former pupil of West Street School. When the Durhams advanced, it was raining and the clinging mud stuck to them like glue. They were held up by concrete machine-gun posts known as pillboxes. Safe inside, the Germans could sweep the ground across which the attackers were advancing with murderous enfilade fire. The only way the infantry could silence them was to creep up and throw grenades

through the firing slot. Neither Private Cox or Private Lees were found and their names are commemorated on the Menin Gate Memorial to the Missing. (Above)

Another soldier wounded on 31st July died on Tuesday, 2nd August. **Sergeant Thomas Reginald Birch** of the 6th Battalion, Royal Berkshire Regiment, was born in Leek but his family later moved to Essex. He was 24 and is buried at Lijssenthoek Military Cemetery, near Ypres.

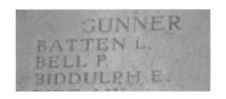

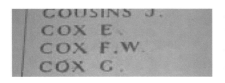

(K. Perrin)

The names of three Leek soldiers as they appear on the Menin Gate Memorial

The driving rain that started on 31st July continued unabated for the next three days making further attacks impossible. One officer in the Royal Field Artillery noted ruefully that he was in more danger of dying from drowning than from hostile fire! The Flanders mud, in places knee-deep, was a nightmare for the unfortunate men expected to fight in these conditions. As the rain poured down, so did the German shells on the British positions. One casualty of the shelling was **Gunner Ernest Biddulph** of the Royal Garrison Artillery who was killed on Friday, 3rd August. He was 28, married, and the father of two young children. He worked at John West's Ironmongers in Derby Street and lived at 73 Shirburn Road. His body was also lost and he is commemorated on the Menin Gate Memorial. Also listed on that impressive memorial is another Leek soldier who was killed by shellfire on Saturday, 4th August. **Private George Arthur Rushton** was 21 and married. He had lived at 46, Fountain Street and was serving with the Machine Gun Corps when he died.

The next day, Sunday, 5th August, **Gunner Herbert Read** from 11, Shirburn Road, was killed. He was a member of a gun team of the Royal Field Artillery. At this stage of the battle, both sides were firing unceasingly at each other in an effort to gain supremacy over the battlefield. When the artillery identified an enemy gun position the consequences were sudden and dreadful for the gunners. Herbert Read was 23, had played for Leek Alexandra Football Club, (later Leek Town) and worked at Wardle and Davenports. His body was recovered and lies buried at New Irish Farm Cemetery, Ypres.

By Friday, 10th August, the rain had eased a little and the British attacked again and captured some ground. The inevitable German counter-attacks came and the assaulting battalions were, in the main, pushed back to their start line. The only real gain was the capture of the Westhoek Ridge. On that day, **Rifleman Harry Malkin**, aged 32 and a father of six, died of wounds. He lived at 1, Buxton Road, Leek, and was serving with the 10th Battalion, King's Royal Rifle Corps. He is also commemorated on the Menin Gate Memorial at Ypres. One of Harry Malkin's sons was a telegram boy in Leek between the wars and went on to fight in the armed forces during the Second World War.

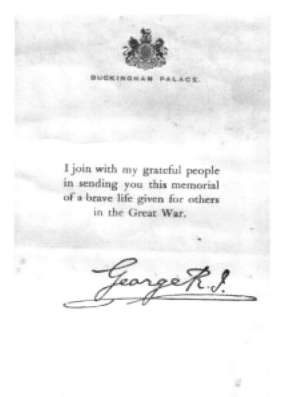

BUCKINGHAM PALACE.

I join with my grateful people in sending you this memorial of a brave life given for others in the Great War.

George R.I.

(Author's Collection)
Bereaved families received this note signed by the King

Private Hezekiah Nowland, aged 34, of the 2nd Battalion, Lincolnshire Regiment, was the next Leek casualty of the Flanders fighting. He was killed by shellfire on Tuesday, 14th August 1917. Private Nowland was married, had worked at Clowes Brothers, Dyers, in Brook Street and lived at 3, Park Road. He is buried at the Divisional Collecting Post Cemetery, Boezinge, Ypres. On the same day, **Private Fred Nelson**, an employee of Brough, Nicholson and Hall's, died of wounds. He came from 2, Church Lane and was serving with the 11th Royal Sussex. Aged 21 when he died, Private Nelson is buried at Dozinghem Military Cemetery, Poperinghe, near Ypres.

On Thursday, 16th August, another major offensive - the Battle of Langemarck - was launched. The conditions by then were so bad that tanks were useless and troops were virtually overwhelmed by the mud. The British artillery had not established superiority and the small gains made that day were at a dreadful cost. Later in the month, more attacks with resulting small gains, pushed the line slowly but bloodily forward towards the Passchendaele Ridge. But now, it is time to return briefly further south to Northern France where the front lines around Loos, Lens and the old Somme battlefields claimed the lives of more Leek soldiers that August.

On Saturday, 11th August, 1917, **Private Charles Partridge** of 2 Court, 18, Ashbourne Road, died of wounds. He was in the 2nd/7th Battalion, Duke of Wellingtons (West Riding) Regiment. His grave is in the Grevillers British Cemetery, two miles west of Bapaume. That same day, **Gunner James Phillips** from 58 Gladstone Street was killed. He was serving with the Leek Battery and is commemorated on the Menin Gate Memorial. The following Wednesday, 15th August, **Lieutenant Harold Swindells** from Ladybank, Leek, was killed near Lens. He was serving with the 1/5th South Staffords and was only 21. His grave is in the Philosophe British Cemetery about 5 miles from Lens. Lieutenant Swindells was a member of the Leek Amateur Operatic Society, the Leek Golf Club and the Congregational Church Choir. Promoted from the ranks, he had seen service in Ireland where he was involved in the quelling of the Sinn Fein rebellion. Before enlisting, Harry Swindells had been in business with his father making bobbins for the textile industry.

(H. Birch)

Harry Swindells

The last Leek casualty in France during that August of 1917 was **Corporal Joshua Marren** of the 4th Royal Fusiliers. He lived at 24 Russell Street and worked as a boot and shoe repairer. Along with Harry Swindells, he was a member of the Congregational Church Choir and was killed by a shellburst on the morning of Tuesday the 21st. Six months before he was killed he had had a narrow escape when a shell burst near his dugout, burying him and causing shell-shock, a condition that took the military authorities some time to recognise as a genuine illness during the First World War. Corporal Marren is buried at Red Cross Corner Cemetery, Beugny, near the town of Bapaume.

Two legacies of war.

The Tyne Cot Cemetery and Memorial to the Missing.

(Below). Rifle bullets and shrapnel balls dug up from the battlefields.

(Author)

Chapter 22

September 1917. Counting the Cost.

"In Flanders fields the poppies blow
Between the crosses, row on row..."

(Dr John McCrae, died 1918.)

For September, 1917, the British High Command hoped for better things in the Ypres salient. Field Marshal Haig decided on a change of plan. It was essential to capture the Gheluvelt Plateau before his overall plans could progress. August had already cost some 68, 000 casualties. He replaced the general responsible for the conduct of the offensive, Sir Hubert Gough, with General Sir Herbert Plumer. Plumer favoured 'bite and hold' tactics which left little to chance and, hopefully, minimised casualties. In the meantime, the Germans had also suffered heavy losses but their defensive positions were very strong.

One very welcome gift for the gunners and infantry facing the German lines that September was good weather for the first half of the month. It was dry and sunny and, perversely, dust and lack of water became a problem for them instead of the mud. Small-scale attacks and raids were made along the enemy lines whilst preparations were continuing for a major offensive later in the month. During this period the shelling continued and three more Leek soldiers were killed.

Gunner Fred Hall, 22, of the Royal Field Artillery was killed on Monday, 10th September, apparently when his gun blew up during firing. He lived at 6, Prospect Road and had worked at Brough, Nicholson and Hall. Three of Fred's brothers also served in the war but all survived. He is buried at Bleuet Farm Cemetery, near Ypres. Bleuet Farm was used as a dressing station during the Passchendaele offensive and the cemetery was started in June 1917 in a corner of the farm. It now contains 442 Great War graves.

On Friday, 14th September, **Major Walter Guy Nicholas Breton** of the Royal Garrison Artillery was killed. He lived at one time in Leonard Street but his parents were living in

Stafford after the war. He is buried at White House Cemetery, near Ypres. Major Breton had won the Distinguished Service Order and was Mentioned in Dispatches during his short career. He was 29 and had qualified as a solicitor. Two days later, **Gunner George Keates**, also of the Royal Garrison Artillery, died of wounds to the left arm and shoulder. He had worked as an assistant rate collector for the Leek Urban District Council and was secretary of the Leek Mechanics Institute. George Keates was 35, married and lived at 9, Junction Road. He is buried at Lijssenthoek Military Cemetery near Ypres.

The next major offensive on the Ypres front commenced on Thursday, 20th September 1917 and became known as the Battle of the Menin Road. This demonstrated that General Plumer's new tactics could work and, although the fighting was hard and the casualties high, the offensive was a success and the line was pushed forward along the whole front for nearly a mile in places. Killed on that day was **Private Edward Smith** from Kiln Lane. He was aged 20 and in the 9th Battalion, Royal Scots. His body was never found and he is commemorated on the Tyne Cot Memorial to the Missing. The following Sunday, 23rd September, **Private Frank Booth**, of the 123rd Company, Machine Gun Corps, was killed. He was born in Huddersfield and his connection to Leek is uncertain. Private Booth is buried at Kemmel No: 1 Cemetery, four miles from Ypres.

(J. Crosby)

Major Fred Davenport

The next major offensive, this time to take Zonnebeke, Polygon Wood and a number of pillboxes known as Tower Hamlets was planned for 26th September 1917. In the meantime, a gruelling battle of attrition was taking place between the British and German gunners and the shells continued their work of killing and maiming. On 25th September, **Major Fred Davenport**, the Chairman of Directors at Wardle and Davenport, was killed whilst serving with the Royal Field Artillery. He was 44, had been awarded the Distinguished Service Order, the Military Cross and had been Mentioned in Dispatches. The Davenport family lived at Woodcroft, Leek, but Fred was married with children and lived at Churnet Grange, between Cheddleton and Basford. Major Davenport was a wealthy man, leaving nearly £180,000 in his will. He is buried at Ypres Reservoir Cemetery.

On the 29th, **Sergeant Sydney Gerald Kelly** of the 16th Battalion, King's Royal Rifle Corps, died of wounds to the head at a casualty clearing station in the Ypres salient. A married man of 30 who had been wounded twice before, Sergeant Kelly lived at 32 Compton, Leek. He is buried at the Lijssenthoek Military

Cemetery, Ypres. Captain L.E. Harris, the company commander, reported that the sergeant had been shot in the head during an attack three days earlier. The next day, **Lance Corporal William Hudson** from 115, Ball Haye Green, was killed along with two other men by shrapnel from a shell or bomb, believed whilst attacking enemy positions. He

(Ashbourne Editions)

Wardle and Davenport's mill in Belle View, 1960

was 24 and serving with the 2/6th Battalion, North Staffords. Formerly a jacquard weaver at Brough, Nicholson and Hall, Private Hudson is buried at Vlamertinghe New Military Cemetery, three miles from Ypres. The inscription on his gravestone reads: "In an Allied country laid, ne'r forgotten though far away." William Hudson's name can also be seen on the memorial board at the former Ball Haye Green Chapel, close to his home.

On the day the battle for the Menin Road was raging, another Leek soldier with the name of Hudson was killed in the Arras sector in France. **Private Albert Hudson** was 20 and lived at 18, Wellington Street. He was in the 1/6th North Staffords and had been in action on the day he was killed, Thursday, 20th September, 1917. That night, he and his comrades were in a recently-dug trench which was under artillery bombardment. One shell killed Private Hudson and three other soldiers. His body was not identified and he is commemorated on the Arras Memorial. This young soldier enlisted in May, 1916 and went to France in August the same year. Three months later he was wounded. In July, 1917, he was suffering from shell-shock. Three months after that, he was dead. Like a number of the soldiers in this book, his third time of becoming a casualty was not lucky.

Back at home, two more local soldiers were buried in Leek Cemetery that September.

(G. Robinson)

Albert Hudson

155

Private Leonard Kirby of the Labour Corps died of 'trench fever' in a London hospital on Monday, 10th September. He was married, the father of two children and lived at 3, London Street. Before transferring to the Labour Corps, Private Kirby had served in the North Staffords. On the 27th, **Sergeant William Doxey** of the Royal Defence Corps died in a Shropshire hospital following a road accident. He had been knocked down and injured by a motor car whilst walking along a lane in Oswestry with two colleagues some days earlier. He was a married man of 56 and had earlier served in the Shropshire Light Infantry, working at a Prisoners Camp in Shrewsbury. His widow, Elizabeth, lived at 84, Prince Street after his death.

Before we leave September, 1917, we visit St Omer in France which, until March, 1916, was the home of the General Headquarters of the British Expeditionary Force. It was also a large hospital centre. Two miles out of the town is the Longuenesse Souvenir Cemetery which contains over 3,000 Great War burials. One of these is 18 year old **Private Cyril Vincent Holden** who served with the Royal Army Medical Corps at the 59th General Hospital, St Omer. He is recorded as dying of wounds on 1st October, 1917, and, although his connection to Leek cannot be established, it is known that he attended St Mary's R.C. Church, Compton. His parents came from Lancaster.

(Commonwealth War Graves Commission)
The Arras Memorial

Chapter 23

Passchendaele - Battle of Mud and Attrition.

*"My dear mother, just a few lines, hoping they find you in the best of health,
as this letter leaves me so at present.........."*

(Private James Donald Whitehouse, aged 19. Severely wounded at Passchendaele
26th October, 1917, died in hospital six weeks later.)

October, 1917, brought more rain for the Allied troops and with it, the hated mud.
On the 4th, British and Anzac forces attacked the Broodseinde Ridge, the Zonnebeke Spur
and Gravenstafel Ridge. Advances were made and ground captured but at a cost of over
20,000 casualties. The Germans also suffered badly and Field Marshal Haig was convinced
that the enemy was about to collapse and that a break-through was still possible. On that
first day of the Battle of Broodseinde, as it became known, two Leek men were killed. **Private Charles Bintcliffe** served with the 2nd Battalion, Border Regiment. He was married
and lived at 9, Cromwell Terrace. His body was never found and he is commemorated on

(Imperial War Museum)

*The devastated ground near Passchendaele. In some places, men and horses simply
disappeared into the mud.*

the Tyne Cot Memorial to the Missing. The second soldier killed that day and also commemorated on the Tyne Cot Memorial was **Private Victor Renshaw** from Leekbrook. He was 25 and serving with the 1st South Staffords.

Private Renshaw had worked at Joshua Wardles and enlisted in May, 1915. He was the uncle of Albert Renshaw who was well-known in Leek for over 30 years as a coach driver.

As the Flanders fighting ground on, conditions were atrocious. Rivers and streams flooded, turning the shell-torn earth into a quagmire. The Somme had been bad enough for mud, but at least the chalky soil there had allowed better drainage than the flat ground of Belgian Flanders did. It was almost impossible to move the British guns forward and many men slipped into slimy, mud-filled shellholes, some of them dying a horrible death. A lot of the soldiers had reached the end of their tether - and it wasn't over yet. Another attack at Poelcappelle on 9th October made little progress in the pouring rain against an influx of German reserves who were well-supplied with mustard gas.

Many miles away in a London hospital, one of the wounded died on Thursday, 11th October. **Company Sergeant-Major Ernest Smith** of the 7th Battalion, King's Royal Rifle Corps was born and raised in Leek but, at some stage, went to live in Derby with his wife. He is buried in the Nottingham Road Cemetery in Derby.

The following day, Friday, 12th October, the British made another push towards the Passchendaele Ridge in what was called the 'First Battle of Passchendaele'. By then, General Plumer's carefully planned 'bite and hold' tactics seem to have been thrown out of the window. Now, it was a matter of throwing in everything and hoping that the Germans would collapse. Again, little progress was made and another 13,000 were added to the growing casualty lists. The morale of the troops was by now very low and few could see any point in continuing the useless slaughter. The men of the 8th Battalion, South Staffordshire Regiment also suffered heavily.

(M. Cope)

Carl Wagstaff

158

They were ready at their start lines at 4.25 that morning and began their attack an hour later. The soldiers did well, capturing German trenches and weapons, killing a number of enemy troops and taking over 100 prisoners. The cost to the Staffords in officers and men killed was 157, including the Commanding Officer, Lt-Colonel Barker and three Leek men.

Lieutenant John Carleton Wagstaff lived at 1, Park Vale (the house is still there, almost opposite Lloyds chemists in Ball Haye Road). He was 28, the eldest of four children and had been a teacher at St Lukes School and later at a school in Stafford. Described by his commanding officer as *"one of the finest men I have ever had the good fortune to know"*, Carl, as he was known, joined the army and served in the

(M. Cope)

Carl Wagstaff's niece visiting his grave

Coldstream Guards prior to being commissioned in the South Staffords. Related to the Wagstaffs who kept the jewellers shop in Russell Street, Lieutenant Wagstaff was shot and killed in the late afternoon of 12th October whilst he and his men were being relieved following the offensive against the Passchendaele Ridge. He is buried close to where he fell, at Poelcapelle British Cemetery in the Ypres salient.

Private Joseph Sheldon was born and raised at Brown Edge. He was 19, one of five children and had worked in his uncle's butcher's shop next to the Lump of Coal pub in the village. It is said that on the day Joseph was killed, his mother declared that she had heard his footsteps in the yard of the family home at Steinfields Cottage, Broad Lane, Brown Edge. His body was never found and he is commemorated on the Tyne Cot Memorial.

(C. Sheldon)

Joseph Sheldon

The third Leek soldier to be killed in action that day was **Private James Arthur Cotterill**, also 19, from 29, Sandon Road. He was the son of a farmer who kept Red Earth Farm on the Macclesfield Road until he died in a tragic accident on the farm when a horse kicked him in the head. The family gave up the farm and moved to Sandon Road (now Cheddleton Road), and, after the war, to 134 Junction Road. Private Cotterill's body was never found and he too is commemorated on the Tyne Cot Memorial. Conditions at Passchendaele at the time were such that many bodies just sank into the mud and were never seen again. Indeed, some have been found, particularly in recent times, but few can be identified. It is likely that Privates Cotterill and Sheldon still lie beneath the Flanders fields somewhere in front of the Passchendaele Ridge but it is just possible that one or both have been found and reburied in a British war cemetery with the headstones engraved: "Known Unto God".

(C. Chell)

James Cotterill

As with the family of Private Joseph Sheldon, there is a similar story handed down in the family that young Jim Cotterill's grandmother was looking into the roaring log fire at Dunwood House Farm where she lived and suddenly announced that she had just seen her grandson "being blown up". The date was the 12th October, 1917, the day he was killed. Her disbelieving family only realised she was right when the War Office telegram arrived a week or so later.

A week later on Thursday, 18th October, 24 year old **Lance Corporal Reginald John Dean** from 8, Shirburn Road, was killed. He was a Lewis Gunner with the 2/5th North Staffords which was a contrast to his job in civilian life - he worked at Skinners in Derby Street. His grave is at Sucrerie Cemetery, Ablain-St Nazaire.

The next Leek soldier to lose his life was **Gunner James Arthur Carter** of the Royal Field Artillery. He was 27 and lived at 'Saundhurst', Longsdon. Gunner Carter was killed on Sunday, 21st October 1917 and is buried at Vlamertinghe New Military Cemetery, 3 miles west of Ypres.

Monday, 22nd October saw the next British offensive at Passchendaele. This was limited to the Poelcappelle sector and yet again, rain and mud made conditions for the gunners and the attacking infantry virtually impossible. Three days later on the 25th, another Leek man was killed. **Lance Corporal John Astles** of the 1st Bedfords was married with one son, lived at 3 Court, 1, Haywood Street and worked at William Hill and Co. He was the brother of Private Arthur Astles who was killed on the Somme in August, 1916. Lance Corporal Astle's body was never found and he is commemorated on the Tyne Cot Memorial.

As the whistles blew at 5.40 on the cold, wet morning of Friday, 26th October, 1917, British and Canadian troops went over the top as the Second Battle of Passchendaele commenced. It was the same story as before. A few hundred yards of mud were captured but at a high cost, some 12,000 were killed, wounded and missing. Three Leek men, all in different battalions, were killed that day.

Private Bernard Wheatley was 24 and serving with the 2/4th Battalion, The Loyal (North Lancashire) Regiment. He was raised at 18, Mill Street and had worked at the Churnet Works before emigrating to America before the war. When war broke out, Bernard Wheatley, like so many other brave young men of his generation, returned to England to volunteer for the army. He served in the Army Service Corps for three years before transferring to The Loyals. Four of his brothers also served their country during the war and all survived. But there is a twist of irony in this young soldier finding himself on the tortured battlefields of Flanders when he could have stayed in America where he was a successful businessman.

During the potato famine in Ireland, many families were forced to leave their homes and settle elsewhere. Amongst those who settled in Leek was a family named Duigan. They were enterprising people and soon opened a lodging house in the Market Place, behind Booth's leather shop, accommodating weary travellers and craftsmen visiting the town. One of their guests was a man named Luke Wheatley, a skilled bricklayer who found work with Thomas Grace and Sons, the builders. Eventually, he married Hannah Duigan, one of the daughters of his host. They had seven children, one of them they named Bernard. Meanwhile, another Irish family named Harrity, had emigrated to America where they built up a business manufacturing umbrellas. The Harritys were cousins of the Duigans. When the time came to expand the business the Harrity family, wishing to keep their success within the family, looked to Luke Wheatley and his wife to provide one of their able young sons to join them. Young Bernard Wheatley was the one chosen and in 1912, set sail for America and a new life. An exiting prospect for a 19 year old stuck in a humdrum job at the Churnet Works. As expected, the young lad prospered but as the nations of Europe began their slide into war, Bernard did what he felt was the right thing, returned to England and joined up. It was to cost him his life.

The men of the 2/4th Loyals had attacked across No Man's Land that Friday morning and captured two enemy strongpoints, Mendlings Farm and Rubens Farm. Further advance was then held up by fire from German pill-boxes but these were overcome and captured when the Loyals received support from another battalion. As the soldiers reached a position on some dominating ground the advance was stopped altogether by withering machine-gun fire from all sides. The Loyals held their ground until relieved late that night. Altogether, the battalion suffered 358 casualties that day, including 61 who were killed or died of wounds. Private Bernard Wheatley was one of them. Lieutenant N.A. Greenough wrote to Bernard's mother: *"......he died gallantly fighting for his King and Country and his loved ones at home.....I deplore the loss of one of my best men.........His death was instantaneous and he suffered little or no pain......"* Comforting words from a young junior officer in the field, trying his best with the one job he would have hated most. From the wording of the letter, it seems that Private Wheatley's body was recovered and buried. Like so many others, however, the grave was lost and he is commemorated on the Tyne Cot Memorial to the Missing.

The second man to die that day was **Private Ernest Hewitt** of the 2/4th Royal Fusiliers. Formerly an air mechanic in the Royal Flying Corps (the forerunner of the Royal Air Force), Ernest Hewitt came from 34, Russell Street and had worked at Bradley's Clothiers in the Market Place before the war. He now lies buried at Cement House Cemetery, Langemarck, in the Ypres salient.

A young officer from Ball Haye Green was the third Leek man to lose his life at Passchendaele on that fateful Friday. **Lieutenant William Cockayne Conley M.C.** of the South Staffordshire Regiment had won the Military Cross for bravery on the Somme. At Passchendaele, he was in charge of a trench mortar battery. It is believed that he was shot through the head during the attack on German positions. His body was never found and he too is commemorated on the Tyne Cot Memorial.

Another example of the postcards so fashionable during the war.

(P.Pickford)

The Cloth Hall, Ypres, in 1918
(Author's Collection)

    The town of Ypres in Belgian Flanders was an important cloth centre in the Middle Ages. During the Great War, Ypres fell to the Allies after the Germans occupied it for one night only. Some five million British and Commonwealth soldiers passed through the town on their way to the Ypres Salient. Under constant bombardment from the Germans, the town was reduced to rubble but restored to its former glory after the war.

(Author's Collection)

The Cloth Hall, Ypres, as it looks today.

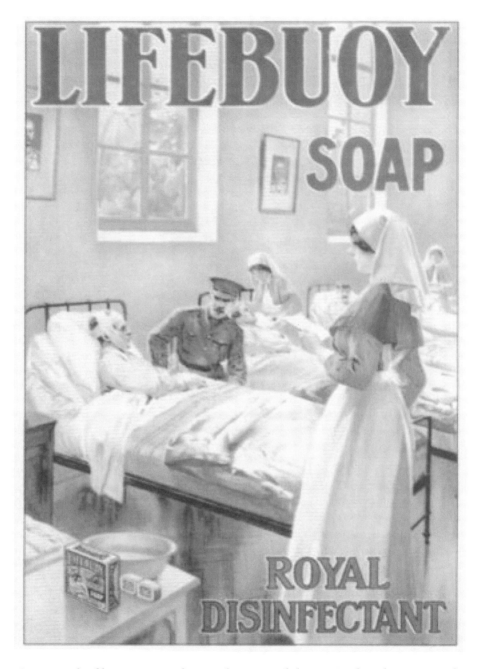

One example of how commercial artists domesticated the war. In this advertisement the artist uses a military hospital to promote Lifebuoy Soap

Chapter 24

Exhaustion at Passchendaele

*"The graves are very well looked after
and his name, etc; will be on his cross..........."*

(From a letter dated 10th November, 1917, sent by the Matron of H.4 Casualty Clearing Station, British Expeditionary Force, France, concerning the death from wounds of Gunner Archie Birch)

After the exhausting battles of October, the British Commander-in-Chief realised that his goal of reaching and capturing the U-boat bases on the coast was now only a dream. But he still felt that one more last effort might yet bring a German collapse and capture the Passchendaele Ridge. He let it be known that he did not want the gigantic sacrifices of his troops during the Third Battle of Ypres to be in vain, so there would be one more offensive. Another reason for continuing this hopeless struggle was to hide the preparations already being made for the next British offensive, many miles south at Cambrai. So, the last desperate push took place on

The original Attestation Paper George Hambleton signed in Canada when he enlisted in August 1915
(National Archives of Canada)

165

Tuesday, 6th November, 1916, when Canadian and British troops finally captured Passchendaele village. By the 10th, the battle was called off. Some 5 miles of ground east of the original British lines had been captured. There were now no reserves left to support the troops who would take part in the Cambrai offensive on 20th November and Field Marshal Haig came in for severe criticism. Two more Leek soldiers were killed before Passchendaele was finally over.

Private George Hambleton was 20 and had lived in York Street, Leek, before emigrating to Canada with his family before the war. From there, he joined the 26th Battalion, New Brunswick Regiment of the Canadian Infantry. He was wounded in the fighting for Passchendaele village on 6th November whilst rescuing a wounded comrade and died the next day. A few days before he was wounded Private Hambleton was on leave in England and visited Leek where he had an uncle living in Talbot Street. He is buried at the Lijssenthoek Military Cemetery, Poperinghe.

(K. Pickford)

Archie Birch - died of wounds

The second soldier to die before the Passchendaele fighting ended was another 19 year-old. **Gunner Archibald Birch** was serving with the 197th Siege Battery, Royal Garrison Artillery, when he died of wounds to the arms, legs and head on Friday, 9th November. He was, like George Hambleton, wounded on the 6th during the attack on Passchendaele village. Archie, as he was known, came from 'Maryville', Broad Street, and worked at Trafford and Co, New Street Mills where his father was the Managing Director. Both Archie and a work colleague, Harvey Hunt, were members of the Leek Methodist Chapel together. Ironically, as Archie Birch died at the end of one great battle, so his close friend died at the start of the next. Harvey Hunt was killed on the first day of the Cambrai offensive, less than two weeks later. (See Chapter 25). Had they not been joined in death this way, the pair would have become brothers-in law; Archie's brother married Harvey's sister in 1918. Such is fate. And it was fate which decreed that the first intimation to Archie's parents that he had been wounded should come from Harvey Hunt's brother, Wilfred, also serving at Passchendaele.

He wrote to Mr and Mrs Birch: *"……..It appears he had just been relieved along with some others and was leaving in a lorry when a shell struck the lorry wounding several of them. They tell me Archie was wounded in many places and rather seriously. I do hope you hear some better news of him shortly...........*" But the better news never came.   Instead, the Matron of the 4th Casualty Clearing Station near the Ypres front wrote on 10th November: "*......although everything possible was done for him he passed away peacefully at 3.15am on 9/11/17......he will be buried with full military honours.......*".

Gunner Archibald Birch is buried at Dozinghem Military Cemetery a few miles from Ypres.

The next Leek soldier to give his life on the Western Front was also only 19 and serving with the 2/5th North Staffords in the Lens area. **Private Percy Carter** from 11, Garden Street, died of wounds to the head on Tuesday, 13th November. A former pupil at West Street School, he was a gardener at Ball Haye Hall. Private Carter is buried at Bruay Communal Cemetery Extension near Bethune in northern France.

(Imperial War Museum)

Canadian troops holding the line at Passchendaele.

167

Chapter 25

The Tanks at Cambrai.

"A pretty mechanical toy, but the war will never be won by such machines".

(Lord Kitchener, on seeing a demonstration of the new tanks.)

The last major offensive in 1917 was the Battle of Cambrai where British tanks were used in large numbers for the first time. The town of Cambrai was part of the German Hindenburg Line and heavily fortified. The area was chosen for a tank offensive because, unlike Passchendaele, the ground here was firm and not too churned up by shell-fire. The secret of the tank, of course, had been given away a year earlier on the Somme in a desperate attempt to support the infantry in achieving a breakthrough and minimising casualties. But there were not enough tanks to make a decisive impact and the Germans did not, at that time, see them as a serious threat.

The plan for the attack at Cambrai was an assault by 378 tanks and 7 divisions of infantry on a frontage of about 6 miles with cavalry in reserve ready to exploit any break-through. Three lines of trenches had to be crossed and captured plus another one just in front of the town itself. The tanks trailed grappling hooks to drag and flatten the barbed wire and then the infantry would follow through. 1,000 guns and nearly 300 aircraft fired on the German positions and at 6.20am on Tuesday, 20th November, 1917, the attack commenced. Surprise was achieved and hundreds of shocked Germans surrendered as the tanks broke through to a depth of some 4 miles. But then the problems started. On the Flesquieres Ridge, the commander of the 51st Division, who had no time for tanks, told his infantry to trail behind the attacking tanks at too great a distance. This caused a delay in getting to grips with the enemy and allowed the Germans time to bring up reinforcements. Although more advances were made the day after the initial attack, there were no reserves to send in. This meant that tired troops could not be relieved and knocked-out tanks could not be replaced. The Germans soon recovered from their shock and quickly learnt how to deal with the tanks - with 77 millimetre field guns, a fearsome weapon of its time. Reinforcements soon blocked further advances by the British and heavy fighting continued until 30th November when the Germans counter-attacked with 20 divisions, pushing the attackers back almost to their start position. By 7th December, the fighting had died down.

Eight Leek soldiers died during the fighting for Cambrai, the first one, a tank driver, on November 20th, the opening day of the attack. **Gunner Harvey Hunt** was 21, one of ten

169

children and lived at 11, Westwood Grove. As described in Chapter 24, he worked at New Street Mills (where Blakemore and Chell is now) with Archie Birch. Harvey was another former pupil of West Street school. He had earlier served in the Royal Army Ordnance Corps, but was now in 'G' Battalion of the Tank Corps. At that time, tanks usually carried an eight man crew who were crowded into the small space around the huge engine. The crew were quickly exhausted by the high temperature and engine fumes inside the lumbering metal monsters. The noise was so loud that the tank commander's orders had to be given by hand signals. The tanks were also liable to break down and over 100 did so at Cambrai. Some 65 tanks, including the one driven by Harvey Hunt, were destroyed by German shellfire. He died alongside his officer, a Captain Muirhead. Both were buried beside the tank but later re-buried, in adjacent graves, at the Flesquieres Hill British Cemetery outside Cambrai.

(K. Pickford)
Harvey Hunt - killed in a tank

(Imperial War Museum)
Tanks lining up for action.

The next Leek man to die in the fighting was **Lance Corporal George Elkin**, who, coincidentally, lived a few doors away from Harvey Hunt at 17, Westwood Grove. He was 25, married and serving with the 9th Battalion, King's Royal Rifle Corps. Lance Corporal Elkin was killed in action on Thursday, 22nd November and is buried at Hermies Hill British Cemetery, 12 miles west of Cambrai. Two days later, during the early hours of the 24th,

Private Samuel Walter Robinson from 6, Broad Street, was admitted to the 48th Casualty Clearing Station, some 18 miles from Cambrai, severely wounded in the chest. He died at 5.45am and was buried in the nearby military cemetery at Manancourt. He served with the 1/8th Battalion, Argyll and Sutherland Highlanders and was only 19. Before joining the army in 1916, Private Robinson had worked in his father's bakery in Haywood Street.

Another former pupil of West Street School was killed on Thursday, 29th November. 21 year old **Private Jesse Lee** from 23, Brook Street, had worked as a braid tenter at Worthington's mill and enlisted in the army in April, 1917. He was serving with the 2/6th North Staffords. His body was never found and he is commemorated on the Cambrai Memorial to the Missing. The next day, Friday, 30th November, the Germans counter-attacked in force along the Cambrai front. Leek-born **Rifleman Arthur William Goodwin** of the 11th Kings Royal Rifle Corps found himself and his mates confronted with swarms of German infantry emerging from the mist. They were supported by low-flying aircraft, machine-guns blazing. The battalion had no time to fall back or reorganise and had to battle it out. Casualties were heavy and included Arthur Goodwin who died of his wounds that day. He is also commemorated on the Cambrai Memorial.

One of the battalions involved in this heavy fighting was the 4th Grenadier Guards. On 1st December, the Guards made a bold attempt to hold the Germans back at the village of Gonnelieu, a few miles from Cambrai, but were forced out, struggling against superior numbers without tank or artillery support. Although they fought bravely and themselves counter-attacked, the Guardsmen were eventually pushed back. One of those killed that day was **Guardsman George Trafford** aged 24, from 7, Nelson Street, Ball Haye Green. His body was never found and he is commemorated on the Cambrai Memorial. By a tragic quirk of fate, George Trafford was not the only soldier of that name from tiny Nelson Street to be killed in the war. Private Albert Trafford from number 4 was killed in August, 1916, on the

(Author)

Nelson Street, Ball Haye Green today. This tiny street lost six men in the war.

Somme. (See Chapter 17). The two families are not thought to have been related.

A former centre-forward with Leek United Football Club became the next victim of the Cambrai fighting when he died of wounds to the head and shoulders on Monday, 3rd December, 1917. **Rifleman George Rogers** came from 13, Prince Street and was serving with the 10th Battalion, King's Royal Rifle Corps. He is buried at Rocqigny-Equancourt Road British Cemetery, nine miles south-east of Bapaume. His name also appears on the memorial board at the former Ball Haye Green Chapel.

Two young Leek soldiers who were gassed during the fighting died later in hospitals behind the lines. **Private George William Peach** of the 2/6th North Staffords came from

Wren Cottage, Ashbourne Road and died at Rouen in north-west France on Wednesday, 5th December. He was 21 and had worked as a postman in Leek. **Private James Bishop**, 28, from 54 Chorley Street, died on Saturday, 8th December at Etaples. He was one of six brothers serving their country, married with three young children, was educated at West Street School and worked for Victor Robinson as a painter and plumber before joining the army. He served in the 2/6th South Staffords. Both soldiers are buried in military cemeteries close to the hospitals where they died.

Sunday, 9th December, saw the death of **Sapper Philip James Goldstraw** who was serving in the 470th Field Company, Royal Engineers. He had also worked as a painter and plumber and lived in Ball Haye Green. His parents later lived at 43, Grove Street. Sapper Goldstraw's grave is at Ribecourt Road Cemetery, Trescault, about 10 miles south-west of Cambrai.

One place where there was particularly heavy fighting in the Cambrai sector was at Bourlon Wood, a few miles west of the town. The British took 4,000 casualties there in two days. Along the whole of the front, the Germans, now with superior numbers, gradually forced the British back more or less to where they had started. Heavy snowfalls on 7th December finally persuaded both sides to call a halt to the fighting. The Battle of Cambrai was over.

Whilst the conflict at Cambrai was raging, the casualties continued on other parts of the Western Front. **Private Reuben Clulow,** serving with the 3rd Battalion, Canterbury Regiment, New Zealand Expeditionary Force, was killed on 22nd November in the Ypres salient, at the age of 30. It is not known if he had emigrated to New Zealand before the war and joined up there, but his mother lived at 77, Shirburn Road. Private Clulow is buried at Buttes New British Cemetery at Polygon Wood, five miles from Ypres.

(J. Crosby)

Bert Willmer

As the exhausted combatants on all sides settled down to face yet another winter of war, another Leek servicemen was buried in Leek Cemetery. **Private Herbert Dudley Willmer** of the 16th Battalion, Manchester Regiment, died from cancer on Friday, 30th November. He was married, lived at 28, Westwood Road and had worked for 17 years as an assistant at Overfields, Cabinet Makers, in Russell Street. The local newspaper of the time reported his death as being due to " *a complaint brought on by soldiering*". This quaint but sad expression was no doubt used to describe anything from trench-foot to pneumonia.

A second soldier buried at Leek that winter was **Private James Donald Whitehouse** from 28, Regent Street. This young lad received horrific shellfire wounds to the chest, right eye and left leg at Ypres on 26th October, 1917, whilst serving with the 15th Battalion, Sherwood Foresters. He was brought back to England and treated at St Bartholomew's Hospital in London. An amputation of the damaged leg failed to save the life of this brave 19 year old and he died on Tuesday, 11th December. Five weeks before he was wounded, Donald, as was known, signed off a letter home with: *"Cheer up Mother. Don't worry about me, I shall be alright"*.

Over six weeks passed before the people of Leek heard of the death on the Western Front of yet another local soldier. **Private Thomas Arthur Cannon** from 4 Court, 1, Compton, was killed in action on Wednesday, 12th December, 1917. He had worked as a dyer at Watson's mill before enlisting in the North Staffords. He was serving with the 13th Battalion, The King's (Liverpool Regiment) when he died and is buried at Favreuil British Cemetery just outside Bapaume.

The last Leek casualty of 1917 apparently died of tuberculosis whilst recovering from wounds sustained in Mesopotamia. **Private Eli Mellor** was 37 and serving with the 6th Battalion, South Lancashire Regiment. He lived in Kiln Lane at one time but his wife moved to 39,

(P. Tomlinson)
Donald Whitehouse - buried in Leek Cemetery.

Ball Haye Green after the war. Private Mellor died on Thursday, 13th December, probably whilst being taken by ship to England for treatment. He is buried in Cape Town Cemetery, South Africa.

Private Mellor was another soldier who had worked for Thomas Grace and Sons. This firm was the major builder in the area at the time and built many of the better-known buildings in Leek, particularly those designed by the Sugden brothers. (Cross Street Mill and the Nicholson Institute are but two examples.) Thomas Street and Grace Street were named after the founder and Geoffrey Avenue after one of the sons.

As 1917 drew to a close, the Allied leaders reflected on the offensives of the past year. They thought of the effect that America, now in the war, might have on the course of future operations. They also acknowledged the strong possibility that a major German offensive on the Western Front was going to take place early in 1918. An ominous sign was the numbers of German troops being released from the Russian Front following the suspension of hostilities after the Russian Revolution. A further problem for the British leaders was the shortage of manpower. This situation was to become the subject of fierce argument in later years but the practical effect was that most infantry divisions were reduced from twelve to nine battalions and more than a hundred battalions were disbanded. What would 1918 hold?

Above: The Stone of Remembrance seen in the larger Commonwealth War Cemeteries.

The Commonwealth War Graves Commission was founded by Sir Fabian Ware during the First World War and his energy established the practises which remain today. These include the principles that headstones and memorials should be permanent, headstones should be uniform and there should be no distinction on account of rank, race or creed. There are war graves in some 150 countries, mostly in the 2,500 or so war cemeteries, but many can be seen in civil cemeteries and churchyards. The Commission has a Debt of Honour Register recording the names of 1,700,000 men and women of the Commonwealth forces who died in the two World Wars. This can be accessed via www.cwgc.org. Alternatively, the Commission can be contacted at 2, Marlow Road, Maidenhead, Berkshire SL6 7DX. (Tel: 01628 634221)

Chapter 26

1918 and the German Spring Offensive

*"We had prepared everything we possibly could knowing it was coming.
It came just like a flood"*

(Unknown officer of the 5th North Staffordshire Regiment which suffered heavy losses
during the German break-through on 21st March 1918.)

All sides in the war used mythical figures in propaganda. This one shows Germanica defending the shores of Germany against the Royal Navy.

1918 was to be the last year of the war but one which cost both sides dearly. The Spring brought a massive offensive by the Germans, designed to finish the war before the Americans built up enough forces in France to tip the balance in favour of the Allies.

Meanwhile, the first Leek fatal casualty of the new year was **Private Peter Booth** of the 17th Battalion, Middlesex Regiment who died of wounds on Monday, 7th January. He was 27 and had worked as a travelling salesman in the family drapers business. Although it is thought that he never actually lived in Leek, Peter married a Leek girl and the couple lived at Frodsham, near Chester. His brother-in-law, Gunner Harold Spearing, was killed in November, 1916. (See Chapter 18). Private Booth is buried at Rocquigny-Equancourt Road British Cemetery, Manancourt, eight miles south east of Bapaume. There are nearly 2,000 First World War burials in that cemetery.

The next soldier to die was 30 year old **Private Edward Hulme** of the 6th Battalion, King's Own Scottish Borderers. He was killed on Wednesday 23rd January whilst his unit was in the area of the old Cambrai battlefield. He is buried at Fins New British Cemetery, some 17 miles south-west of Cambrai. Private Hulme was married and lived at Court 1, No: 5, Horton Street. The next soldier, by coincidence, shared the same surname but it is not known if they were related. **Private William Hulme** of the 8th South Staffords was captured on the Western Front by the Germans and died, apparently from dysentery, on Friday 1st February, 1918, in a prisoner-of-war camp in Germany. His grave is at Cologne Southern Cemetery, where over a thousand Allied prisoners who died in captivity are buried. Private Hulme was 24, came from 22, Gladstone Street and was another ex-pupil of West Street School.

For the first time in many months of war a full four weeks elapsed before the next Leek soldier died. This period seems to be the 'calm before the storm', at least for the soldiers from Leek, as we shall see in the following paragraphs. **Private George Cope** from 210, Mill Street, died of gunshot wounds to the chest on Friday, 1st March, 1918. He was a stretcher bearer with the 4th North Staffords. Private Cope is buried at Cement House Cemetery, Langemarck, near Ypres. This is a large military cemetery with 3,553 graves of First World War soldiers, over 2,000 of which are unidentified. The cemetery was named after a nearby fortified farm building. A fortnight later on 16th March 1918, a young soldier of 19 was killed many miles further south. **Private Herbert Brindley** from Broad Street was killed on Saturday, 16th March whilst serving with the 2nd Sherwood Foresters. He is buried at Favreuil British Cemetery, just outside Bapaume. His mother lived at 15, Shirburn Road after the war.

The tired and battle-weary soldiers holding the line on the Western Front had endured yet another winter in the trenches but worse was to come. At 4.40 on the morning of Thursday, 21st March, 1918, several thousand German guns opened up on the British lines on a fifty-mile front south of Arras. The flashes burned through the fog and the ground trembled. By 9.40am, the German infantry, spearheaded by their best troops, attacked and thus began the last great battle of the First World War. The fears of the British commanders had been realised and the German Spring Offensive was a reality. By the evening, over 7,000 British soldiers lay dead and many more were wounded or captured. Six of those killed were Leek men.

For a brief period in early 1918 the Germans actually outnumbered the British and French forces by 192 divisions to 156. Britain was surviving the U-boat campaign due to the convoy system and, for Germany, a decisive victory on the Western Front was needed which would end the war before the Americans could make their presence felt. If the British were beaten, the planners argued, then the French would collapse. The offensive was called 'Operation Michael' and was to be an all-out effort. When the attack came, the 59th (2nd North Midland) Division comprised of men from Staffordshire, Derbyshire and Nottinghamshire, suffered particularly heavy losses.

(Imperial War Museum)

German troops marching to the front in readiness for the Spring Offensive

The 1/5th Battalion, North Staffordshire Regiment, as we saw earlier in this book, was heavily involved in some of the major campaigns of the war. By January, 1918, however, the battalion became one of the casualties of the cut-backs and was disbanded. The officers and men were despatched to four other North Stafford battalions, including the 2nd/5th and that battalion now became known as the 5th Battalion. On 21st March, the 5th North Staffords were in the line at the village of Bullecourt, roughly half-way between Arras and Cambrai. We shall return to 'The Potters' in a moment.

By this stage of the war, the British had designed their defensive lines differently. Much had been learned from the deep German defence systems at Passchendaele. The front line was now known as the Forward Zone and regarded as an outpost line. This was defended in sufficient strength to force the enemy to bombard and attack it with infantry but flexible enough to allow a withdrawal by the defenders to the second and main line of defence, the Battle Zone. This zone held a strong set of defences sited in the best possible position and was far enough back to escape the first enemy attack on the Forward Zone. Any German troops who made it through the Forward Zone would have to run the gauntlet of the machine gun and artillery fire from the Battle Zone before they even reached its front wire. But, as fate would have it, the morning of 21st March was foggy and this proved to be a bonus for the Germans. In many places, the stormtroopers, hidden from the defenders by the heavy mist, infiltrated through the Forward Zone and bypassed the strongpoints. Consequently, whole units of British officers and men were cut off and surrounded. Many were killed or wounded in the fighting and the rest taken prisoner.

The fate of the 5th North Staffords perhaps typifies what happened to many of the British battalions in the Forward Zone that day. For several hours that morning their front line was bombarded with gas shells followed by an infantry attack. The troops held the line and resisted the German onslaught. Later in the day, however, the sound of battle was heard in two nearby villages to the Staffords' rear. The Germans had broken through to the right of the Staffords and, before long, the defenders found themselves surrounded. With no hope of rescue or receiving reinforcements, the Staffordshire men fought bravely, two companies holding out until late afternoon. Inevitably, their ammunition eventually ran out and those still alive had no option but to surrender. Only 35 escaped back to the rear to fight another day. A total of some 560 officers and men had been killed or captured. Many of those taken prisoner were wounded. Two of the 5th North Staffords soldiers killed that day were Leek men.

Private John James Johnson was a stretcher bearer with the battalion and came from Junction Road. His body was never found. **Private John Chawner** was 22 and lived at 20, Nunn Street. He was never found either and the names of both men are commemorated on the Arras Memorial.

Some two miles to the south of Bullecourt and the 5th North Staffords' positions, the line was held by the 7th Battalion, Sherwood Foresters. A young officer attached to that unit was also killed during the German attack. **Lieutenant George Ball** was 24 and one of the 171 officers and men from the battalion killed that day. Again, his connection to Leek has not been established and it is known that his parents lived in Derby after the war. Lieutenant Ball is commemorated on the Arras Memorial.

Some 30 miles to the south, the men of the 1st North Staffords were holding the line in the Forward Zone near to St Quentin. They were attacked by the German 66th Regiment which, history shows, suffered the worst casualty rate for the attackers on that day - 182 killed and nearly 600 wounded and missing. By contrast, casualties amongst the 1st North Staffords and the four other battalions holding the line amounted to 167 killed. Amongst the British dead was Leek-born **Private William Prince**, thought to have lived in Moorhouse Street, a signaller with the battalion. His body was never found and he is commemorated on the Pozieres Memorial.

The remaining two Leek soldiers killed on that tragic day were **Private James Prince** of the 3rd Worcesters and **Private Edward Carter** of the 4th East Lancashires. James Prince lived at 7, Rosebank Terrace and was only 19. It is not known if he was related to William Prince although it is likely. He is commemorated on the Arras Memorial. Private Carter had earlier served in the North Staffordshire Regiment and he is commemorated on the Pozieres Memorial. No other details are known about him.

As the first day of the Spring Offensive came to a close, the Germans had taken nearly 100 square miles of ground from the British. By comparison, almost exactly the same amount of ground had been taken by the British and French in 140 days of hard fighting during the Battle of the Somme and at a cost of over half a million casualties. But what no-one would realise then is that this was the beginning of the end of the First World War although, at the time, it was one of the worst crises of the war for Field Marshal Douglas Haig. Although the Germans made further advances over the following weeks, including seizing back the old Somme battlefields where so much blood had been spilt in 1916, the offensive petered out in June, 1918. By then, German forces had reached the River Marne, much the same as they had during the first offensive in 1914, but were turned back, their supply lines overstretched and their soldiers exhausted. From then on, the Allies held the initiative until the Armistice in November.

By 23rd March, 1918, the Germans had driven back parts of the British Army over twelve miles. The next day, Sunday the 24th, the Somme town of Bapaume fell. On that day, **Private John Fowler** from Ball Lane was killed. He served with the 17th Battalion, Royal Fusiliers, and was the brother of Private William Fowler who died in Mesopotamia in 1917. (See Chapter 18). Private Fowler is commemorated on the Arras Memorial.

Three days later on Tuesday 26th March, two more Leek soldiers fell. **Private Harry Barber**, a former pupil at West Street School, was killed whilst serving with the 9th Battalion, Royal Sussex Regiment, and **Private Charles Bishop** who was with the 1/4th Battalion, Northumberland Fusiliers. Both men are commemorated on the Pozieres Memorial. On the same day, the town of Albert, where virtually all Kitchener's cheery young hopefuls had marched through on their way to the Somme front in 1916, was taken by the Germans.

The Albert Basilica, badly damaged during the war. At the top, the golden figure of the Virgin Mary holding the Infant Jesus. The statue was knocked over by a German shell in 1915 and hung at a precarious angle for the next three years. It was said that if the statue fell, then the war would end. It did fall, in the Spring of 1918, when Albert fell to the Germans.

Above: The Basilica as it is today

On Wednesday, 27th March, as the German advance pushed on, **Private Stephen Arthur Goodwin** was killed, believed by gas poisoning, at the age of 23 whilst in action with the 9th Battalion, Royal Fusiliers. He was born and lived in Leek and his name also appears on the Pozieres Memorial.

Another major German offensive, called 'Operation Mars', was launched against the town of Arras on Thursday, 28th March but was repelled with heavy losses. By now, it was evident that the power of the offensive was declining. The mobility of the Germans was governed by the pace of their foot soldiers; there were few tanks and little in the way of transport. Casualties amongst the stormtroopers had been heavy and the infantrymen who followed were not of the same quality. Two Leek soldiers died in the fighting that day. **Private John William Owen** from 4, Smithfield Cottages was serving with the 7th Battalion, Royal West Kent Regiment. He was 31 and is also commemorated on the Pozieres

(J. Crosby)
Stephen Goodwin - gassed

180

Memorial. **Guardsman Henry Slater** of the 2nd Battalion, Grenadier Guards, was also 31 and lived at 4, Pickwood Road. He had been a warehouseman at the Churnet Works. His body was recovered and is buried at Douchey Les Ayette British Cemetery, nine miles south of Arras.

Ten days into the Spring Offensive and on the last day of March, another Leek soldier was killed in action. **Lance Corporal Walter Ashley** from 25, James Street served with the 1/5th Battalion, Gloucestershire Regiment. He was never found or identified and is commemorated on the Pozieres Memorial.

Left: The Pozieres Memorial and Cemetery on the Somme. Several of the Leek soldiers killed during the German Spring Offensive are commemorated here.
(Commonwealth War Graves Commission)

*The main churches in Leek also honoured
the war dead of the parish.*

*Below. The memorial plaque in
St. Luke's Church*

*Above. The memorial outside
All Saint's Church*

*The plaque in
St. Edwards
Parish Church*

Chapter 27

'Backs to the Wall'

".....believing in the justice of our cause each one of us must fight on to the end".

(Field Marshal Sir Douglas Haig, April, 1918)

April, 1918, brought a change of tactics in the German offensives on the Western Front. On the 4th, troops forged ahead with a limited attack to capture Amiens but were blocked by British and Australian forces. The next day, the German army commander, Ludendorff, called off Operation Michael and ordered fresh attacks towards Flanders between Armentieres and Givenchy, and at Messines. During that first week of April, two more Leek soldiers died.

Private William Lowe of the 5th Battalion, Lincolnshire Regiment, died of wounds on Monday the 1st. His address is uncertain but his brother lived at 141, Mill Street. Private Lowe is buried at Roisel Communal Cemetery Extension, a few miles east of the Somme town of Peronne. On Sunday, 7th April, **Gunner Samuel Salt** serving with the 235th Brigade, Royal Field Artillery, was killed by shrapnel wounds to the head when

The little prayer book issued to servicemen in the war

a German shell exploded close to his gun position. He came from 36, Livingstone Street, had worked in the packing warehouse at Wardle and Davenports and was 20 when he died. He is buried at Couin New British Cemetery between Amiens and Arras where there are 350 burials from the First World War.

A young soldier who was born in Leek but later moved to Bridgenorth, Shropshire, where he enlisted, was killed on Tuesday, 9th April. **Private Harold Glenn** was serving with the 1/10th King's (Liverpool Regiment). He was never found and this 19 year-old is another Leek lad commemorated on the Loos Memorial.

The German assaults in the Flanders area were known as the Lys Offensive, after the River Lys which runs through the area. By 11th April, the situation for the British was serious and the Germans were only five miles from Hazebrouck, an important rail and communications centre. Field Marshal Haig issued his famous order: *"There is no other course open to us but to fight it out. Every position must be held to the last man; there must be no retirement. With our backs to the wall and believing in the justice of our cause each one of us must fight on to the end".*

The next Leek soldier to lose his life on the Western Front was **Private Antony Graham**, the brother of Arthur Graham who was killed three years earlier (see Chapter 5). Antony lived at 46 Grove Street and was serving with the 1/6th Battalion, South Staffords, when he died from the effects of poison gas on Monday, 15th April, 1918. It is believed that the Grahams, at one time the only family of that name in Leek, originated from Scotland, moved to Ireland, then to Manchester and finally to Leek. Antony Graham's body was never found or identified and he is commemorated on the Arras Memorial. The following day, as the Germans pushed forwards to the Ypres Salient, 24 year old **Gunner William Edward Brandrick**, an employee of Brough, Nicholson and Hall was killed near to the Ypres-Menin road when a shell burst in a dug-out entrance. A machine-gunner in the Machine Gun Corps, he lies buried at Voormezeele Enclosure Cemetery, near Ypres.

(P. Kirk)

Antony Graham - died of gas poisoning

As the Germans continued their assaults in Flanders, the British commanders reluctantly decided to withdraw from the Passchendaele Ridge losing the ground so desperately fought for in the November battles. This part of the German offensive was called off on 29th

April but not before another four Leek soldiers lost their lives in the Ypres Salient.

Private Thomas Robinson was a married man of 30 and lived at 99, Shirburn Road. He was killed on Saturday, 20th April, 1918 serving with the 11th Battalion, Lancashire Fusiliers. He is commemorated on the Tyne Cot Memorial. The next day, Lance Corporal Arthur Morris from 58, Grove Street, died of his wounds at a Casualty Clearing Station near Poperinghe. Serving in the 2/5th Sherwood Foresters, he was a former pupil at West Street School. Lance Corporal Morris is buried at Haringhe (Bandaghem) Military Cemetery, Poperinghe.

Also buried at Haringhe Cemetery is Gunner William Baddeley from Junction Road. He was killed on Thursday, 25th April serving with the 319th Siege Battery, Royal Garrison Artillery. Killed on the same day was 19 year old Private Ernest Nelson of 2 Court, 8, Ball Lane. He was serving with the 1/5th Battalion, West Yorkshire Regiment. His body was never found and descendants of his family recall that his mother kept her front door open for years afterwards in the hope that he had

(P. Pickford)
Ernest Nelson

been perhaps shell-shocked and would one day return home. Private Nelson is commemorated on the Tyne Cot Memorial.

During that last April of the war, three more Leek soldiers died in other countries. Private John Kirkham DCM of 38, Pickwood Road, died at the age of 30 in the United Kingdom on Tuesday, the 9th. He was serving with the 1st Battalion, Royal Irish Fusiliers. This soldier had won the Distinguished Conduct Medal in 1915 for conspicuous gallantry. His citation reads: "When all the (telephone) wires had been cut, Private Kirkham volunteered to carry an important message. He had to pass over about a thousand yards of ground swept by rifle fire and, although wounded, he successfully accomplished the task". Private Kirkham is buried in Leek Cemetery.

(Author)
John Kirkham's grave in Leek Cemetery

Thousands of miles away on the Palestine Front where British and Commonwealth forces were fighting the Turks, **Lieutenant Ernest William Gould** of the 4th Battalion, South Lancashire Regiment, was killed in action on Thursday, 11th April. He was a native of Wirksworth and his direct connection with Leek has not been established. After the war, his parents were living in Sussex. Lieutenant Gould was only 19 when he was killed. He is buried at Ramleh War Cemetery in Israel not far from Tel-Aviv. The cemetery contains over 3,500 burials from the First World War and is a stark reminder of the fact that the four year conflict was not confined to the Western Front. The British interests in this part of the world were, of course, focussed upon the Suez Canal. Back in Europe, in a different theatre of war, **Private Percy Goodfellow**, from 113, Mill Street was killed on Monday, 15th April, on his 29th birthday. A baker at Leek Co-op before the war, he was serving with the 2nd Battalion, Cheshire Regiment in Salonika, Greece. British, French, Serbian and some Russian troops were stationed at this strategically important port on the Aegean coast to counter the threat from Bulgaria. The conditions in this area were bad for the troops. Although the Allies suffered less than 20,000 battle casualties during the whole campaign, almost 450,000 men were struck down with malaria. Private Goodfellow is commemorated on the Doiran Memorial in Greece.

SOMEBODY KNOWS, SOMEBODY CARES (2).

Somebody knows, somebody cares, somebody's sad like me,
Somebody sighs, somebody cries for sympathy, sweet sympathy;
Some fond heart aches, some fond heart breaks, now that we
two are apart,
But somebody someday will find Paradise in the garden of
somebody's heart.

(P.Pickford)

Chapter 28

The Turning of the Tide

"Happy are men who yet before they are killed
Can let their veins run cold............."

(War Poet, Lieutenant Wilfred Owen. Killed in action, November, 1918)

With May came Ludendorff's next gamble and the third phase of the German Spring Offensive. On the 27th, his troops attacked at the River Aisne (where they had been in 1914) and, within a few hours, had crossed the river and destroyed the best part of eight British and French divisions. An advance of

(Imperial War Museum)
Blinded British troops awaiting treatment

twelve miles was made that day and by early June, the Germans had reached the River Marne, 56 miles from Paris. But, before the offensive commenced, five more Leek soldiers lost their lives on French soil.

On Monday, 6th May, **Corporal Reginald Wood**, serving with the Machine Gun Corps, was killed in action. He was 20 and came from 41, Junction Road. His body was never found or identified and he is commemorated on the Loos Memorial. Nine days later on Wednesday, 15th May, **Private Joseph Henry Bratt**, from Pool End, Macclesfield Road, died in hospital at Rouen after being gassed two days earlier. He was serving with the 9th North Staffords and was 24. His father was a wheelwright and the family lived where the Robin Hood garage now is. Private Bratt is buried at St Sever Cemetery Extension, Rouen and is also commemorated on the Meerbrook memorial. Buried in the same cemetery is another Leek soldier from the 9th North Staffords who probably suffered the same fate as Joseph Bratt. **Lance Corporal Harry Stockton** died in hospital on Wednesday, 22nd May. He had lived at 26, Ball Haye Road.

Private **John William Goldstraw** of the 1/6th North Staffords was the next Leek casualty. He died of his wounds on Friday, 24th May, 1918 and is buried at Pernes British Cemetery, about 20 miles west of Loos. On Sunday, 26th, ex-boy scout **Private Reginald Davies** from 12, Britannia Street, also died of wounds at the tender age of 18. He was in the 2/4th Kings Own Yorkshire Light Infantry and is buried at Bienvillers Military Cemetery some 14 miles south-west of Arras.

As the Germans launched their attack on the Aisne, two more Leek soldiers died. **Sergeant Harold Birchenough** serving with the 15th Battalion, Durham Light Infantry was killed on Monday, 27th May. He was born in Leek and attended West Street School, enlisting in the Royal Fusiliers when war broke out. His body was never found or identified and he is commemorated on the Soissons Memorial on the River Aisne. This memorial commemorates those who fell between May and August, 1918 in the areas of the Aisne and the Marne and who have no known grave. There are nearly 4,000 names recorded on the memorial walls. On Wednesday, 29th, another 18 year-old was lost. **Private George Henry James Brindley** served with the 2nd Battalion, Essex Regiment and died of his wounds after being shot in the chest. One of four children, he had worked at Wardle and Davenports and lived at 52 Derby Street where his parents kept a fruit and vegetable shop. Private Brindley is buried at Gonnehem British Cemetery, a few miles north of Bethune.

Yet more Leek servicemen died in the United Kingdom during May, 1918, and one died in Mesopotamia.

Able Seaman William Mitchell from 10, St Georges Street had been a crew member of one of the ships which took part on a raid on the Belgian post of Zeebrugge on 22/23rd

(Imperial War Museum)

Zeebrugge Harbour after the raid

April, 1918. The port was in German hands and used as a U-boat base. The raid, which involved plans to sink old British ships filled with concrete to block the entrances, achieved little but was useful for the British propaganda machine. William Mitchell survived the raid only to be killed in an accident in England two weeks later on 6th May. He was 41 and serving on HMS Attentive. His grave is at Plaistow, Essex.

Lance-Corporal Frank Malkin was 46 when he died of illness on Friday, 17th May whilst serving with the Royal Engineers in England. He was married and lived at 18, Britannia Street, a few doors away from Private Reginald Davies, killed a few weeks earlier in France. Lance-Corporal Malkin is buried in Leek Cemetery. Not far from his grave is that of **Sergeant Samuel Stretch** from Rosebank. He had served for over three years with the 2nd Battalion, (Duke of Wellingtons) West Riding Regiment and gone through some rough times before being badly wounded on the Western Front. He was brought back to England for treatment but died of his wounds on Tuesday, 21st May. He was 28. A week later Leek Cemetery officials prepared for the burial of another local soldier who died on the 28th May. **Gunner John Arthur Johnson** was 20 and came from 39, Nelson Street. He served with a Reserve Brigade of the Royal Field Artillery.

A soldier attached to the Australian Corps of the Army Service Corps was killed on Friday, 31st May. **Driver Sydney William Leckenby** was 29 and born in Yorkshire. At the time of his death he was living with his wife in Worksop. His connection to Leek cannot be established although he probably worked and lived here for some time prior to his marriage. Driver Leckenby is buried at Daours Communal Cemetery, seven miles east of Amiens. His surname appears to have been misspelt as 'Leckenbury' on the Leek Monument.

The one Leek soldier who died in Mesopotamia that May was **Private John William Plant** who was born and enlisted in Leek. He died, believed from disease, on Saturday, 18th May whilst serving with the 7th Battalion, North Staffords. He is buried at Baghdad War Cemetery.

In early June, 1918, as the German armies reached the River Marne, so the casualties on both sides mounted. On the 2nd, a Sunday, 19 year old **Private David Birchenough** was killed. He lived at 5, Garden Street, attended the nearby West Street School and was serving in France with the 5th Battalion, Kings Own Yorkshire Light Infantry. His grave is at Bienvillers Military Cemetery, about 13 miles south-west of Arras. On Monday, 10th June, **Private John Fleet** from 5, Railway Cottages, Leekbrook, was killed. He was in the 24th Battalion, Royal Fusiliers and was also19. Private Fleet is buried at Douchy-Les-Ayette British Cemetery, France, 9 miles south of Arras. The following day, Tuesday, 11th June, 28 year old **Private William Ernald Bond** of the 18th Lancashire Fusiliers died of wounds. He was a married man and a native of Tean but his address in Leek is unknown. Private Bond is buried at Doullens Communal Cemetery between Amiens and Arras.

Another member of the Leek Battery was killed in action in France on Wednesday, 12th June, 1918. **Gunner Charles Owen Ball** came from 13, North Avenue and was 24. Another ex-pupil of West Street School, he is buried at Fouquieres Churchyard Extension,

Bethune. There are 387 Commonwealth burials here, 249 of them from the 46th (North Midland) Division.

Further to the north, another Leek gunner died of his wounds on Sunday, 16th June. **Gunner Henry Malkin**, aged 32, was married and lived at one time at 94, Mill Street. He was serving with the 251st Siege Battery, Royal Garrison Artillery. His grave is in the Hoogstade Belgian Military Cemetery, Alveringem. The remaining two Leek soldiers who died in June, 1918, are thought to have been Prisoners-of-War, captured during the German advances after 21st March. **Private George Smith,** a married man from Gaunt Street, was serving with the 1st Sherwood Foresters and died on Wednesday, 12th June. He is buried at Premont British Cemetery, France, 14 miles south-east of Cambrai. As this cemetery was not started until October, 1918, it is believed that Private Smith was brought there from another cemetery in a German-held sector where he was first buried. The second soldier was 20 year-old **Private Frank Pointon** from 40, Livingstone Street. He was wounded in France whilst serving with the 13th Battalion, Yorkshire Regiment and captured. Taken to a hospital in Germany, Frank Pointon died there on Saturday, 22nd June. He is buried at Niederzwehren War Cemetery in Germany. His neighbour from two doors away, Samuel Salt, had already been killed two months earlier.

As July, 1918, got under way the military situation in France was similar to that of 1914 with German forces preparing to attack on the River Marne. In the meantime, a young Leek soldier who was posthumously awarded the Military Medal for bravery lost his fight for life after being badly wounded in France. **Private Sidney Simpson M.M.** was serving with the Royal Army Medical Corps and frequently went out into No Man's Land to carry in wounded soldiers. This was a dangerous task and, inevitably, his luck ran out on 28th June when he went into No Man's Land under fire to rescue wounded men near Bethune. He himself became a casualty when he was shot in the leg by sniper-fire. He was evacuated to England where his badly damaged leg had to be amputated at a military hospital in Dover. Unfortunately, gangrene set in, his condition worsened and Sidney died at the hospital on 5th July, aged 21. He never

(B. Simpson)
Sidney Simpson- Awarded the Military Medal

knew that he had been awarded the Military Medal for his courage on the day he was wounded. Sidney was brought back to his home town and buried in Leek Cemetery. He had lived at 43, Shoobridge Street, was one of seven children and worked in the Leek silk mills before enlisting in 1915. His brother, Harry, was killed at Arras in May, 1917. (See Chapter 19).

(Daily Mail)

The photograph published in the Daily Mail in 1916. Private Simpson is carrying the front right-hand of the stretcher.

Sidney Simpson kept a diary which survived and is now a prized possession of his nephew. He gives some interesting accounts of life on the Western Front. One entry, written at the height at the Battle of the Somme (but obviously not in that sector), gives an idea of one way troops were kept occupied out of the line - running races. " *.........I went on to win 3 francs in the quarter mile race on 12th July, 10 francs in the half mile race (2nd place) - all to the accompaniment of an army band. Went to bed at 7pm, tired out but 13 francs richer*". Another entry on 21st July 1916 was a different story. Sidney was at the Somme front then. "*..........Germans shell us heavy, dug-out smashed in a dozen yards away. 3 killed, 2 wounded. Many horses killed. At night Germans shell us heavy with gas shells, they send so many we are ordered to wear gas helmets*". Early in September 1916, a photographer from the Daily Mail visited Montauban on the Somme front and photographed Sidney Simpson and other stretcher-bearers carrying a wounded man over the muddy wastes of the battlefield. Entries in the diary stopped on the 18th June, 1918, ten days before he was wounded.

Private Sidney Simpson, his brother Harry and another brother, Fred, are also commemorated on an interesting brass plaque in All Saints Church, erected by a fourth brother, William.

On the same day that Sidney Simpson died at Dover, a 51 year old soldier in the Royal Defence Corps died of a heart attack in Leek. **Private Edmund McLeavy** lived at No: 1, Court 9, Mill Street. He was a silk weaver by trade. Private McLeavy is buried in Leek Cemetery.

The fate of the next Leek soldier to die is not so clear. **Private Norman Riley** was the son of Edwin and Clara Riley of 7, Westwood Road. He died in England on 7th July, 1918, at the age of 18. A former pupil at West Street School, Private Riley was attached to the Sherwood Foresters. He was probably still in training for eventual transfer to the Western Front. His grave is also in Leek Cemetery.

Lance Corporal Sam Hunt was another Leek soldier captured by the Germans during the Spring Offensive of March, 1918. He was serving with the 2/5th North Staffords who put up a brave resistance in the front lines against the enemy onslaught and suffered heavy casualties. He died in captivity, on 12th July, possibly of wounds or from the Spanish 'flu

(Commonwealth War Graves Commission)
Cologne Southern Cemetery, Germany. Over 1,000 allied prisoners-of-war are buried here.

epidemic which was starting to ravage young and old alike around the world. Lance Corporal Hunt is buried at Cologne Southern Cemetery, Germany, not far from Private William Hulme who died the previous February whilst in German hands. As referred to earlier, this cemetery contains over a thousand Allied servicemen who died whilst in captivity.

The last Leek soldier to be killed in July, 1918, was 20 year old **Gunner Thomas William Malkin** from 74, Mill Street. He was serving with the 46th Battalion, Machine Gun Corps when he was killed by a shell explosion during the early hours of the 24th. A former employee at Goodwin and Tatton's mill, he is buried at the military extension of Fouquieres Churchyard just outside Bethune, France.

The Germans attacked on the Marne on July 15th 1918, but three days later, Allied forces, including the Americans, counter-attacked and not only stopped, but reversed the German advances. By the end of July, the tide had turned in the fortunes of the Allied forces and what had been a crisis for them in the last few months was now one for Germany. German soldiers were becoming demoralised and in many cases, the will to fight was fast waning. Field Marshal Haig sensed that the war would be finished before the winter set in and history would prove him right. Nevertheless, there was still a long, hard struggle ahead before Germany would give up the fight and the casualties on both sides continued to mount. The exhausting counter-attack on the Marne ended on August 4th by which time several miles of territory had been recovered by the Allies. Undoubtedly, this was the beginning of the end for Germany.

There is a British war cemetery a few miles from Soissons called Raperie British Cemetery which contains, amongst its 600 burials, the graves of 100 officers and men of the 9th Battalion, Royal Scots who fell in the opening days of August, 1918 during the victorious advance of the Scottish Divisions in this area. One of these is that of **Private Harold Pickford** from 25, York Street, Leek, a former employee at Clemesha Brothers and Birch. He was killed at the age of 21 on Thursday, 1st August.

Eighty miles to the north, at Douchy-Les-Ayette British Cemetery near Arras, lies another Leek soldier killed on the 1st August. **Private Thomas Charles Yates** of the 2nd South Staffords

Tom Yates

(I. Ward)

came from 9, Duke Street and was only 19. Descendants of this boy's mother recall how, in the heady days of late 1914, he rushed off to join the army in response to Kitchener's call. He was 15 at the time. How far he got through the recruitment and training process is not known but what is certain is that his mother, Jane Yates, soon caught up with him and had him sent back home quite smartly! Tom rejoined later in the war, presumably at the right age, but was not destined to survive it. His family always put a small cross in Tom's memory on the Monument every Remembrance Sunday.

It was not uncommon for under-age lads to try and join up, particularly in the early months of the war and this applied to Leek as much as anywhere else. With the passage of time, it has become virtually impossible to identify those who did actually manage to enlist whilst still under the required age. A soldier had to be 19 before he could go on <u>active service abroad</u> but this was reduced after the Spring Offensive in March, 1918 to the age of 18 because of the manpower shortage in the British Army. Some of the commanders of the Territorial battalions, however, are thought not to have been too fussy about a lad's age providing the parents had no objection to their son serving abroad. There is strong evidence of 16, 17 and 18 year old Territorials (Terriers, or 'Week-End soldiers' as they were sometimes irreverently called) serving on the Western Front in the early part of the war.

On Thursday 8th August, 1918, British and French divisions launched a massive counter-offensive against the German Army east of Amiens on the Somme. Australian and Canadian units, known for their fighting quality, played a crucial role. The build-up to the offensive was kept secret from the enemy by clever use of deception and much use was made of tanks, heavy artillery and aircraft. The tactical ability of the BEF had now vastly improved since the 1916 days, of that, there was no doubt. That day, later described by Ludendorff as the "*blackest* day *of the German Army in the history of the war*", Allied troops advanced some nine miles, despite the summer heat and the exhaustion of the tank crews sweating in their steel boxes. Over the next two days the advance gradually slowed to a halt as fatigue set in and German reserves were brought up to stiffen the resistance.

One of the British battalions involved on the 8th August was the 7th Royal Sussex and its soldiers made an extraordinary and courageous assault on German-held territory on the Morlancourt Ridge. Gassed and shelled whilst marching along the Corbie to Bray road on the way to the jumping-off trenches and knowing little of the terrain over which they were to attack, they and the men of another battalion advanced under heavy fire and reached their first objective. Between them, the two battalions lost 520 officers and men killed or wounded and were unable to advance further due to the ferocity of the machine gun and artillery fire coming from German positions in a wood. The 7th Royal Sussex were also involved in the fighting the next day but were then pulled out of the line for rest and recuperation. One of the battalion casualties was 26 year old **Private Percy Belfield** from 24, Union Street, Leek. He had worked at Joshua Wardles, Leekbrook, was married and the father of four sons with a fifth on the way. Private Belfield is buried at Beacon Cemetery, Sailly-Laurette, some 6 miles from Albert and is recorded as having died on the 13th August. It is believed that he

(G. Belfield)

Percy Belfield with his wife and children

was mortally wounded during the attacks of the 8th or 9th August when his battalion was in action but did not die until the 13th. There are some 40 graves of men from the 7th Royal Sussex in Beacon Cemetery. They were relocated there from a small battlefield cemetery known as 'Sussex Cemetery' just over half a mile away and most were killed in the advance of 8th August. Percy Belfield's five sons all served during the Second World War but survived.

The British War Medal. The standard medal issued to members of all forces of the Empire who had served in uniform or who rendered 'approved' service.

195

*The statue of Field Marshal Douglas Haig (later Earl Haig) at Edinburgh Castle.
There is still controversy today over this commander's conduct of the war.*

Chapter 29

Advance to Victory

"Risks which a month ago would have been criminal to incur, ought now to be incurred as a duty. It is no longer necessary to advance in regular lines and step by step............."

(Field Marshal Sir Douglas Haig, disappointed in his Army Commanders' caution and rigidity of plans, August, 1918.)

By late August, 1918, the Allies had reached the Somme town of Albert, determined to take back the town which featured so prominently in the 1916 battles. The advance began on 21st August. The next day, Thursday, 22nd, two soldiers from the town were killed in action and a third died of his wounds.

Lance Corporal John Richards had exchanged one uniform for another when he enlisted in the army. He was a police constable at the old Leek Police Station in Leonard Street.

The old Leek Police Station in Leonard Street.
From a painting by the author.

Originally joining the Military Police, he was later transferred to the 10th Battalion, King's Shropshire Light Infantry and was killed when his battalion advanced on enemy positions south of the Lys canal, near Bethune. The troops attacked through a cornfield which, at the height of summer was full of high, standing corn. The Germans had concealed themselves well and when the battalion was only a hundred yards away, opened up with devastating fire. This was followed up by a determined counter-attack and the Shropshire men were forced back to their start lines. 179 officers and men were killed, wounded or taken prisoner. Lance-Corporal Richards is buried at Vielle-Chapelle New Military Cemetery, north-east of Bethune. He was 26.

On the same day but further to the south on the old Somme battlefields, **Private Percy Hammersley** of the 12th Battalion, Gloucestershire Regiment was killed, apparently whilst his company was moving across a valley to repel a German counter-attack. He came from Junction Road and was 28. His body was not found or identified and he is commemorated on the Vis-en-Artois Memorial between Arras and Cambrai. This memorial records the names of over 9,000 men who fell between August 1918 and the Armistice in November between the Somme and Loos and who have no known grave.

The third Leek soldier to die that Thursday was a 29 year old driver with the Royal Field Artillery. **Driver Thomas Mowbray Missen** was married with one child and lived at 17, Horton Street. He was reportedly injured by a bomb from a German aircraft and died from his wounds. He had been wounded twice and gassed once already during the war. Driver Missen is buried at Villers-Bretonneux Military Cemetery, situated on the main road from Amiens to St Quentin.

The following day, Friday 23rd August, the fighting for Albert claimed the lives of two more Leek soldiers. **Private Arthur Robinson** from 138, Mill Street was serving with the 10th Battalion, Essex Regiment. He was an ex-pupil at West Street School. Private Robinson is buried at Albert Communal Cemetery Extension, France. **Private Harold Tatton** was serving with the 7th Battalion, Royal West Surrey Regiment. He came from 70, Southbank Street and was only 18. His family always believed that he lied about his age when enlisting. Private Tatton is buried at Becourt Military Cemetery, just outside Albert. Both battalions these soldiers were serving in were involved on the assault on Morlancourt earlier in the month when Private Percy Belfield was killed.

By 23rd August, the British had captured Albert and were pushing on towards Bapaume, reaching the outskirts by the 26th. That day, a Monday, **Private Harold Bould** from 137, Ball Haye Road, Leek, died of wounds in a hospital at Rouen. He was 33 and serving with the 1st Bedfords. His grave is at the St Sever Cemetery, within two miles of Rouen Cathedral.

Another Leek soldier died of his wounds in hospital at the large military base of Etaples on Saturday, 31st August, 1918. **Lance-Corporal John William Ainsworth** of the 1st North

Staffords lived with an aunt at 17, Regent Street. He was a single man of 28, a devout Methodist and had worked in the knitting department at Wardle and Davenport's. Jack had been wounded twice before on the Western Front and the last time he returned to the front from hospital, after the March Offensive, he found most of his comrades killed, captured or wounded. The injury which killed Lance-Corporal Ainsworth was a gunshot wound to the spine. He is buried at the Etaples Military Cemetery.

By early September, 1918, the town of Peronne had fallen to the seemingly unstoppable Allies. That and other successes persuaded Ludendorff to pull his forces back to the Hindenburg Line but, by now, growing numbers of German soldiers had lost faith in their leaders.

Jack Ainsworth

(J. Burrows)

On Monday, 2nd September, **Private Henry Peacock** of the 1st Battalion, Cheshire Regiment, was killed in action. He was 39 and worked on the railways at Mansfield before enlisting. His brother, Joseph, lived at Court 2, No: 2, New Street, Leek. Private Peacock had been invalided home on two previous occasions, once with shell-shock and later with enteric fever. Unfortunately, his place of burial or commemoration cannot be found in official records.

On Tuesday the 3rd, Leek-born **Private Frederick William Clay** of the 1/6th Sherwood Foresters was killed. He is buried at Fouquieres Churchyard just outside Bethune. The next day, **Private James William Ball** aged 24 and from 20, Langford Street, was killed in action fighting with the 1st Battalion, Hertfordshire Regiment. He is buried at Hermies Hill British Cemetery, mid-way between Bapaume and Cambrai.

Over in the Middle East where, as we saw earlier, the 7th North Staffords had been in action in Mesopotamia, two more Leek servicemen, a captain and a lance-corporal, were killed on Saturday, 14th September. By this time, the battalion had taken part in the operations to capture Baghdad and were now advancing through northern Persia (now Iran) where it was in action against the Turks near Baku on the coast of the Caspian Sea. Turkish troops, in large numbers, attacked the British and most of the Staffords, fighting to the last, became casualties. **Captain Eric Minor Spink** was 24 and the son of a vicar, the Reverend Edmund Spink who, ironically, conducted the funeral of at least one of the Leek soldiers who died in the war. Captain Spink was seen directing his men against the enemy moments before he fell. He is commemorated on the Haidar Pasha Memorial, Istanbul, Turkey. **Lance-Corpo-**

ral **Edgar Birch**, was 26 and lived at 3, Portland Street. His younger brother, Harry, was killed in Palestine in 1917. (See Chapter 19). Lance-Corporal Birch is commemorated on the Tehran Memorial, Iran.

The next Leek soldier to be killed on the Western Front that September was 24 year old **Private Harry Mathias Keates**. He was born in Portland Street but his parents later moved to 33, Ball Haye Green. Harry served in the 1/4th Kings Own Scottish Borderers and was a former member of the Salvation Army in Leek. He was missing in action on the 20th and is commemorated on the Vis-en-Artois Memorial.

History shows that amongst the finest fighting formations in the British Expeditionary force were those of Australia and Canada. They both played a crucial role in the offensives of 8th August, 1918, and afterwards. The Canadians were later moved to the Arras area and on Friday, 27th September, took part in a major assault on the Hindenburg Line, the main German line of defence. They had the task of crossing the Canal du Nord, a formidable obstacle, and advancing beyond the opposite bank into heavily defended territory. This was achieved and although several days hard fighting followed the breakthrough had been achieved. The way was paved for the capture of Cambrai in early October. One of the soldiers killed in the assault on 27th September was Leek-born **Corporal James Knowles**. He was a married man of 26 and had been raised at 16A, Ball Haye Green. In 1911, after marrying, James and his new wife emigrated to Canada to start a new life there. After war broke out, he joined the 8th Battalion, Canadian Infantry (Manitoba Regiment), and found himself crossing the Atlantic once more. But this time, he would

(B. Bailey)

James Knowles is the soldier pictured standing in the centre

not return. Corporal Knowles is buried at Sancourt British Cemetery, near Cambrai. After his death, his wife, Millicent, returned to Leek and lived at 2, Prospect Place.

A second Leek-born soldier killed on the same day as Corporal Knowles had also emigrated before the war, not to Canada but to New Zealand where his mother lived. **Lance-Corporal Frank Mansell** was thought to be an engineer in Leek but his address here is not known. When he was killed, he was serving with the 1st Battalion, 3rd New Zealand Rifle Brigade which fought for four days to capture the town of Bapaume from the Germans. Lance-Corporal Mansell, (a relative of the late Ken Willshaw), is commemorated on the Grevillers (New Zealand) Memorial, just west of Bapaume.

The next day, Saturday, 28th September, Allied forces attacking in the Ypres salient, drove the Germans off the Passchendaele Ridge. Killed that day was **Private Thomas Henry Wood** from 67, Portland Street. He was serving with the 20th Battalion, Middlesex Regiment and was 19. Harry, as he was known, had worked for Frank Foster, the butcher, in Cawdrey Buildings, Fountain Street and had five sisters. A soldier with Harry when he was killed told the family that their son was shot by a sniper just before or as he was 'going over the top' in the attack on enemy positions. The letter was accompanied by Harry's bible. As happened so often, his body was lost and he is commemorated on the Tyne Cot Memorial to the Missing. A nephew of Harry's who is now 92 remembers seeing his uncle's poor mother breaking her heart in the street near her home whilst bells were pealing and people celebrating after the armistice in November, 1918, six weeks after her son's death. This unfortunate lady was, of course, but one of over 400 mothers in the town who were going through the same agonies. On that same Saturday, **Private Thomas Robinson** was killed in action. He was in the 1/5th South Staffords and had enlisted at Leek. No other details are known about this soldier who was never found, he is commemorated on the Vis-en-Artois Memorial, France.

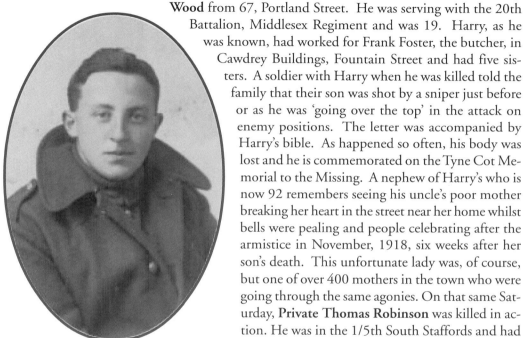

(A. Wood)
Harry Wood - shot by sniper

Sunday, 29th September 1918, was the day which saw a magnificent performance by the Staffordshire Brigade of the 46th (North Midland) Division. The Territorials of the 5th North Staffords, the 5th and 6th South Staffords who had fared so badly at Gommecourt on 1st July, 1916, stormed the defences of the St Quentin Canal at Bellenglise, overwhelmed the German defenders and won well-deserved praise from the highest quarters for successfully breaching the Hindenburg Line. The 46th Division captured 4,200 out of the day's total of 5,300 enemy soldiers that day. The Staffordshire men, following a daring and dangerous but well-prepared plan, crossed the 35 foot wide canal, up to 15 feet deep in places, on ropes, make-shift rafts, collapsible boats, and footbridges which the Germans had failed to destroy. They and follow-up units made inroads three to four miles deep into enemy-held territory. The nearby Riqueval Bridge, some 15 miles south of Cambrai, was captured intact and the famous photograph of the Staffordshire Brigade triumphantly lining the steep embankment by the bridge is frequently published in historical accounts of the First World War. (See page 205.) For three days prior to the assault, a heavy bombardment of the enemy positions across the canal had crashed down. The Leek Battery was one of the artillery units involved, firing 150 rounds daily from their 4.5" howitzers. Bellenglise, a small but heavily fortified village, is one of the places named on the top section of the Monument.

Killed in action on the day of the Staffords' success, but further to the north, was **Private Joe Collins**, 20, of the 2/4th Battalion, West Riding Regiment. He had worked at Brough, Nicholson and Hall and lived at 14, Wood Street. He is buried at Grand Ravine British Cemetery, seven miles from Cambrai.

Three more Leek soldiers died the following day, Monday, 30th September, 1918, all in different theatres of war. **Private James Gilman**, 28, of the1st Battalion, Coldstream Guards, died of wounds at a casualty clearing station in the Bapaume area. He is buried at Grevillers British Cemetery, just west of Bapaume. Private Gilman was married and lived at 19, Queen Street. He was educated at West Street School and later worked at the Alexandra Mill, rising to a managerial position. Miles to the north in Belgian Flanders, **Private William Henry Clayton** from 12, Frith Street, was killed in action serving with the 1st Battalion, Lancashire Fusiliers. He was 21 and another ex-pupil at West Street School. Before enlisting, Private Clayton worked at the Ball Haye Green Co-op. He is buried at Vichte Military Cemetery, 30 miles east of Ypres

(A. Wood)

Richard Cantrell

The third soldier to die on 30th September was **Private Richard Cantrell**, aged 23, of the 8th Battalion, Kings Shropshire Light Infantry. He lived and worked at Gutter Farm, Bradnop where his father was the tenant farmer. Private Cantrell, who enlisted in the North Staffordshire Regiment against his mother's wishes, (later transferring to the Shropshires), was badly injured during the Allied offensives against the Bulgarians in September, 1918, at Salonika, Greece, and died of his wounds on the 30th. He is buried at Mikra British Cemetery, a few miles from Thessalonika (formerly Salonika).

October, 1918, was, of course, the penultimate month of conflict on the Western Front. Still the casualties continued but the menace of the so-called Spanish 'Flu was also taking its dreadful toll across the world. In all, some 70 million people died from this viral infection in 1918 and 1919. When it died away, the disease was still unexplained and no treatment had been found for it. One Leek soldier who died in England may have been a victim. **Private Charles Victor Fenton** was 41 and serving with the 9th Battalion, Northamptonshire Regiment when he died on Wednesday, 2nd October. His parents lived at 102, Westwood Road, next door to Lieutenant Hubert Gwynne who, as we saw, was killed on the Somme in November, 1916. Private Fenton is buried in Leek Cemetery.

Let us return now to the activities of the Leek Battery which had been firing on targets in what was known as the Battle of Ramicourt between 3rd and 5th October, 1918. Ramicourt, one of the place-names carved into the top section of the Leek Monument is a small village some five miles northeast of Bellenglise. By Saturday, 5th October, the Battery gunners were laying down a creeping artillery barrage and smoke shells near the village of Montbrehain, a couple of miles from Ramicourt. It was on that day that the Battery lost a brave and dedicated member, **Sergeant Percy Pickford M.M.** He was killed by shellfire whilst running to the assistance of a wounded man, one of the Battery drivers, whose horse had been killed beneath him. Sergeant Pickford was 24 and one of 12 children raised at 20, North Street, now the North Stores. Before the war he had worked at Brough, Nicholson and Hall and was a keen footballer, captaining the Leek Territorial Football Team. He won his Military Medal in July, 1917, at the same time as Lieutenant Lewthwaite won his Miltary Cross and for the same reasons. In a letter to his mother, the Battery commander praised her son, describing him as *"the most popular man in the Battery......I have lost one of my best friends"*.

Sergeant Percy Pickford M.M. is buried at Bellicourt British Cemetery, about eight miles west of Montbrehain where he fell. The rather touching inscription on his headstone, chosen by his family, reads: *"To live in hearts we leave behind is not to die"*.

The next Leek soldier to lose his life was **Private William Atkinson** from 11, Nelson Street. He was serving with the 1st Staffordshire Imperial Yeomanry on the Palestine Front when he died, believed from disease, on Monday, 7th October, 1918. He is buried at Kantara War Memorial Cemetery, Egypt, where there was a hospital. The village of Kantara was an important fortified area in the defence of the Suez Canal against Turkish attacks.

(K. Pickford)

Percy Pickford - killed whilst assisting a wounded man.

The breaching of the Hindenburg Line undoubtedly convinced the German High Command that the war was lost. Already, peace overtures were being made to the United States but still the resistance to the Allied advance continued. By 9th October, Canadian patrols had entered Cambrai, the prize fought over in the tank offensive of the previous November but, within 48 hours, the Germans had made a stand on the line of the River Selle near Le Cateau. The village of St. Aubert, some 10 miles east of Cambrai, was captured as the Allies continued to pound their enemy. Buried in the cemetery there is **Corporal Harry Golby** of the 3rd Battalion, Rifle Brigade. He had driven a delivery van for Brough, Nicholson and Hall before joining the colours and was a former pupil of West Street School. Corporal Golby, only 19 when he was killed on Friday 11th October, reportedly whilst firing a Lewis machine gun in action against the enemy, had lived with his sister at 3, Alma Street, Leek. The next day, Saturday, 12th October, **Private James Thomas Smith** from 28, Compton, was killed. He was 34, had worked as a bricklayer's labourer and was married with two children. Private Smith served with the 11th Battalion, Essex Regiment and is buried at Brancourt le Grand Military Cemetery, between Le Cateau and St Quentin.

Imperial War Museum

Above and opposite page: Two photographs of men of the North and South Staffordshires at Riqueval Bridge over the St. Quentin Canal near Bellenglise, after their success in breaching the Hindenburg Line. This magnificent performance restored faith in the 46th (North Midland) Division.

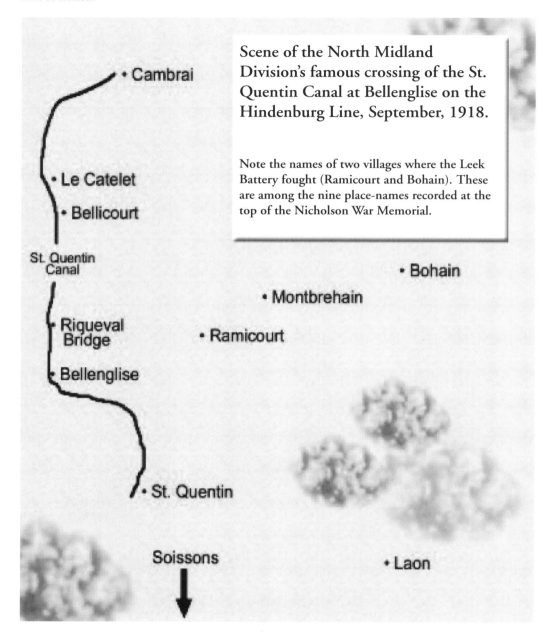

Scene of the North Midland Division's famous crossing of the St. Quentin Canal at Bellenglise on the Hindenburg Line, September, 1918.

Note the names of two villages where the Leek Battery fought (Ramicourt and Bohain). These are among the nine place-names recorded at the top of the Nicholson War Memorial.

• Cambrai

• Le Catelet

• Bellicourt

St. Quentin Canal

• Riqueval Bridge

• Bellenglise

• Bohain

• Montbrehain

• Ramicourt

• St. Quentin

Soissons

• Laon

Chapter 30

The End in Sight

".......I don't think it will last much longer, he is falling back all along the line"

(Private Thomas Fowell in a letter to his mother, a few weeks before
he was killed in action.)

Whilst the Allies drew breath and prepared to launch another large offensive, known as the Battle of the River Selle, the 1st North Staffords and other units attacked across the river to try to gain a foothold on the other side. The Staffordshire men were forced back by a heavy German artillery barrage followed by gas shells and lost three-quarters of their complement. One Leek soldier who was shot through the back and lung during the attack was **Private George Ball** from 20, Field Street. He died from his wounds on Thursday, 17th October and is buried at Delsaux Farm Cemetery, Beugny, 13 miles south-west of Cambrai. George Ball was 27 and had worked in the Braid Department at A.J. Worthington's. Another Leek soldier with the same name died in hospital the following Tuesday, 22nd October, but this time of pneumonia brought on by wounds. **Private Harry Ball** was 32 and had lived in Garden Street. A former pupil at West Street School, he was serving with the 8th Royal Berkshires when he died. He is buried at the Villers Bretonneux Military Cemetery, east of Amiens, where the main memorial to the Australians is sited.

(D. Ball)
Harry Ball

Only two Leek men are recorded as being killed during the First World War in aeroplanes, unlike the Second World War where eleven Leek airmen lost their lives. Although the development of the aircraft as a fighting weapon between 1914 and 1918 was quite dramatic, its real potential was seen during the Second World War, particularly with the air forces of all combatant nations carrying the air war to the towns, cities and shipping of their enemies. We saw in Chapter 18 where Lieutenant Ellis from Kniveden Hall was killed in his aeroplane in 1916. The second Leek man to die in this way was **Air Mechanic (1st Class)**

Harold Keates, 24, from 7, Westwood Grove. He was killed on Wednesday, 23rd October, 1918, in an aircraft which crashed at Hornchurch airfield, north London. The pilot, 2nd Lieutenant W.J. Cole, had taken Harry Keates in the air, probably on a test-flight. It was common practice to do this – it helped to focus the minds of mechanics when servicing or repairing aeroplanes if they knew they were likely to be flying in the machines afterwards. The Board of Enquiry into the crash, which also claimed the life of Lieutenant Cole, decided that the pilot had deliberately put the aircraft, an Avro 504, into a spin, but for reasons unknown, failed to correct it in time.

Harry Keates was brought back to Leek and buried in the cemetery here. His wife later remarried and moved to Aberystwyth. Hornchurch airfield became famous during the Battle of Britain in 1940; Spitfires and Hurricanes were flown from there.

On the same day that Harold Keates was killed in England, **Private Charles Marriott Wood** from Junction Road was killed in action with the 1/8th Lancashire Fusiliers during fighting in the Battle of the Selle. The village of Romeries, some 10 miles east of Cambrai, was captured on that day. The village is close to the River Selle which gave its name to the battle and Private Wood is buried in the Communal Cemetery there. One of nine children, he came from a railway family and his father was at one time the stationmaster at Leek. He was only 19. The next day, Thursday 24th October, 1918, **Private James Lovatt** of the 2/6th North Staffords died in the Ypres Salient. It is not known where he lived but he was born at Thorncliffe and later lived in Leek. Private Lovatt is buried at Cement House Cemetery, Langemarck, near Ypres.

Terlincthun British Cemetery is situated on the northern outskirts of Boulogne and was used by British hospitals in the area during the later months of the war. One Leek soldier buried there is 33 year-old **Gunner James William Lazenby** of the Royal Field Artillery. He came from 17, Waterloo Street and died on Friday, 25th October. It is not known if he died from wounds or illness. Another soldier buried in that cemetery is **Private Arnold Hambleton** from Lowe Hill Cottage, off the Ashbourne Road. He died of wounds in one of the Boulogne hospitals on Tuesday, 29th October, 1918. He had worked as a braid tenter at Brough, Nicholson and Hall and was another 19 year-old. He was serving with the 20th Battalion, Durham Light Infantry and his family always believed that he had lied about his age when he enlisted.

(T. Hambleton)

*The girlfriend of Arnold Hambleton
visiting his grave in 1920*

The next Leek soldier to die was the son of Thomas and Eliza Jane McKenzie, the first couple to be married at All Saints church after it was opened in 1889. **Private Harry McKenzie** from 84, Grove Street was serving with the Royal Army Medical Corps in France when he contracted pneumonia and died on Saturday, 2nd November. He was 21 and had worked at Wardle and Davenports. Harry was one of eleven children, three of whom died in infancy within a week of each other. He had a dog which was at Grove Street when Harry died in a French hospital. It is said that the poor animal howled all night long on 2nd November and would not be pacified. The notification of Harry's death came days later. Private McKenzie is buried at Tourgeville Military Cemetery, France.

LEFT: Silk bookmark printed in memory of Harry McKenzie. These were made by Brough, Nicholson and Hall and proved quite popular during the war as a permanent tribute to a fallen serviceman

(P. Potter)

Harry McKenzie's case is but one example of how difficult it has been to trace and identify many of the servicemen named on the Monument. He enlisted under the name of 'Kinzey' and his official record of death is under that name. It seems that his grandparents were named, or called themselves, Kinzey but the name had been changed to McKenzie at some stage. Had his niece not done some excellent detective work to ensure her uncle's rightful place in this book, poor Harry would have been relegated to the appendix at the back which lists the servicemen I have not been able to identify.

At long last, November 1918 had arrived and for the war-weary troops the long months and years of fighting would end in less than two more weeks. However, the mammoth task the Allied forces had set themselves four years earlier, was not yet quite finished. Early November saw the last major British offensive on the Western Front. After successes by the American, Canadian and New Zealand forces in their respective sectors, Field Marshal Haig ordered an attack on a thirty-mile front from the northern French town of Valenciennes to the Sambre, on either side of the Forest of Mormal. It was on the opening day of the Sambre offensive, Monday, 4th November, that an 18 year old Leek soldier, looking forward eagerly to the end of hostilities and to going home again, was killed. **Private Thomas Fowell** was a battalion runner in the 10th Sherwood Foresters with the dangerous job of carrying messages to and from the front, often under fire. He lived at Court 16, 2, Ashbourne Road and was the oldest of four children. His mother, Mary Fowell, was widowed in 1915 and Tom, with his job at the Compton Mill of White and Davis, had to support the family.

Tom Fowell and his family were clearly very close and letters sent home by Tom show how much he missed those he had left behind. That he should be killed so close to the end of the war and after only three months on active service was particularly tragic. The perceptions of the war by an 18 year old in 1918 would be quite different from those young men and boys of 1914 who saw the opportunity to get into uniform and take up a rifle as an exiting adventure. In one letter to his mother from the training camp on Cannock Chase in February 1918, Tom wrote: *"I am a bit down, I would sooner be at home. ....Never tell anyone to go for a soldier under 19, it is rotten".* A month later, having heard the news from home that his younger brothers and sister had put

(P. Webb)
Tom Fowell

weight on and were looking generally healthier, he wrote: *"....glad brothers and sisters are getting fatter....."*. Not a comment that would be welcomed today, perhaps, but an indication of the poor conditions and relative poverty many families found themselves in during those times.

Tom's concern for the financial survival of his family is also reflected in his letters, a responsibility not so many young men of that age today would have to worry about. His mother was widowed and Tom was the breadwinner. Mrs Fowell was reminded of the danger her son was in when he wrote to her from the West-

Standard postcard used by troops at the front

ern Front in September, 1918, describing a near-miss from a bursting shell which had left him dazed but unhurt and another soldier wounded. She was cheered up, however, by another letter in which Tom wrote: *".......I don't think it will last much longer, he (the enemy) is falling back all along the line."* In another letter, written only two weeks before his death Tom said: *".........I hope it will stop soon as I can come home and help you at home as I left you very poor and my money was missed at home."* Some comfort at the time but the poor lady's worst fears were realised when she received a letter from an Army Chaplain dated 12th November delivering the news she never wanted to hear. *" It is with deep regret that I write to tell you the sad news that Pte T Fowell 103698, Sherwood Foresters, was killed in action on Nov 4th..............I came to perform the last rites...........his body has received a Christian burial and lies in a grave which will be preserved. It is in an orchard on the North eastern outskirts of the village of Ghissignies. May God help you to bear this burden, especially at a time when all around seem to be rejoicing at the cessation of hostilities...................."* A few weeks later, the officer commanding Tom's company wrote to confirm the sad facts, adding that the young soldier was killed whilst acting as battalion runner in the fighting in and around the Forest of Mormal.

Private Thomas Fowell is buried at Ghissignies British Cemetery, France, where half of the burials there fell on 4th November.

(F. Prime)
Claude Prime - won the Military Medal for Gallantry

The last Leek soldier recorded as 'killed in action' in the closing days of the war was **Corporal Claude Prime M.M.** of the Leek Battery and the brother of Gunner George Virgil Prime who was killed on the opening day of the Battle of the Somme in 1916. (See Chapter 15). Corporal Prime was killed on Wednesday, 6th November. He had won the Military Medal for "gallant conduct" in July, 1917, when he jumped in to a gun pit which was on fire from a direct hit and put out the flames. His actions had saved the gun and some 100 rounds of high-explosive ammunition from being blown sky-high. This brave soldier was one of ten children and lived at 5, Kiln Lane. The Leek Battery was in action in the vicinity of the Sambre-Oise Canal east of Cambrai at the time Claude Prime was killed. He is buried, however, at Nechin Communal Cemetery, Hainaut, Belgium, some 60 miles to the north. No explanation can be found for this but it is perhaps fitting that the last Leek soldier to be killed in action during the war belonged to Leek's very own locally-raised artillery unit and had demonstrated, as so many other Leek men had, bravery above and beyond the call of duty.

Chapter 31

The Eleventh Hour of the Eleventh Day of the Eleventh Month

".....in a German military hospital near Stettin, Corporal Adolph Hitler, recovering from a British gas attack, raged in his heart over Germany's humiliation, and dreamed of the part he might play in her resurgence"

(From 'The Great War' by the author and historian Correlli Barnett.)

At 11am on Monday, 11th November, 1918, after 1,568 days of war and six hours after the Armistice was signed, the sound of gunfire ceased and peace at last descended on the Western Front. Hours earlier, Canadian troops had cleared the Belgian town of Mons of the remaining German troops there. It had been a long time since Private Edward Merriman became the first Leek soldier of the war to die in action, at Mons, in August, 1914. Things had turned full circle. The Kaiser had abdicated, the sailors of the German High Seas Fleet

(Imperial War Museum)
Staffordshire soldiers celebrating the Armistice at the front

had mutinied and political upheaval was taking place in a defeated Germany. There was wild rejoicing in London, Paris and other towns and cities around the world but on the battle-fields most fighting men welcomed the Armistice with feelings of weary relief rather than excitement. They would go home of course, but many of their friends who fell in battle would not. Sadly, even though hostilities had ceased that day, other names would be added to the already too long 'Roll of Honour' for the small market town of Leek. These were the names of soldiers who died after the guns had ceased their roar, either from wounds, illnesses or accidents.

The families of the next three soldiers must have felt particularly cheated by fate as their loved ones died just one day after the Armistice, on Tuesday, 12th November, 1918. It was almost as though they had waited to see it through but they were just too exhausted to carry on now the job was finished. The first one was Leek-born **Lance Bombardier Nathan Goodfellow** of the Royal Field Artillery. The cause of his death is not

(V. Webb)

Above - Ralph Vernon
Left - Percy Osborne

(F. Rogers)

known but he is buried in Leek Cemetery. Also buried there is **Private Ralph Vernon** who was serving with the Army Veterinary Corps. Aged 50, he loved animals, joining the army in 1915 where he would have found plenty of work caring for the sick and injured horses which were used in great numbers by the army. Private Vernon was the father of ten children and lived at 39, Broad Street. He died from influenza at Aldershot Barracks in Hampshire. The third soldier died in hospital in France, believed from pneumonia brought on by earlier wounds. **Private Percy Osborne** from 10, Fountain Street was 23 and serving with the Royal Army Service Corps. One of 22 children, (his father had married twice) he worked for the Potteries Electric Traction Company at Stoke, the forerunner of the PMT. Private Osborne is buried at Etaples Military Cemetery, France.

On Wednesday, 13th November, **Private Victor Henry Wilson** of the 28th Battalion, Durham Light Infantry died, believed from illness. He is buried in Leek Cemetery. Also buried there is **Corporal Ernest Poole** of the West Yorkshire Regiment who died in a Leek hospital on 26th November. It is thought that he had been discharged from the army, through ill-health, some time before. He was 49 and lived at 9 Garden Street,

Also buried at Leek is **Sergeant Samuel Birch Vigrass** of the Royal Army Ordnance Corps. He died on Monday 2nd December, 1918, from pneumonia. A former pupil at West Street School, Sergeant Vigrass had worked at Wardle and Davenport's as a cashier before the war. His wife lived at Little Birchall Farm and the couple had bought a house in Shirburn Road. It is thought that he contracted pneumonia after travelling back from France in

(J. Scott)

Above - Sam Vigrass
Left - and with his wife on their wedding day

an open truck. Less than a week earlier on Wednesday 27th November, **Private Charles Murfin** of the 19th Garrison Battalion, Hampshire Regiment, had died in Belgium. It is believed that he lived in Wood Street, Leek, and worked in the silk mills. Private Murfin is buried at Kortrijk Communal Cemetery, Belgium, some 18 miles east of Ypres.

Another Leek-born prisoner of war died in Germany on Monday, 23rd December, 1918. **Corporal Ralph Goldstraw** was captured by the Germans in April 1917 whilst serving with the Royal Marine Light Infantry. He was 22 and lived at 13, Grove Street. He was seriously ill when his POW Camp was liberated by the Allied Forces and died in hospital. He is buried at Hamburg War Cemetery, Germany. The next day, Christmas Eve, **Driver William Herbert Rhead** of the Royal Army Service Corps died in Greece where he had served with the British forces at Salonika. He was 32 and married. His address in Leek is not known but his widow moved to Hanley after the war. Driver Rhead, the last Leek serviceman to die in 1918, is buried at Bralo British Cemetery, Greece, where a large proportion of the burials were victims of the Spanish 'flu epidemic.

As in every other town, local people celebrated the end of the war with mixed emotions. There was relief and joy tinged with sadness and grief. Hundreds of families in the town would never be the same again. Hundreds more saw their menfolk return wounded or ill. Without doubt, one and all must have hoped that the Great War, as they called it, was surely the 'war to end all wars'.

The Victory Medal. Nearly 6 million were issued along with the British War Medal

Before we move on to the years after the war ended and the Leek servicemen who died then, let us look briefly at an overview of the losses street by street, during, and just after the war. Leek was then a tight knit community and undoubtedly, most people would know one another, particularly their neighbours. The effect on these families can only be imagined.

The table below shows the streets where losses were three or more.

ROAD/STREET	SERVICE DEATHS	ROAD/STREET	SERVICE DEATHS
		Compton	5
Mill Street	17	Duke Street	5 (includes 3 brothers)
Ashbourne Road	9	Fountain Street	5
Shirburn Road	9	Kiln Lane	5
Ball Haye Green	8	London Street	5
Junction Road	8	North Avenue	5
Grove Street	7	Portland Street	5
Westwood Road	7	Sandon Road	4 (now Cheddleton Road)
Nelson Street	6	Broad Street	4
Picton Street	6	Garden Street	4

ROAD/STREET	SERVICE DEATHS	ROAD/STREET	SERVICE DEATHS
Leonard Street	4	Grosvenor Street	3
Livingstone Street	4	High Street	3
Parker Street	4	Horton Street	3
Pickwood Road	4	John Street	3
Shoobridge Street	4	Nab Hill Avenue	3
Southbank Street	4	Prince Street	3
Ball Haye Road	3	Queen Street	3
Ball Lane	3	Regent Street	3
Brunswick Street	3	St. Edward Street	3
Buxton Road	3	Wellington Street	3
Chorley Street	3	Wood Street	3
Gladstone Street	3		

(I am grateful to my colleague, David Ball, for the above analysis)

(R. Poole)

Mill Street, around 1900. Could any of the little boys in this picture be one of the seventeen from these cramped houses who fell in the Great War?

Chapter 32

1919 and Beyond

"The Chairman reported an offer by Sir Arthur Nicholson to lay out the ground in the cattle market between Ashbourne Road and Cawdry Buildings as an open space and to erect thereon a Clock Tower as a Memorial to those from Leek who have fallen in the war"

(Leek Times report on a meeting of the Leek Urban District Council, March, 1919)

Many servicemen who had endured the horrors of war, were of course, still in the service of the Crown in 1919 and afterwards. A number of Leek men died during 1919 both before, and after, the signing of the Treaty of Versailles which officially ended the war and laid the blame for it at Germany's feet. Several more died in 1920, 1921 and 1922 and their names were included on the Monument plaques.

Corporal Arthur Davenport was 23 and serving with the 7th North Staffords. Raised in Grove Street, he had enlisted in 1914, serving in Gallipoli, Mesopotamia and Salonika. He died of pneumonia in Iran on Sunday, 12th January, 1919 and is buried at Tehran War Cemetery.

(J. E. Blore)

Victory celebrations in Leek

February, 1919, was clearly a bad month in the British Isles and Europe. Six Leek soldiers died in a three-week period, almost certainly from chest-related diseases.

Private John James Pickford from 29, King Street, was also 23 and fell victim to pneumonia. He died on Thursday, 6th February whilst serving with the Labour Corps. He is buried in Leek Cemetery.

On Tuesday, 11th February, **Private Harry Platt Hulme** a Leek-born soldier attached to the Royal Garrison Artillery died in France. His age and address are not known but he is buried at Doullens Communal Cemetery on the Somme. **Private Walter Percy Connolly** also died that Tuesday, but in Shrewsbury. He was 23 and serving with the 8th Battalion, London Regiment (Post Office Rifles). It is believed that his family lived in Leek before or during the war although his parents later moved to Shrewsbury. Private Connolly is buried in that town's General Cemetery.

Another Leek soldier buried abroad in 1919 was **Private George Albert Hibbert** from 49, Rose Bank. He was 28, married and serving with the 8th Battalion, Seaforth Highlanders when he died on Monday, 17th February. His grave is at Belgrade Cemetery, Belgium.

46 year old **Private Harry Geston**, a married man from 5, Brunswick Street died in France on Saturday, 22nd February, whilst serving with the Labour Corps. He is buried at Pont-Remy Cemetery on the Somme. Three days later on Tuesday, 25th February, **Sergeant Richard Hill** of the Royal Army Veterinary Corps, attached to the New Zealand Field Artillery, died of influenza. The son of Leek's Doctor Robert Hill and thought to have lived in Leonard Street, he is buried at Tidworth Military Cemetery, Wiltshire, close to the Army Training base on Salisbury Plain.

On 7th March, **Driver Harry Peacock** of the Royal Field Artillery died in Leek of influenza and pneumonia. He was 29 and lived at 7, Westwood Terrace. His grave is in Leek Cemetery. A week later, on 14th March, **Corporal Frederick Ernest Stanmore** of the Oxford and Buckinghamshire Light Infantry died in England of a stroke. He lived at 25, John Street and was the father of six children. Aged 56, Corporal Stanmore was a regular soldier who met and married his wife whilst serving in Dublin. His grave is also in Leek Cemetery.

The next local casualty was killed in a motor cycle accident. **Lieutenant Basil Edward Cresswell Boucher** of the 1st Battalion, Royal Welsh Fusiliers,

(P. Stanmore)

Frederick Stanmore

died on Saturday, 10th May, 1919, at the Royal Salop Hospital in Shrewsbury. He lived at The Heath House, Cheddleton, and is buried in Cheddleton churchyard. His cousin, Arthur, was killed in Belgium in 1917. (See Chapter 20). Boucher Road, Cheddleton, is named after this family. Five days later, on 15th May, **Driver Colin Rider** of the Royal Army Service Corps, died in Leek of tuberculosis. He was 24 and lived at 19, King Street. He is buried at Leek Cemetery.

The next two Leek soldiers both died in July, 1919, and are buried in Leek Cemetery.

Private Reginald Charles Riches of the Royal Army Service Corps was 26 and died on Wednesday, 2nd July. His address in the town is not known. A week later, on Wednesday, 9th July, **Private Rupert Tatton** died from acute gastritis. He came from 89 Mill Street and had

(J. Crosby)

Basil Boucher

served in the King's Own (Royal Lancaster) Regiment until transferring to the Labour Corps. He had served throughout the war and was wounded in France in 1915. He was the brother of Arthur Tatton, killed on the Somme in July, 1916.

The last Leek soldier to die in 1919 succumbed to disease 12 months after the Armistice, on 19th December. **Pioneer Alfred Thomas Walker** was 44 and serving with the Royal Engineers, still out in France. He was married and lived at 14, Kiln Lane, Leek. His grave is at Aire Communal Cemetery, some ten miles south of St Omer where there was a large hospital centre during the war. Alfred Walker and the other 893 souls from the Great War buried in that cemetery could have had no way of knowing that history would repeat itself and that they would be joined in the cemetery in 1940 by twenty-one more British servicemen who fell in the withdrawal to Dunkirk.

In 1920, **Corporal James Edward Gee**, 21, of 128, Mill Street, died of tuberculosis at home on 9th February. He had served in the Royal Welsh Fusiliers and worked at one time as an assistant librarian at the Nicholson Institute. He is buried at Leek Cemetery. Later that year, **Lance Corporal James Doxey** from 84, Strangman Street, Leek, died from natural causes on 23rd November at the age of 29. He had served with the Machine Gun Corps in the war and was a keen cricketer. His son, who now lives in Shropshire, was only four weeks old when his father died. Before war broke out, Lance Corporal Doxey had worked at Brough, Nicholson and Hall. He is also buried in Leek Cemetery.

In 1921, **Private James Weaver** of the Royal Defence Corps, died on 12th April. He was 54 and served, for some part of the war at least, in the South Staffordshire Regiment. He lived at 13, South Street and was working as a labourer after discharge from the forces. He is buried in Leek Cemetery. **Air Mechanic (1st Class) Thomas Irwin** of the Royal Air Force, died on Friday, 26th August, in Canada, whilst attached to the Canadian Air Force. He is buried at Toronto Cemetery in Ontario. He was 47.

Names of former soldiers who died after the war were still recorded, (for the purpose of inclusion on the Monument plaques), as late as 1922, albeit only one can be identified for that year. **Private John Swarbrook** of 10, Westwood Grove, Leek, served with the Royal Fusiliers and was wounded in the left arm during the opening phase of the Battle of the Somme. As a result, he was unfit for further active service and was transferred to the Labour Corps. Records show that he was discharged from the army in December, 1917. He died on 6th December, 1922 and is buried in Leek Cemetery. He was 41 and working as an overlocker in one of the Leek silk mills but there is little doubt that his earlier wound contributed to his eventual death.

(E. Foster)

What every wartime serviceman looked forward to - his de-mobilisation papers.
These belonged to William Foster, who survived the war.

Sir Arthur Nicholson's pledge to build a 'Clock Tower' came to fruition in 1925 and the Monument, as we know it, has stood proudly for nearly eighty years as a prominent reminder of the courage and fortitude of a past generation.

Souvenir programme courtesy of G. Wardle

George Wardle, the son of Private John Thomas Wardle who was killed in 1917, was at the Unveiling Ceremony in August, 1925. He recalls:

"The ceremony was a grand affair. The streets around the monument were crowded and it was a beautiful, sunny day. All widows and orphans

of the men killed were allocated front row seats and I sat between my mother and sister. My mother had pinned my father's medals on my jacket and I felt very proud of him, but also very sad that he had been killed. There were a lot of dignitaries and senior army officers there and it was all very impressive. I shall never forget that day".

So that is the story of the young, (and some not so young), men of Leek who died during the Great War and soon afterwards, whose names are recorded on the Nicholson War Memorial. This account, albeit patchy in places - necessarily so because of the passage of time and consequent lack of information - is our town's tribute to these men. It is an unfortunate fact that I have not been able to correctly identify all the 420 men listed on the Memorial. This means that forty of the men who fell are now, sadly, just names and despite extensive research, cannot be linked to official records. Nevertheless, their names, (listed in Appendix 4) will not be forgotten. We should also remember those thousands of local men (and women) who served their country during those dreadful years and who came home, many wounded, others scarred in mind if not in body. To all those from our small town who gave their lives or were wounded or suffered as a result of the Great War, this book is dedicated.

(Brampton Publications)

The Unveiling Ceremony at the Nicholson War Memorial, 20th August, 1925.

Another Casualty of War

Mrs Ellen Wilson, mother of R.S.M. Arthur Wilson,
killed on the Somme in 1916,
lays a wreath in his memory at the unveiling ceremony in 1925

Sir Arthur Nicholson J.P., C.C.

Sir Arthur funded the building of the Memorial Clock Tower,
officially the Nicholson War Memorial, but known locally as the 'Monument'

Acknowledgements

The author is grateful for the help and information provided by the the following organisations and people. Many people have assisted in this project and apologies are sincerely offered to anyone omitted in error.

Historical Sources

The Commonwealth War Graves Commission
Imperial War Museum
Leek Library
Leek Post and Times
Leek Town Council
National Army Museum
Parish Churches of St.Luke, St.Edward and All Saints.
Royal Naval Historical Branch
Royal Air Force Museum, Hendon

Regimental Museums:

Lancashire Fusiliers
Northumberland Fusiliers
Royal Green Jackets
Staffordshire Regiment
Sherwood Foresters

Individual contributions

E. Ash. D.Baldwin. I.Bailey. R.Bailey. B.Bailey. A.Ball. D.Ball. G.Ball J.Band.
V.Beech. G.Belfield. M.Bibby. I.Billing. P.Booth. H.Bostock. P.Bowcock. D.Bowcock
M.Bowyer. J.Bratt. J.Bridgett. H. Brown. L.Brown. J.Burrows. C.Chell. J.Clarke
N.Clarke. M.Clowes. M.Cope. M.Cope. J.Crosby. M.Derry. K.Dickens. R.Duffet.
M.Emery. H.Fletcher. N.Fogg. J.Glancey. B.Hall. A.Hambleton. T.Hambleton.
K.Harrison. H.Henshaw. J.Holden. C.Hunt. N.Hunt. D.Irving. J.Jablonska.
B.Johnson. D.Johnson. B.Keates. M.Keeling. P.Kirk. C.Lomas. R.Lovatt. S.Malkin.
G.Massey. B.Mellor. A.Murfin. M.Myatt. D.Norman. M.D.Nowland. H.Owen.

V.Pegg. K.S.Perrin. E.Pickford. K.Pickford. S.Pickford. B.Podmore. R.Poole. D.Porter.
P.Potter. C.Poyser. A.Prime. D.Rhead. C.Robinson. G.Robinson. F.Rogers. D.Salt.
J.Scott. W.Serrell. C.Sheldon. M.Sheldon. P.Sheldon. J.Sheldon. B.Shenton. M.Sigley.
B.Simpson. H.Spearing. P.Stanmore. I. Steele. P.Tomlinson. M.Toy. I.Ward. G. Wardle.
P.Webb. M.Webb. V.Webb. T.Wheatley. G.Whiteman. R.Wilson. A.Wood. J.Wood.
S.Wood.

Select   bibliography

Bennett, G. The Battle of Jutland. 1964.
Blore, J.E. and Sherratt, J.R. Over There. 1991.
Cole, C. Royal Flying Corps, 1915-1916. 1969.
Evans, M.M. Over The Top. 2002.
Gilbert, M. First World War. 1994.
Gliddon, G. The Battle of The Somme. 1987.
Holmes, R. The Western Front. 1999.
Leek Sailors and Soldiers Comforts Society. Roll of Honour. 1915.
Livesey, A. The Viking Atlas of WW1. 1994.
Macdonald, L. They Called it Passchendaele. 1978.
Mair, C. Britain at War, 1914-1919. 1982.
McCarthy, C. The Somme. The Day By Day Account. 1993.
Middlebrook, M. The First Day on The Somme. 1971.
Middlebrook, M. The Kaiser's Battle. 1978.
Poole, R. A History of Leek. 2002.
Pope, S. and Wheal, E. MacMillan Dictionary of The First World War. 1995.
Robbins, K. The First World War, 1984.
Simkins, P. Chronicles of the Great War 1999.
Stedman, M. and Skelding, E. Great Battles of the Great War. 1999.
Warner, P. The Battle of Loos. 1976.
Winter, J.M. The Experience of World War 1.

Appendices

The following is divided in to four appendices:

Appendix 1 gives the servicemen, in alphabetical order, who have been identified and are included in the main text of this publication.

Appendix 2 lists the cemeteries and memorials where the Leek servicemen are buried or commemorated, with their locations.

Appendix 3 lists the cemeteries and memorials and corresponding names of servicemen buried or commemorated there.

Appendix 4 lists the forty names which cannot be linked to known or officially listed casualties.

Appendix I

Page	NAME		RANK	NUMBER/UNIT	DIED	BURIED/COMMEMORATED
198	Ainsworth	J.	Private	12065 North Staffords	31.8.1918	Etaples Mil Cem.
119	Alcock	U.	Private	G/15134 Royal Sussex	21.10.1916	Thiepval Memorial
94	Allard	S.	Private	16810 Sherwood Foresters	1.7.1916	Thiepval Memorial
71	Arrowsmith	E.	Sergeant	12370 North Staffords	6.11.1915	Browns Road, Festubert
181	Ashley	W.	L/Corporal	242014 Gloucesters	31.3.1918	Pozieres Memorial
101	Ashworth	H.	L/Corporal	11138 Royal Fusiliers	16.7.1916	Pozieres British Cem.
108	Astles	A	Private	11009 North Staffords	13.8.1916	Flatiron Copse Cem.
136	Astles	F	Private	201347 Northumberland Fus.	3.5.1917	Arras Memorial
160	Astles	J	L/Corporal	21118 Bedfordshire Reg't.	25.10.1917	Tyne Cot Memorial
122	Atkinson	J	Private	40559 North Staffords	18.11.1916	Connaught Cem.
203	Atkinson	W	Trooper	300843 Staffs Imp. Yeomanry	7.10.1918	Kantara Cem, Egypt
185	Baddeley	W	Gunner	64242 Royal Garrison Artillery	25.4.1918	Haringhe Cem,Ypres
130	Bailey	H	Corporal	805431 Royal Field Artillery	10.1.1917	Bienvillers Mil Cem.
134	Bailey	I	Private	16995 Bedfordshire Reg't.	15.4.1917	Arras Memorial
189	Ball	C.O.	Gunner	805468 Royal Field Artillery	12.6.1918	Fouquieres Cem.
207	Ball	G	Private	241725 North Staffords	17.10.1918	Delsaux Farm Cem.
178	Ball	G.	Lieutenant	- Sherwood Foresters	21.3.1918	Arras Memorial
207	Ball	H	Private	44768 Royal Berkshire Reg't.	22.10.1918	Villers-Bretonneux Cem
199	Ball	J.W.	Private	39547 Hertfordshire Reg't.	4.9.1918	Hermies Hill Cem.
143	Barber	H	Private	202028 North Staffords	1.7.1917	Arras Memorial
179	Barber	H	Private	G/15150 Royal Sussex Reg't.	26.3.1918	Pozieres Memorial
51	Barks	W	Private	10995 North Staffords	9.8.1915	Fld amb Cem, Gallipoli
138	Barnett	A	Private	41210 Suffolk Reg't.	8.6.1917	Arras Memorial

230

	Surname	Initial	Rank	Service No. & Regiment	Date	Cemetery/Memorial
50	Baskerville	W	Private	G/11021 Royal Fusiliers	25.6.1915	Twelve Tree Cps, G'poli
194	Belfield	P	Private	G/15156 Royal Sussex Reg't.	13.8.1918	Beacon Cem.
138	Bestwick	G	Sergeant	805420 Royal Field Artillery	8.6.1917	Fosse No: 10 Cem.
115	Bestwick	R	Private	4648 Durham Light Infantry	16.9.1916	Thiepval Memorial
148	Biddulph	E	Gunner	127598 Royal Garrison Artillery	3.8.1917	Menin Gate Memorial
54	Biddulph	J	Private	15949 North Staffords	10.1.1916	Alexandria Cem, Egypt
82	Billing	A	A.B.	J/26661 HMS Invincible, R.N.	31.5.1916	Portsmouth Memorial
95	Billing	H	L/Corporal	200680 South Staffords	1.7.1916	Thiepval Memorial
157	Bincliffe	C	Private	20208 Border Reg't.	4.10.1917	Tyne Cot Memorial
166	Birch	A	Gunner	151379 Royal Garrison Artillery	9.11.1917	Dozinghem Cem.
200	Birch	E	L/Corporal	13052 North Staffords	14.9.1918	Tehran Memorial
134	Birch	H	Private	201366 Norfolk Reg't.	19.4.1917	Gaza War Cem, Israel
148	Birch	T.R	Sergeant	12907 Royal Berkshire Reg't.	2.8.1917	Lijssenthoek Cem.
189	Birchenough	D	Private	50699 K.O.Y.L.I.	2.6.1918	Bienvillers Mil Cem.
188	Birchenough	H	Sergeant	91909 Durham Light Infantry	27.5.1918	Soissons Memorial
179	Bishop	C	Private	201344 Northumberland Fus.	26.3.1918	Pozieres Memorial
172	Bishop	J	Private	32374 South Staffords	8.12.1917	Etaples Mil Cem.
83	Bloor	T	Boy	J/35047 HMS Hampshire, R.N.	5.6.1916	Portsmouth Memorial
42	Bloore	F	Private	G/4584 Royal Sussex Reg't.	9.5.1915	Le Touret Memorial
189	Bond	W.E.	Private	20829 Lancashire Fusiliers	11.6.1918	Doullens Cem.
154	Booth	F	Private	29119 Machine Gun Corps	23.9.1917	Kemmel No: 1 Cem.
175	Booth	P	Private	G/42640 Middlesex Reg't.	7.1.1918	Rocquigny-Eq'crt Rd. Cem.
69	Booth	T	Private	21338 Canadian Infantry	30.9.1915	Leek Cemetery
114	Booth	W	Guardsman	23044 Grenadier Guards	15.9.1916	Thiepval Memorial
74	Bostock	E	Private	8470 North Staffords	21.2.1916	Divisional Cem.
144	Boucher	A.G.	Lieutenant	- King's Royal Rifle Corps	10.7.1917	Nieuport Memorial
219	Boucher	B.E.	Lieutenant	- Royal Welsh Fusiliers	10.5.1919	Cheddleton Churchyard
198	Bould	H	Private	19323 Bedfordshire Reg't.	26.8.1918	St Sever Cem.
109	Bowyer	S	Private	23565 D.C.L.I.	18.8.1916	Thiepval Memorial

137	Bowyer	W	Private	8555 Royal Defence Corps	10.5.1917	Leek Cemetery
184	Brandrick	W.E	Gunner	2660 Machine Gun Corps	16.4.1918	Voormezeele Cem.
187	Bratt	J.H.	Private	202034 North Staffords	15.5.1918	St Sever Cem.
52	Brennan	J.J.	L/Corporal	10469 North Staffords	14.8.1915	Helles Memorial
153	Breton	W.G.	Major	- Royal Garrison Artillery	14.9.1917	White House Cem.
188	Brindley	G	Private	42784 Essex Reg't.	29.5.1918	Gonnehem Brit. Cem.
176	Brindley	H.	Private	93549 Sherwood Foresters	16.3.1918	Favreuil Brit.Cem.
132	Brookes	J.	Private	201584 North Staffords	14.3.1917	Thiepval Memorial
71	Broome	J.	Gunner	RMA/7422 Royal Marine Artillery	8.11.1915	Leek Cemetery
96	Cade	H.E.	Driver	810184 Royal Field Artillery	1.7.1916	Thiepval Memorial
173	Cannon	T.A.	Private	235127 Kings Liverpool Reg't.	12.12.1917	Favreuil Brit. Cem.
202	Cantrell	R	Private	20686 K.S.L.I.	30.9.1918	Mikra Cem., Greece
178	Carter	E	Private	2919 East Lancashire Reg't.	21.3.1918	Pozieres Memorial
160	Carter	J.A.	Gunner	1526828 Royal Field Artillery	21.10.1917	Vlamertinghe Cem .
167	Carter	P	Private	201623 North Staffords	13.11.1917	Bruay Communal Cem.
56	Carter	W.H.	Private	16301 West Riding Reg't.	27.6.1915	Voormezeele Cem.
72	Cartlidge	J.	Private	7647 North Staffords	8.11.1915	Menin Gate Memorial
131	Chappells	E.C.	Private	- Sherwood Foresters	3.2.1917	Leek Cemetery
178	Chawner	J.	Private	14318 North Staffords	21.3.1918	Arras Memorial
144	Cheshire	J.	Private	19300 North Staffords	23.7.1917	Baghdad Cem. Iraq
117	Cheshire	S	Private	15498 Cheshire Reg't.	1.10.1916	Regina Trench Cem.
101	Clarke	J.	Private	11141 Royal Fusiliers	16.7.1916	Thiepval Memorial
199	Clay	F.W.	Private	93551 Sherwood Foresters	3.9.1918	Fouquieres Cem.
202	Clayton	W.H.	Private	54017 Lancashire Fusiliers	30.9.1918	Vichte Mil. Cem.
137	Clowes	E.H.	Private	G/44302 Royal Fusiliers	10.5.1917	Arras Memorial
172	Clulow	R	Private	32124 N.Z. Exp. Force	22.11.1917	Buttes New B/Cem.
202	Collins	J	Private	22334 West Riding Reg't.	29.9.1918	Grand Ravine Cem.
162	Conley	W.C.	Lieutenant	- South Staffords	26.10.1917	Tyne Cot Memorial
219	Connolly	W.P.	Private	372029 London Reg't	11.2.1919	Shrewsbury Cem. UK

No.	Surname	Initial	Rank	Service No. & Regiment	Date	Cemetery / Memorial
138	Constantine	W	Private	241784 North Staffords	8.6.1917	Tournai Cem.
176	Cope	G	Private	35831 North Staffords	1.3.1918	Cement House Cem.
160	Cotterill	J.A.	Private	32321 South Staffords	12.10.1917	Tyne Cot Memorial
148	Cox	F.W.	Private	36193 Sherwood Foresters	31.7.1917	Menin Gate Memorial
130	Crabtree	H	Bombardier	805444 Royal Field Artillery	10.1.1917	Bienvillers Mil. Cem.
116	Crombie	R	Private	24158 Manchester Reg't.	26.9.1916	Regina Trench Cem.
98	Dale	A.W.	Lieutenant	– Northumberland Fusiliers	1.7.1917	La Laiterie Mil. Cem.
218	Davenport	A	Corporal	15726 North Staffords	12.1.1919	Tehran War Cem. Iran
154	Davenport	F.	Major	– Royal Field Artillery	25.9.1917	Ypres Reservoir Cem.
188	Davies	R	Private	39347 K.O.Y.L.I.	26.5.1918	Bienvillers Mil. Cem.
160	Dean	R.J	L/Corporal	201926 North Staffords	18.10.1917	Sucrerie Cem.
119	Desborough	J.J.	Private	27356 Loyal North Lancs	25.10.1916	Thiepval Memorial
102	Dickenson	J.	Private	23794 Royal Welsh Fusiliers	20.7.1916	Caterpillar Valley Cem.
34	Doody	C.H.	L/Corporal	9171 Royal Lancaster Reg't	19.3.1915	Strand Mil. Cem.
109	Doxey	J	Private	5011 North Staffords	26.8.1916	De Cusine Ravine Cem.
220	Doxey	J.	L/Corporal	– Machine Gun Corps	23.11.1920	Leek Cemetery
156	Doxey	W	Sergeant	12463 Royal Defence Corps	27.9.1917	Leek Cemetery
21	Drury	J.	Private	9390 South Staffords	20.9.1914	Braine Cem.
65	Dunn	C	L/Corporal	8826 Royal Fusiliers	29.9.1915	Loos Memorial
52	Eaton	A	Private	10515 North Staffords	10.8.1915	Helles Memorial
132	Edge	A.E.	Col.Sergeant	– Royal Marine L.I.	12.2.1917	Caister on Sea Cem. U.K.
130	Edge	H.	Private	46000 Northumberland Fus.	19.1.1917	Ration Farm Mil. Cem.
170	Elkin	G	L/Corporal	R/39530 King's Royal Rifle Corps	22 11.1917	Hermies Hill Cem.
118	Ellis	P.C.	Lieutenant	– H.L.I./ Royal Flying Corps	17.10.1916	Pont du Hem Mil. Cem.
53	Farnell	W	L/Corporal	G/11342 Royal Fusiliers	23.9.1915	Helles Memorial
203	Fenton	C.V.	Private	60515 Northamptonshire Reg't.	2.10.1918	Leek Cemetery
69	Flanagan	G	Private	20088 South Staffords	1.10.1915	Leek Cemetery
189	Fleet	J.	Private	81525 Royal Fusiliers	10.6.1918	Douchy-Les-Ayette Cem.
94	Flower	E	Private	8999 Manchester Reg't.	1.7.1916	Thiepval Memorial

No.	Surname	Initial	Rank	Number / Regiment	Date	Memorial / Cemetery
120	Fogg	J.	Private	43232 Bedfordshire Reg't.	16.11.1916	Thiepval Memorial
129	Fogg	J.	Sapper	1165 Royal Engineers	5.1.1917	Warlincourt Halte Cem.
131	Fogg	T	Private	31192 South Lancashire Reg't.	18.2.1917	Puchevillers Cem.
87	Ford	R	Corporal	9399 South Staffords	26.6.1916	Gommecourt Wood Cem.
142	Foster	W	Private	201568 North Staffords	1.7.1917	Arras Memorial
209	Fowell	T	Private	103698 Sherwood Foresters	4.11.1918	Ghissignies Brit. Cem.
179	Fowler	J.	Private	G/11094 Royal Fusiliers	24.3.1918	Arras Memorial
127	Fowler	W	Private	14083 North Staffords	25.2.1917	Basra Memorial Iraq
220	Gee	J.E.	Corporal	- Royal Welsh Fusiliers	9.2.1920	Leek Cemetery
219	Geston	H	Private	368819 Labour Corps	22.2.1919	Pont-Remy Cem.
100	Gibson	E	Private	9180 Royal Fusiliers	7.7.1916	Thiepval Memorial
116	Giddings	J.	Private	16992 Bedfordshire Reg't.	28.9.1916	Thiepval Memorial
202	Gilman	J.	Private	2154 Coldstream Guards	30.9.1918	Grevillers Cem.
184	Glenn	H	Private	57187 King's (Liverpool) Reg't.	9.4.1918	Loos Memorial
78	Godwin	J.	Private	16535 North Staffords	29.5.1916	Amara War Cem. Iraq
204	Golby	H.	Corporal	S/32302 Rifle Brigade	11.10.1918	St. Aubert Cem.
108	Goldstraw	B	Private	12140 North Staffords	13.8.1916	Flatiron Copse Cem.
37	Goldstraw	G.O.	Private	12113 Royal Fusiliers	26.4.1915	Menin Gate Memorial
188	Goldstraw	J.W.	Private	241597 North Staffords	24.5.1918	Pernes Brit. Cem.
172	Goldstraw	P.	Sapper	486861 Royal Engineers	9.12.1917	Ribecourt Road Cem.
215	Goldstraw	R	Corporal	PO/16513 Royal Marine L.I.	23.12.1918	Hamburg Cem.
58	Goodfellow	A	Gunner	66889 Royal Field Artillery	9.8.1915	Ramparts Cem, Ypres
214	Goodfellow	N	Bombardier	204949 Royal Field Artillery	12.11.1918	Leek Cemetery
186	Goodfellow	P.	Private	25898 Cheshire Reg't.	15.4.1918	Doiran Mem. Greece
171	Goodwin	A.W.	Rifleman	A/200236 King's Royal Rifle Corps	30.11.1917	Cambrai Memorial
112	Goodwin	G	Private	16993 Bedfordshire Reg't.	3.9.1916	Guillemont Road Cem.
24	Goodwin	J	Private	11031 Scottish Rifles	5.11.1914	Ploegsteert Memorial
180	Goodwin	S.A.	Private	43416 Royal Fusiliers	27.3.1918	Pozieres Memorial
186	Gould	E.W.	Lieutenant	- South Lancashire Reg't	11.4.1918	Ramleh War Cem. Israel

No.	Surname	Initials	Rank	Regiment	Date	Location
184	Graham	A	Private	42496 South Staffords	15.4.1918	Arras Memorial
34	Graham	A	Private	13590 Worcestershire Reg't.	12.3.1915	Estaires Com. Cem.
20	Graham	G.H.	Corporal	8788 Royal Irish Reg't.	26.8.1914	Bethencourt Cem.
70	Greatbatch	J.J.	Private	12788 Ox and Bucks L.I.	17.10.1915	Menin Gate Memorial
101	Green	C.E.	Lieutenant	-K.S.L.I.	15.7.1916	Thiepval Memorial
56	Green	D.J.	Rifleman	R/6249 King's Royal Rifle Corps	30.6.1915	Bedford House Cem.
125	Green	N.	Lieutenant	- North Staffords	25.1.1917	Amara War Cem. Iraq
122	Gwynne	H.L.	Lieutenant	- North Staffords	18.11.1916	Thiepval Memorial
153	Hall	F	Gunner	31405 Royal Field Artillery	10.9.1917	Bleuet Farm Cem.
49	Hall	J.	Private	1545 Manchester Reg't.	5.6.1915	Helles Memorial
208	Hambleton	A	Private	82138 Durham Light Infantry	29.10.1918	Terlincthun Cem.
166	Hambleton	G	Private	123015 Canadian Infantry	7.11.1917	Lijssenthoek Cem.
74	Hammersley H.	H.	Private	3911 Royal Fusiliers	18.2.1916	Loos Memorial
198	Hammersley P.	P.	Private	38036 Gloucestershire Reg't.	22.8.1918	Vis-en-Artois Memorial
110	Hammond	W	Private	25915 Cheshire Reg't.	12.8.1916	Salonika Cem Greece
44	Hampson	S	Private	R4/065701 R.A.S.C.	18.5.1915	Bristol Cem. U.K.
137	Harrod	W	Gunner	L/23563 Royal Field Artillery	18.5.1917	Duisans Brit. Cem.
131	Heath	G.W.	Sapper	5927 Royal Engineers	27.1.1917	Leek Cemetery
162	Hewitt	E	Private	G/68400 Royal Fusiliers	26.10.1917	Cement House Cem.
219	Hibbert	G.A.	Private	S/12563 Seaforth Highlanders	17.2.1919	Belgrade Cem.
140	Higginbotham F.L.	F.L.	L/Corporal	46667 Northumberland Fus.	19.6.1917	Menin Gate Memorial
44	Higginbotham W	W	Private	9116 Royal Fusiliers	10.5.1915	La Chapelle Com. Cem.
141	Hill	C.E.	L/Corporal	242523 North Staffords	30.6.1917	Arras Memorial
132	Hill	G.T.	Gunner	65876 Royal Garrison Artillery	22.3.1917	Habarcq Com. Cem.
219	Hill	R	Sergeant	171347 Royal Army Vet. Corps	25.2.1919	Tidworth Cem, U.K.
56	Hilton	W.T.	Bombardier	78822 Royal Field Artillery	16.7.1915	Poperinge New Cem.
156	Holden	C.V.	Private	91868 R.A.M.C.	1.10.1917	Longuenesse Cem.
122	Hollinshead	S	Private	19322 North Staffords	18.11.1916	Thiepval Memorial
35	Howard	W.S	Gunner	844 Royal Field Artillery	7.4.1915	Longuenesse Cem.

155	Hudson	A	Private	23352 North Staffords	20.9.1917	Arras Memorial
113	Hudson	J.J.	Private	16444 Bedfordshire Reg't.	4.9.1916	Thiepval Memorial
155	Hudson	W	L/Corporal	241732 North Staffords	30.9.1917	Vlamertinghe Cem.
176	Hulme	E	Private	28585 K.O.S.B.	23.1.1918	Fins New Brit. Cem.
135	Hulme	H.	Private	15741 Royal Sussex Reg't.	22.4.1917	Vlamertinghe Cem.
219	Hulme	H.P.	Private	T4/219384 R.A.S.C.and R.G.A.	11.2.1919	Doullens Com.Cem.
117	Hulme	J A	Corporal	G/4581 Royal Sussex Reg't.	3.10.1916	Thiepval Memorial
78	Hulme	J.J.	Private	7445 North Staffords	27.4.1916	Dranouter Mil. Cem.
176	Hulme	W	Private	42035 South Staffords	1.2.1918	Cologne Southern Cem.
169	Hunt	H	Gunner	69979 Tank Corps	20.11 1917	Flesquieres Hill Cem.
192	Hunt	S	L/Corporal	201850 North Staffords	12.7.1918	Cologne Southern Cem.
221	Irwin	T	Air Mechanic	70646 Royal Air Force	26.8.1921	Toronto Cem. Canada
102	Johnson	H.P.	Private	15247 North Staffords	22.7.1916	Thiepval Memorial
189	Johnson	J.A	Gunner	240571 Royal Field Artillery	28.5.1918	Leek Cemetery
178	Johnson	J.J.	Private	200470 North Staffords	21.3.1918	Arras Memorial
85	Johnson	R	Private	8624 North Staffords	7.6.1916	Bailleul Com. Cem.
82	Johnson	R	Boy	J/37132 HMS Barham, R.N.	31.5.1916	Plymouth Memorial
66	Johnson	R.T.	Captain	- North Staffords	13.10.1915	Loos Memorial
137	Keates	F.W.	Private	41099 Royal Inniskilling Fus.	19.5.1917	Arras Memorial
154	Keates	G	Gunner	151089 Royal Garrison Artillery	16.9.1917	Lijssenthoek Cem.
208	Keates	H.	Air Mechanic	21953 Royal Air Force	23.10.1918	Leek Cemetery
200	Keates	H.M.	Private	202193 K.O.S.B.	20.9.1918	Vis-en-Artois Memorial
78	Keates	J.E.	Private	15575 North Staffords	22.4.1916	Basra Memorial, Iraq
93	Kelk	J.H.	Private	12/1481 York and Lancs Reg't	1.7.1916	Thiepval Memorial
154	Kelly	S.G.	Sergeant	C/395 King's Royal Rifle Corps	29.9.1917	Lijssenthoek Cem.
156	Kirby	L.	Private	196392 Labour Corps	10.9.1917	Leek Cemetery
114	Kirkham	E	Private	4021 Northumberland Fus.	15.9.1916	Thiepval Memorial
185	Kirkham	J.	Private	8809 Royal Irish Fusiliers	9.4.1918	Leek Cemetery
200	Knowles	J	Corporal	2378440 Canadian Infantry	27.9.1918	Sancourt Brit. Cem.

208	Lazenby	J.W.	Gunner	25903 Royal Field Artillery	25.10.1918	Terlincthun Cem.
104	Leadbeater	J.	Captain	- Australian Infantry	25.7.1916	Villers-Bretonneux Mem.
74	Lear	J.W.	Sergeant	23117 South Lancashire Reg't	12.2.1916	Leek Cemetery
189	Leckenby	S.W.	Private	M/274359 R.A.S.C.	31.5.1918	Daours Com. Cem.
148	Lees	E	Private	23431 Durham Light Infantry	31.7.1917	Menin Gate Memorial
171	Lee	J	Private	40900 North Staffords	29.11.1917	Cambrai Memorial
145	Lewthwaite	C.G.	Lieutenant	- Royal Field Artillery	29.7.1917	Fosse No: 10 Cem.
140	Lillie-Mitchell	J.E.	Corporal	93175 Royal Garrison Artillery	20.6.1917	Cite Bonjean Mil. Cem.
143	Lovatt	G	Private	201585 North Staffords	1.7.1917	Arras Memorial
208	Lovatt	J	Private	202464 North Staffords	24.10.1918	Cement House Cem.
126	Lowe	T.E.	Private	18592 North Staffords	25.2.1917	Basra Memorial, Iraq
72	Lowe	W	Private	8018 North Staffords	8.11.1915	Menin Gate Memorial
183	Lowe	W	Private	49527 Lincolnshire Reg't.	1.4.1918	Roisel Com. Cem.
24	Machin	J.	Private	9041 South Staffords	7.11.1914	Menin Gate Memorial
189	Malkin	F	L/Corporal	33402 Royal Engineers	17.5.1918	Leek Cemetery
149	Malkin	H	Rifleman	R/15158 King's Royal Rifle Corps	10.8 1917	Menin Gate Memorial
190	Malkin	H.	Gunner	46613 Royal Garrison Artillery	16.6.1918	Hoogstade Mil. Cem.
38	Malkin	P	Private	2941 East Surrey Reg't.	8.5.1915	Menin Gate Memorial
193	Malkin	T.W.	Gunner	86286 Machine Gun Corps	24.7.1918	Fouquieres Cem.
201	Mansell	F	L/Corporal	23/1513 N.Z. Rifle Brigade	27 9.1918	Grevillers N.Z. Memorial
150	Marren	J	Corporal	9705 Royal Fusiliers	21.8.1917	Red Cross Corner Cem.
131	Mayers	J.W.	Private	40745 Worcestershire Reg't.	11.2.1917	Queens Cem. Puisieux
209	McKenzie	H	Private	94258 Alias Kinzey. R.A.M.C.	2.11.1918	Tourgeville Mil. Cem
192	McLeavy	E.	Private	- Royal Defence Corps	5.7.1918	Leek Cemetery
100	Meakin	T	Private	14473 Loyal North Lancs Reg't	7.7.1916	Pozieres British Cem.
173	Mellor	E.S.	Private	36857 South Lancashire Reg't.	13.12.1917	Capetown Cem S.A.
115	Mellor	F.J.	Lieutenant	- Sherwood Foresters	19.9.1916	Grove Town Cem.
64	Mellor	T	Private	16584 South Staffords	25.9.1915	Loos Memorial
19	Merriman	E	Private	8282 Royal Irish Reg't.	23.8.1914	La Ferte-S-J Mem.

	Surname	Initials	Rank	Service No. & Regiment	Date	Cemetery/Memorial
85	Messham	H.J.	Private	467037 Canadian M.G.C.	17.6.1916	Boulogne Eastern Cem.
198	Missen	T.M.	Driver	59650 Royal Field Artillery	22.8.1918	Villers-Bretonneux Cem.
188	Mitchell	W	A.B.	172225 Royal Navy	6.5.1918	East London Cem.
137	Moorcroft	F	Private	41731 Sherwood Foresters	12.5.1917	Thiepval Memorial
185	Morris	A	L/Corporal	106196 Sherwood Foresters	21.4.1918	Haringhe Cem., Ypres
110	Moss	W	Sergeant	SE/8959 Army Vet. Corps	1.9.1916	Amara War Cem, Iraq
215	Murfin	C	Private	- Hampshire Reg't.	27.11.1918	Kortrijk Com. Cem.
71	Murray	P.V.	Private	10578 Royal Fusiliers	4.11.1915	Spoilbank Cem.
135	Mycock	H	Private	11182 Royal Fusiliers	24.4.1917	Dickebusch New Cem.
185	Nelson	E	Private	51326 West Yorkshire Reg't.	25.4.1918	Tyne Cot Memorial
149	Nelson	F	Private	G/15122 Royal Sussex Reg't.	14.8.1917	Dozinghem Cem.
58	Nicholson	B.L.	Lieutenant	- Royal Field Artillery	24.7.1915	Dranouter Churchyard
125	Noble	A	Private	16818 North Staffords	27.1.1917	Amara War Cem, Iraq
109	Nowland	A	Private	8851 East Surrey Reg't.	16.8.1916	Thiepval Memorial
149	Nowland	H	Private	25602 Lincolnshire Reg't	14.8.1917	Div Collecting Post Cem
134	Oakes	W.E.	Private	38536 Northumberland Fus.	9.4.1917	Arras Memorial
214	Osbourne	P	Private	M2/031683 R.A.S.C.	12.11.1918	Etaples Mil Cem.
78	O'Shaughnessy	W	Private	16108 North Staffords	5.4.1916	Basra Memorial, Iraq
180	Owen	J.W	Private	204459 Royal West Kent Reg't.	28.3.1918	Pozieres Memorial
150	Partridge	C	Private	305334 West Riding Reg't.	11.8.1917	Grevillers Cem.
171	Peach	G.W.	Private	241596 North Staffords	5.12.1917	St Sever Cem.
219	Peacock	H	Driver	- Royal Field Artillery	7.3.1919	Leek Cemetery
199	Peacock	H	Private	- Cheshire Reg't	2.9.1918	Not Known
150	Phillips	J.	Gunner	837268 Royal Field Artillery	11.8.1917	Menin Gate Memorial
119	Pickford	D	C/Sgt-Maj	9031 Sherwood Foresters	23.10.1916	Leek Cemetery
85	Pickford	D	Sergeant	- Royal Field Artillery	2.6.1916	Leek Cemetery
144	Pickford	E	Gunner	152263 Royal Field Artillery	23.7.1917	Lijssenthoek Cem.
137	Pickford	F	Private	29254 East Lancashire Reg't.	12.5.1917	Arras Memorial
193	Pickford	H	Private	352859 Royal Scots	1.8.1918	Raperie Brit. Cem.

	Surname	Initials	Rank	Number & Regiment	Date	Cemetery/Memorial
219	Pickford	J.J.	Private	11162 Labour Corps	6.2.1919	Leek Cemetery
203	Pickford	P.	Sergeant	805429 Royal Field Artillery	5.10.1918	Bellicourt Cem.
110	Plant	H.	Private	26584 Sherwood Foresters	3.9.1916	Thiepval Memorial
189	Plant	J.W.	Private	29994 North Staffords	18.5.1918	Baghdad Cem, Iraq
144	Plant	S	Gunner	151494 Royal Garrison Artillery	6.7.1917	White House Cem.
105	Plant	W	Private	16854 Bedfordshire Reg't.	27.7.1916	Thiepval Memorial
190	Pointon	F	Private	43694 Yorkshire Reg't	22.6.1918	Neiderzwehren Cem.
215	Poole	E	Corporal	- West Yorkshire Reg't	26.11.1918	Leek Cemetery
37	Poyser	J.W	Private	3640 East Surrey Reg't.	27.4.1915	Menin Gate Memorial
31	Price	C.H.	Lieutenant	- Canadian Light Infantry	24.1.1915	Voormezeele Cem.
211	Prime	C	Corporal	805739 Royal Field Artillery	6.11.1918	Nechin Com. Cem.
96	Prime	G.V.	Gunner	398 Royal Field Artillery	1.7.1916	Thiepval Memorial
105	Prince	E	Private	16994 Bedfordshire Reg't.	27.7.1916	Thiepval Memorial
178	Prince	J	Private	42383 Worcestershire Reg't.	21.3.1918	Arras Memorial
178	Prince	W	Private	7738 North Staffords	21.3.1918	Pozieres Memorial
71	Prosser	W	Private	3971 North Staffords	17.10.1915	Lillers Com. Cem.
52	Quinn	P	Private	11037 North Staffords	10.8.1915	Helles Memorial
149	Read	H	Gunner	101586 Royal Field Artillery	5.8.1917	New Irish Farm Cem.
158	Renshaw	V	Private	43011 South Staffords	4.10.1917	Tyne Cot Memorial
118	Rhead	F	Private	14761 Royal Fusiliers	7.10.1916	Thiepval Memorial
215	Rhead	W.H.	Driver	T4/186340 R.A.S.C.	24.12.1918	Bralo Brit. Cem. Greece
197	Richards	J.	L/Corporal	31869 K.S.L.I.	22.8.1918	Vielle-Chapelle Cem.
131	Richardson	E	Private	3042 Royal Fusiliers	6.2.1917	Bouzincourt Com. Cem
220	Riches	R.C.	Private	M/321671 R.A.S.C.	2.7.1919	Leek Cemetery
220	Rider	C	Driver	- R.A.S.C.	15.5.1919	Leek Cemetery
54	Rider	W	Q.M.S.	8728 North Staffords	7.1.1916	Helles Memorial
192	Riley	N	Private	TRG/51569Sherwood Foresters	7.7.1918	Leek Cemetery
198	Robinson	A	Private	44112 Essex Reg't.	23.8.1918	Albert Com. Cem.
124	Robinson	C.C.	Sergeant	3/3957 Black Watch	2.12.1916	Perth Cem. U.K.

No.	Surname	Initial	Rank	Service No. & Regiment	Date	Cemetery/Memorial
60	Robinson	C.W.	Corporal	16948 Hampshire Reg't.	12.9.1915	Hamel Mil. Cem.
78	Robinson	E	Guardsman	22313 Grenadier Guards	9.5.1916	Ypres Reservoir Cem.
133	Robinson	J	Private	808287 Canadian Infantry	9.4.1917	Vimy Memorial
115	Robinson	J.H.	Private	G/6849 East Kent Reg't.	25.9.1916	Thiepval Memorial
170	Robinson	S.W.	Private	201841 Argylls	24.11.1917	Rocquigny-Eq'crt Rd. Cem.
185	Robinson	T	Private	0793 Lancashire Fusiliers	20.4.1918	Tyne Cot Memorial
201	Robinson	T	Private	41060 South Staffords	28.9.1918	Vis-en-Artois Memorial
171	Rogers	G	Rifleman	R/38033 King's Royal Rifle Corps	3.12.1917	Rocquigny-Eq'crt Rd. Cem.
149	Rushton	G.A.	Private	60955 Machine Gun Corps	4.8.1917	Menin Gate Memorial
55	Rushton	J	Private	16443 Bedfordshire Reg't.	2.6.1915	Menin Gate Memorial
144	Sales	V	Rifleman	267778 West Yorkshire Reg't.	3.7.1917	Laventie Mil. Cem.
107	Salt	C	Sergeant	5331 North Staffords	4.8.1916	De Cusine Ravine Cem.
183	Salt	S	Gunner	174175 Royal Field Artillery	7.4.1918	Couin New Brit. Cem.
64	Salt	S	Private	8423 North Staffords	25.9.1915	La Brique Mil. Cem.
145	Scotton	W	Private	49668 King's (Liverpool) Reg't.	26.7.1917	Bethune Town Cem.
78	Sharratt	J	Private	17811 North Staffords	20.4.1916	Basra Memorial
140	Shaw	H	Private	54530 Royal Welsh Fusiliers	22.6.1917	Bard Cottage Cem. Ypres
159	Sheldon	J	Private	41473 South Staffords	12.10.1917	Tyne Cot Memorial
87	Shenton	H	Private	5251 North Staffords	24.6.1916	Thiepval Memorial
134	Shute	H	Bombardier	76684 Royal Field Artillery	12.4.1917	Nine Elms Mil. Cem.
78	Sigley	F	Private	23189 Royal Welsh Fusiliers	30.4.1916	Lindenhoek Chalet Cem.
121	Sigley	R.J.	Private	18297 K.O.Y.L.I.	18.11.1916	Thiepval Memorial
37	Sillito	M	Private	16391 Royal Fusiliers	26.4.1915	Menin Gate Memorial
38	Simister	C.R.	Private	4765 Royal Fusiliers	2.5.1915	Bailleul Com. Cem.
135	Simpson	H	Private	241995 West Yorkshire Reg't.	3.5.1917	Arras Memorial
190	Simpson	S	Private	15561 R.A.M.C.	5.7.1918	Leek Cemetery
57	Sims	S	Private	2960 R.A.M.C.	16.7.1915	Etaples Mil Cem.
181	Slater	H	Guardsman	28809 Grenadier Guards	28.3.1918	Douchy-Les-Ayette Cem.
101	Slater	J.T	Private	11095 Royal Fusiliers	9.7.1916	Thiepval Memorial

No.	Surname	Initials	Rank	Service	Date	Memorial / Cemetery
43	Smethurst	J.V.	Private	G/4585 Royal Sussex Reg't.	9.5.1915	Le Touret Memorial
135	Smith	A	Private	200756 Durham Light Infantry	23.4.1917	Arras Memorial
158	Smith	E	C.S.M.	5924 King's Royal Rifle Corps	11.10.1917	N/ham Rd Cem. Derby
154	Smith	E	Private	352863 Royal Scots	20.9.1917	Tyne Cot Memorial
190	Smith	G	Private	53167 Sherwood Foresters	12.6.1918	Premont Brit.Cem
118	Smith	H.	Guardsman	20793 Grenadier Guards	16.10.1916	Etaples Mil Cem.
204	Smith	J.T	Private	50134 Essex Regt.	12.10.1918	Brancourt-le-Grand Cem.
89	Smith	S	Private	4438 R.A.M.C.	29.6.1916	Kirkee Memorial, India
59	Smith	T	Private	13584 East Lancashire Regt.	22.8.1915	Merville Com. Cem.
51	Smith	W	Private	27114 Royal Welsh Fusiliers	8.8.1915	Helles Memorial
141	Smith	W.T.	Private	201958 North Staffords	27.6.1917	Arras Memorial
120	Spearing	H	Gunner	119389 Royal Field Artillery	8.11.1916	Thiepval Memorial
199	Spink	E.M.	Captain	- North Staffords	14.9.1918	Haidar Pasha Mem. Turkey
78	Sproson	A	Private	17066 Lincolnshire Reg't.	21.5.1916	Warloy-Baillon Com.Cem.
219	Stanmore	F.E.	Corporal	- Ox and Bucks L.I.	14.3.1919	Leek Cemetery
137	Stannard	H	Private	234936 Canadian Infantry.	9.5.1917	Vimy Memorial
187	Stockton	H.	L/Corporal	12244 North Staffords	22.5.1918	St Sever Cem.
134	Street	J.H.H	Private	10221 North Staffords	12.4.1917	Chipping Barnet Cem.
189	Stretch	S	Corporal	3/16255 West Riding Reg't.	21.5.1918	Leek Cemetery
221	Swarbrook	J	Private	- Royal Fusiliers	6.12.1922	Leek Cemetery
107	Sweetmore	H.	Private	1196 Royal Fusiliers	9.8.1916	Thiepval Memorial
150	Swindells	H.	Lieutenant	- South Staffords	15.8.1917	Philosophe Brit. Cem.
102	Tatton	A	Private	11120 Royal Welsh Fusiliers	20.7.1916	Thiepval Memorial
198	Tatton	H.	Private	G/72320 Royal West Surreys	23.8.1918	Becourt Mil.Cem.
220	Tatton	R	Private	11342 Labour Corps	9.7.1919	Leek Cemetery
95	Taylor	T	Private	201621 North Staffords	1.7.1916	Thiepval Memorial
113	Thornton	T	Private	10551 Royal Fusiliers	14.9.1916	La Neuville Cem.
27	Tomkinson	G	A.B.	SS/805 HMS Good Hope. R.N.	1.11.1914	Portsmouth Memorial
101	Tomkinson	H	Sapper	10692 Royal Engineers	15.7.1916	Mericourt L'Abbe Cem.

No.	Surname	Initials	Rank	Regiment	Date	Cemetery/Memorial
143	Tomlinson	W	Private	14115 Royal Fusiliers	1.7.1917	Lijssenthoek Cem.
107	Trafford	A	Private	5500 North Staffords	11.8.1916	Warlincourt Halte Cem.
171	Trafford	G	Guardsman	23899 Grenadier Guards	1.12.17	Cambrai Memorial
53	Trafford	H.E.	Private	15126 North Staffords	21.10.1915	Helles Memorial
85	Trafford	H.S.B	Rifleman	C/12262 King's Royal Rifle Corps	24.6.1916	Berks Cem. Ext.
23	Trafford	W.R.	L/Corporal	7970 K.S.L.I.	5.11.1914	Leek Cemetery
132	Travis	J	Private	201567 North Staffords	14.3.1917	Rossignol Wood Cem.
65	Tudor	H.A.	Private	2767 North Staffords	13.10.1915	Vermelles Brit. Cem.
108	Turner	J	Private	12262 North Staffords	13.8.1916	Flatiron Copse Cem.
214	Vernon	R	Private	TT/0936 Royal Army Vet. Corps	12.11.1918	Leek Cemetery
215	Vigrass	S.B.	Sergeant	22748 R.A.O.C.	2.12.1918	Leek Cemetery
159	Wagstaffe	J.C.	Lieutenant	- South Staffords	12.10.1917	Poelcapelle Brit. Cem.
220	Walker	A.T.	Pioneer	604982 Royal Engineers	19.12.1919	Aire Com. Cem.
21	Walker	J.E	W/Officer	- R.C.A.S.	29.8.1914	Dover Cem. U.K.
113	Wallis	R	Private	16991 Bedfordshire Reg't.	5.9.1916	Thiepval Memorial
124	Walwyn	P	Sergeant	TT/02467 Royal Army Vet.Corps	6.12.1916	Curragh Mil. Cem. Ireland.
141	Warbrick	J.E.	Private	201644 North Staffords	15.6.1917	Noeux-le-Mines Com. Cem.
136	Wardle	J.T.	Private	242673 North Staffords	9.5.1917	Hargicourt Brit. Cem.
137	Watson	C.C.	Lieutenant	- Royal Field Artillery	1.6.1917	Fosse No: 10 Cem.
220	Weaver	J	Private	- Royal Defence Corps	12.4.1921	Leek Cemetery
161	Wheatley	B	Private	28513 Loyal North Lancs Reg't	26.10.1917	Tyne Cot Memorial
87	Wheeldon	E	Private	9800 Machine Gun Corps	25.6.1916	Bois-de-Noilette Brit. Cem.
100	Wheeldon	W.F.	L/Corporal	4783 Manchester Reg't.	7.7.1916	Thiepval Memorial
64	White	H.G.	Guardsman	13231 Grenadier Guards	27.9.1915	Loos Memorial
173	Whitehouse	J.D	Private	330122 Sherwood Foresters	11.12.1917	Leek Cemetery
172	Willmer	H.D.	Private	47159 Manchester Reg't.	30.11.1917	Leek Cemetery
122	Wilson	A	R.S.M.	9274 North Staffords	18.11.1916	Connaught Cem.
74	Wilson	R	Private	16600 Scottish Rifles	27.1.1916	Loos Memorial
215	Wilson	V.H.	Private	106658 Durham Light Infantry	13.11.1918	Leek Cemetery

43	Winckle	J.G.	Private	G/4583 Royal Sussex Reg't.	11.5.1915	Choques Mil. Cem.
208	Wood	C.M.	Private	57107 Lancashire Fusiliers	23.10.1918	Romeries Com. Cem.
52	Wood	F	Corporal	41826 Royal Garrison Artillery	14.8.1915	Helles Memorial
187	Wood	R	Corporal	60480 M.G.C.	6.5.1918	Loos Memorial
201	Wood	T.H.	Private	G/96300 Middlesex Reg't.	28.9.1918	Tyne Cot Memorial
125	Wrench	T	Corporal	8511 North Staffords	12.1 1917	Amara War Cem. Iraq
67	Yates	H	Private	12107 Royal Fusiliers	19.10.1915	Lapugnoy Mil. Cem.
124	Yates	S	Private	S/8190 Rifle Brigade	23.12.1916	Leek Cemetery
193	Yates	T.C.	Private	235395 South Staffords	1.8.1918	Douchy-Les-Ayette Cem.

Appendix 2

MILITARY AND CIVIL CEMETERIES AND MEMORIALS MAINTAINED BY THE COMMONWEALTH WAR GRAVES COMMISSION WHERE LEEK SERVICEMEN ARE BURIED OR COMMEMORATED.

Details of the precise grave location or Memorial panel listing an individual name can usually be found in the C.W.G.C. registers kept at Military Cemeteries or Memorials. Alternatively, particulars are available from the Commonwealth War Graves Commission.

This list is only intended as a basic guide to cemetery and memorial locations and visitors are advised to plan routes carefully and check on access suitability of the various sites.

Aire Communal Cemetery Extension, Somme, France.   (1 Leek burial)
(Situated 14km south east of St. Omer, just north of Aire town)

Albert Communal Cemetery Extension, Somme, France.   (1 Leek burial)
(On the junction of the D938 Peronne Road and the D329 Bray sur Somme Road, Albert.)

Alexandria (Chatby) Military and War Memorial Cemetery, Egypt.   (1 Leek burial)
(On the eastern side of Alexandria on the road to Sharia Anubis.)

Amara War Cemetery, Iraq.   (5 Leek burials)
(East of the town of Amara, between the left bank of the Tigris and the Chahaila Canal.)

Arras Memorial, France.   (21 Leek names commemorated)
(Located in the Faubourg-d'Amiens Cemetery, on the Boulevard du General de Gaulle, Arras.)

Baghdad (North Gate) War Cemetery, Iraq.   (2 Leek burials)
(Located 800 metres beyond the North Gate of the city of Baghdad on the road to Baguba.)

Bailleul Communal Cemetery Extension, Nord, France.   (2 Leek burials)
(On the Ypres (Ieper) road out of the town.)

Bard Cottage Cemetery, Ypres (Ieper), Belgium.   (1 Leek burial)
(Located on the N369 in the direction of Boezinge.)

Basra Memorial, Iraq.   (5 Leek names commemorated)

Beacon Cemetery, Sailly-Laurette, Somme, France. (1 Leek burial)
(Village is 19km east of Amiens. Cemetery located on the D1 in the direction of Amiens-Corbie.)

Becourt Military Cemetery, Becordel-Becourt, Somme, France. (1 Leek burial)
(Village is 2km to the east of Albert, cemetery is on the south side of the road from Becourt to Albert.)

Bedford House Cemetery, Ypres (Ieper), Belgium. (1 Leek burial)
(Located 2.5km south of the town centre on the N365 road to Armentieres.)

Belgrade Cemetery, Namur, Belgium. (1 Leek burial)
(Located on the N4 (Chaussee De Waterloo) in the town of Belgrade.)

Bellicourt British Cemetery, Aisne, France. (1 Leek burial)
(Bellicourt village is 13km north of St.Quentin. Cemetery is off the D331 in the direction of Peronne.)

Berks Cemetery Extension, Ploegsteert, Belgium. (1 Leek burial)
(Located 12km south of Ieper town centre on the N365.)

Bethencourt Communal Cemetery, Nord, France. (1 Leek burial)
(Village is north of Le Cateau. Cemetery is off the road from Cauchy, to Solesmes.)

Bethune Town Cemetery, Pas de Calais, France. (1 Leek burial)
(Located in the centre of the town.)

Bienvillers Military Cemetery, Pas de Calais, France. (4 Leek burials)
(Cemetery located south of the village on the D2 leading to Soustre.)

Bleuet Farm Cemetery, Ypres (Ieper), Belgium. (1 Leek burial)
(Located near the village of Elverdinge off the N8 road.)

Bois-de-Noulette British Cemetery, Aix-Noulette, Pas de Calais, France. (1 Leek burial)
(Village is 8km from Bethune on the road to Arras. Cemetery is in the hamlet of Noulette, 1.5km south of Aix-Noulette.)

Boulogne Eastern Cemetery, Pas de Calais, France. (1 Leek burial)
(Located on the eastern side of the town on the road to St. Omer.)

Bouzincourt Communal Cemetery Extension, Somme, France. (1 Leek burial)
(Village is 3km north-west of Albert. Cemetery is on northern side, signposted from D938.)

Braine Communal Cemetery, Aisne, France.   (1 Leek burial)
(The town of Braine is reached via the D14. The Cemetery is off the town centre on the D1320.)

Bralo British Cemetery, Greece.   (1 Leek burial)
(Cemetery is located on the main road from Amfissa to Lamia and is between the villages of Gravia and Bralo.)

Brancourt-le-Grand Military Cemetery, Aisne, France.   (1 Leek burial)
(Cemetery is in the south-east corner of the village. Brancourt lies between Le Cateau and St.Quentin.)

Bristol (Arnos Vale) Cemetery, England.   (1 Leek burial)

Brown's Road Military Cemetery, Festubert, Pas de Calais, France.   (1 Leek burial)
(Located 8km east-north-east of Bethune, off the D166 road from Festubert to Cuinchy.)

Bruay Communal Cemetery Extension, Pas de Calais, France.   (1 Leek burial)
(Village situated 6km south-west of Bethune. Cemetery is off the N41, in the direction of Berck.)

Buttes New British Cemetery, Polygon Wood, Zonnebeke, Belgium.   (1 Leek burial)
(Located 8km from Ieper town centre on the Lange Dreve, a road leading from the N8, connecting Ieper to Menen)

Caister on Sea Cemetery, Great Yarmouth, Norfolk, England.   (1 Leek burial)

Cambrai Memorial, France.   (3 Leek names commemorated)
(Located in Louvewal Cemetery, on the N30, 16km south-west of Cambrai.)

Capetown Cemetery, South Africa   (1 Leek burial)

Caterpillar Valley Cemetery, Longueval, Somme, France.   (1 Leek burial)
(Village is 13km east of Albert. Cemetery is west of the village on the road to Contalmaison.)

Cement House Cemetery, Langemarck-Poelkapelle, Belgium.   (3 Leek burials)
(Located north of Ieper off the N313.)

Cheddleton Churchyard, Leek, Staffordshire.   (1 Leek burial)
(Located off the Leek to Cheadle road in the village of Cheddleton, adjacent to the church of Saint Edward the Confessor.)

Chipping Barnet Churchyard, Chipping Barnet, Hertfordshire.   (1 Leek burial)

Choques Military Cemetery, Pas de Calais, France.   (1 Leek burial)
(Town is 4km north-west of Bethune on the Lillers road. Cemetery is in the town on the road to Gonnheim.)

Cite Bonjean Military Cemetery, Armentieres, Nord, France.   (1 Leek burial)
(Situated off the D945 road to Estaires.)

Cologne Southern Cemetery, Germany.   (2 Leek burials)
(Located 5km south of the cathedral on the Honningerweg.)

Connaught Cemetery, Thiepval, Somme, France.   (2 Leek burials)
(Village is 8km north-east of Albert. Cemetery is lkm north-west of village on the D73.)

Couin New British Cemetery, Pas de Calais, France.   (1 Leek burial)
(Village is 15km east of Doullens. Cemetery is on the D2 road just outside Couin.)

Curragh Military Cemetery, County Kildare, Ireland.   (1 Leek burial)
(Located in Curragh Military Camp, 4 miles south-east of Kildare.)

Daors Communal Cemetery Extension, Somme, France.   (1 Leek burial)
(Village is 10km east of Amiens. Cemetery is off the D115 in the direction of Pont-Noyelle.)

De Cusine Ravine British Cemetery, Pas de Calais, France.   (2 Leek burials)
(Near the village of Basseux, 12km south-west of Arras, off the D1 road.)

Delsaux Farm Cemetery, Beugny, France.   (1 Leek burial)
(Beugny is 19km south-west of Cambrai on the RN30. Cemetery is located off the RD20 a kilometre from the village in the direction of Haplincourt.)

Dickebusch New Military Cemetery, Ypres, (Ieper), Belgium.   (1 Leek burial)
(The village, now spelt Dikkebus, is on the N375 south west of Ypres. Cemetery is near the village church.)

Divisional Collecting Post Cemetery and Extension, Belgium.   (1 Leek burial)
(Located to the north-east of Ypres (Ieper) off the A19.)

Divisional Cemetery, Dickebusch Road. Belgium.   (1 Leek burial)
(Located 2km west of Ypres town centre on the Omloopstraat.)

Doiran Memorial, Greece.   (1 Leek name commemorated)
(Located near Doiran Military Cemetery in the north of Greece close to the Yugoslav border and close to Lake Doiran.)

Douchey-Les-Ayette British Cemetery, Pas de Calais, France.　　(3 Leek burials)
(Village is some 14km south of Arras on the Amiens road.)

Doullens Communal Cemetery Extension No: 2, Somme, France.　　(2 Leek burials)
(The town is 30km north of Amiens on the N25 road to Arras. Cemetery is on the eastern side of Doullens, off the road to Arras.)

Dover (St. James) Cemetery, Kent.　　(1 Leek burial)

Dozinghem Military Cemetery, Belgium.　　(2 Leek burials)
(Located 12km west of Ypres on the Leeuwerikstraat, a road leading from the N308 connecting Ypres (Ieper) to Poperinge.)

Dranouter Churchyard and Dranouter Military Cemetery, Belgium.　　(2 Leek burials, 1
(Village is 1km south of Ypres on the N375.)　　in each)

Duisans British Cemetery, Etrun, Pas de Clais, France.　　(1 Leek burial)
(Duisans and Etrun villages are 9km west of Arras. Cemetery is in Etrun on the D339)

East London Cemetery, Plaistow, Essex, England.　　(1 Leek burial)

Estaires Communal Cemetery, Nord, France.　　(1 Leek burial)
(Town is 11km west of Armentieres. Cemetery is on the eastern outskirts, on the road to Bailleul.)

Etaples Military Cemetery, Pas de Calais, France.　　(5 Leek burials)
(Town is 27km south of Boulogne. Cemetery is to the north of the town on the road to Boulogne.)

Favreuil British Cemetery, Pas de Calais, France.　　(2 Leek burials)
(Cemetery is on the D.lOE, 2km north of Bapaume.)

(7th) Field Ambulance Cemetery, Gallipoli.　　(1 Leek burial)
(Located off the Anzac-Suvla road.)

Fins New British Cemetery, Sorel-le-Grand, Somme, France.　　(1 Leek burial)
(Fins is a village on the road from Cambrai to Peronne. Cemetery is outside Fins on the road to Heudicourt.)

Flatiron Copse Cemetery, Mametz, Somme, France.　　(3 Leek burials)
(Located on the D929, 10km east of Albert.)

Flesquieres Hill British Cemetery, Cambrai, France.   (1 Leek burial)
(Flesquieres village is 5km south-west of the Cambrai to Bapaume road. Cemetery is east of the village on the D92 road to Cantaing.)

Fosse No: 10 Communal Cemetery Extension, Sains-en-Gohelle, France. (3 Leek burials)
(Located 20km north of Arras on the road to Bethune.)

Fouquieres Churchyard Extension, Pas de Calais, France.   (3 Leek burials)
(Village is lkm south-west of Bethune. Churchyard is on the road to Bruay.)

Gaza War Cemetery, Israel.   (1 Leek burial)
(Cemetery is 2km north of the city near the Bureir Road and close to the railway station.)

Ghissignies British Cemetery, Nord, France.   (1 Leek burial)
(Village is south-west of Le Quesnay. Cemetery is on the D86 road to Le Quesnay.)

Gommecourt Wood New Cemetery, Foncquevillers, France.   (1 Leek burial)
(Village is 18km south-west of Arras on the D3. Cemetery is on the D6.)

Gonnehem British Cemetery, Pas de Calais, France.   (1 Leek burial)
(Village is 7km north-west of Bethune. Cemetery is on the D182 Lillers road.)

Grand Ravine British Cemetery, Havrincourt, France,   (1 Leek burial)
(Village is 10km south-west of Cambrai. Cemetery is in the nearby Havrincourt Wood.)

Grevillers British Cemetery, Pas de Clais, France.   (2 Leek burials)
(Village is 3km west of Bapaume. Cemetery is on the RD29.)

Grevillers (New Zealand) Memorial, Pas de Clais, France.   (1 Leek name commemorated)
(Located in Grevillers British Cemetery)

Grove Town British Cemetery, Meaulte, Somme, France.   (1 Leek burial)
(South of Albert, 3km beyond Meaulte on the Bray-sur-Somme road.)

Guillemont Road Cemetery, Guillemont Road, Somme, France.   (1 Leek burial)
(Village is 12km east of Albert. Cemetery is on the D64, out of the village on the Montauban Rd.)

Habarcq Communal Cemetery Extension, Pas de Calais, France.   (1 Leek burial)
(Village is 12km west of Arras. Cemetery is on north side of village on the D61 road to Haute-Avesnes.)

Haidar Pasha Memorial, Istanbul, Turkey.   (1 Leek name commemorated)
(Situated in the suburb of Haidar Pasha, in the cemetery of the same name.)

Hamburg Cemetery, Gemmany.   (1 Leek burial)
(Located within the city at the junction with the Alsterdorfer and Fuhlsbuttlerstrasse.)

Hamel Military Cemetery, Beaumont-Hamel, Somme, France.   (1 Leek burial)
(Village of Hamel is 6km north of Albert. Cemetery is in the village.)

Hargicourt British Cemetery, Aisne, France.   (1 Leek burial)
(Village is 16km north-west of St Quentin. Cemetery is on the Peronne road.

Haringhe (Bandaghem) Military Cemetery, Belgium.   (2 Leek burials)
(Village of Haringe located 18km north-west of Ypres, off the N308 road.)

Helles Memorial, Gallipoli, Turkey.   (9 Leek names commemorated)
(Situated on the tip of the Gallipoli Peninsula.)

Hermies Hill British Cemetery, Pas de Calais, France.   (2 Leek burials)
(The town of Hermies is situated 3km south of the N30 Bapaume to Cambrai road Cemetery is off the D34 and D5E roads.)

Hoogstade Belgian Military Cemetery, Belgium.   (1 Leek burial)
(Village is south of Veume on the N8 road. Cemetery is in the village.)

Kantara War Memorial Cemetery, Egypt.   (1 Leek burial)
(Located 30km north of Ismailia on the main Ismailia to Port Said road.)

Kemmel No: 1 French Cemetery, Belgium.   (1 Leek burial)
(Located off the N331 Ypres to Kemmel road, 6km south-west of Ypres.)

Kirkee 1914-1918 Memorial, India.   (1 Leek name commemorated)
(Kirkee adjoins the university town of Poona on the plateau above Bombay.)

Kortrijk (St Jan) Communal Cemetery, Kortrijk, Belgium.   (1 Leek burial)
(Located 28km east of Ypres town centre on the N8 road.)

La Brique Military Cemetery, Ypres (leper), Belgium.   (1 Leek burial)
(Located in the north-east of the town in the Pilkemseweg.)

La Chapelle d'Armentieres Communal Cemetery, Nord, France.   (1 Leek burial)
(Village is 1.5km west of Armentieres. Cemetery is on the road towards Houplines.)

La Ferte-sous-Jouarre Memorial, Seine-et-Marne, France.   (1 Leek burial)
(La Ferte is a small town 66km east of Paris. Memorial is in a small park on the River Marne on the Paris road.)

La Laiterie Military Cemetery, Belgium.   (1 Leek burial)
(Located 7km south of Ypres (Ieper) on the N331.)

La Neuville British Cemetery, Corbie, Somme, France.   (1 Leek burial)
(Corbie is 15km south-west of Albert. Cemetery is to the west of the village.)

Lapugnoy Military Cemetery, Pas de Calais, France.   (1 Leek burial)
(Village is 6km west of Bethune. Cemetery is off the D70 towards Marles-les-Mines.)

Laventie Military Cemetery, La Gorgue, Nord, France.   (1 Leek burial)
(Cemetery is located to the north-east of Laventie off the D166.)

Le Touret Memorial, Pas de Calais, France.   (2 Leek names commemorated)
(Located in the Le Touret Military Cemetery on the main Bethune to Armentieres road, the
D171.)

Leek Cemetery, Staffordshire, England.   (39 Leek burials)
(Situated off the main Leek to Cheadle road, Leek.)

Lijssenthoek Military Cemetery, Poperinge, Belgium.   (6 Leek burials)
(Located 12km west of Ypres (Ieper) town centre on the Boescheepseweg a road leading from
the N308 Ieper to Poperinge road.)

Lillers Communal Cemetery, Pas de Calais, France.   (1 Leek burial)
(Town is 15km west-north-west of Bethune. Cemetery is to the north of the town, off the
D182.)

Lindenhoek Chalet Military Cemetery, Belgium.   (1 Leek burial)
(Located 9km south-west of Ypres, off the N331.)

Longuenesse (St Omer) Souvenir Cemetery, Pas de Calais, France.   (2 Leek burials)
(Longuenesse is an area of St Omer, cemetery is off the D928 Abbeville road.)

Loos Memorial, Pas de Calais, France.   (8 Leek names commemorated)
(Located in Dud Corner Cemetery, on the N43, 1km west of Loos on the Lens-Bethune road.)

Menin Gate Memorial, Ypres (Ieper).   (16 Leek names commemorated)
(Situated at the eastern end of the town on the road to Menin and Courtrai.)

Mericourt L'Abbe Communal Cemetery Extension, Somme, France.   (1 Leek burial)
(Village is 6km south-east of Albert on the road to Amiens. Cemetery is to the east of the
village.)

Merville Communal Cemetery, Nord, France.   (1 Leek burial)
(Town is 15km north of Bethune. Cemetery is off the D38 road to Neuf-Berquin.)

Mikra British Cemetery, Kalamaria, Greece.   (1 Leek burial)
(Located 8km south of Thessalonika on the road to the airport.)

Nechin Communal Cemetery, Hainaut, Belgium.   (1 Leek burial)
(Located centrally between the towns of Lille, Kortrijk and Tournai, off the N518.)

Neiderzwehren Cemetery, Kassel, Hessen, Gemmany.   (1 Leek burial)
(Located 10km south of Kassel and 2km from the main Kassel to Marburg road.)

New Irish Farm Cemetery, Ypres (Ieper), Belgium.   (1 Leek burial)
(Located to the north-east of Ypres off the road to Kortrijk.)

Nottingham Road Cemetery, Derby, England.   (1 Leek burial)

Nieuport Memorial, Belgium.   (1 Leek name commemorated)
(Located on the road from Nieuport docks where it joins the Lombardsijde.)

Nine Elms Military Cemetery, Thelus, Pas de Calais, France. (1 Leek burial)
(Thelus is 6km north of Arras, off the main Arras to Lens road. Cemetery is 1.5km south of the village.)

Noeux-le-Mines Communal Cemetery, Pas de Calais, France.   (1 Leek burial)
(Town is 6km south of Bethune on the Arras road. Cemetery is on the northern side of the town.)

Pernes British Cemetery, Pas de Calais, France.   (1 Leek burial)
(Pernes-en-Artois is a town on the main Lillers to St Pol road. Cemetery is lkm west of the town.)

Perth (Wellshill) Cemetery, Perthshire, Scotland.   (1 Leek burial)

Philosophe British Cemetery, Mazingarbe, Pas de Calais, France. (1 Leek burial)
(Cemetery is located between Bethune and Lens, off the D165E.)

Ploegsteert Memorial, Comines-Warneton, Hainaut, Belgium.
                                        (1 Leek name commemorated)
(Located in Berks Cemetery Extension, 12km south of Ypres on the N365.)

Plymouth Memorial, Plymouth, Devon, England.   (1 Leek name commemorated)

Poelcapelle British Cemetery, Langemark-Poelkapelle, Belgium.　　(1 Leek burial)
(Situated 10km north-east of Ypres on the N313.)

Pont-du-Hem Military Cemetery, La Gorgue, Nord, France.　　(1 Leek burial)
(Located on the D947 road from La Bassee to Estaires, 5km from Estaires.)

Pont-Remy British Cemetery, Somme, France.　　(1 Leek burial)
(Village is 11 km south-east of Abbeville, on the northem bank of the River Somme.
Cemetery is north of the village.)

Poperinghe New Military Cemetery, Poperinge, Belgium.　　(1 Leek burial)
(Town is 10km west of Ypres. Cemetery is off the N33 road.)

Portsmouth Naval Memorial, Southsea Common, Portsmouth, Hampshire.
　　(3 Leek names commemorated)

Pozieres British Cemetery, Somme, France.　　(2 Leek burials)
(Located on the D929 Albert to Bapaume road, 6 km from Albert.)

Pozieres Memorial, Somme, France.　　(7 Leek names commemorated)
(Location as for Cemetery; the Memorial encloses the Cemetery.)

Premont British Cemetery, Aisne, France.　　(1 Leek burial)
(Village is 19km south-east of Cambrai. Cemetery is south-east of village on the road to
Bohain.)

Puchevillers British Cemetery, Somme, France.　　(1 Leek burial)
(Village is situated on the D11 19km north-east of Amiens. Cemetery is west of village.)

Queens Cemetery, Puisieux, Pas de Calais, France.　　(1 Leek burial)
(Village situated 15km north of Albert. Cemetery is on the old front line of July, 1916,
and is south of Mark Copse, facing the Sheffield Memorial Park.

Ramleh War Cemetery, Israel.　　(1 Leek burial)
(Town, (now Ramla) is 12km south-east of Jaffa. Cemetery is close to Ramla Prison.)

Ramparts Cemetery, Ypres (leper), Belgium.　　(1 Leek burial)
(Located in the town, close to the Lille Gate.)

Raperie British Cemetery, Villemontoire, Aisne, France.　　(1 Leek burial)
(Village is to the west of the N2 Chateau-Thierry to Soissons road, 10km from Soissons.
Cemetery is off the D1280 road to Vierzy.)

Ration Farm Military Cemetery, La Chapelle-d'Armentieres, Nord, France. (1 Leek burial)
(Located 2.5km south of the village on the road to Fleurbaix.)

Red Cross Corner Cemetery, Beugny, Pas de Calais, France. (1 Leek burial)
(Beugny is 5km north-east of Bapaume on the N30. Cemetery is on the west side of the village.)

Regina Trench Cemetery, Grandcourt, Somme, France. (2 Leek burials)
(Cemetery is approached from the direction of Courcelette (off the D929). Located 1.5km north-west of Courcelette.)

Ribecourt Road Cemetery, Trescault, Pas de Calais, France. (1 Leek burial)
(Village is 13km south-west of Cambrai. Cemetery is to the north-east of Trescault.)

Rocquigny-Equancourt Road British Cemetery,
Manancourt, Somme, France. (3 Leek burials)
(Located between the two villages of Rocquigny and Equancourt, 13km north of Peronne.)

Roisel Communal Cemetery Extension, Somme, France. (1 Leek burial)
(Town is 11km east of Peronne. Cemetery is on the Villers-Faucon road.)

Romeries Communal Cemetery Extension, Nord, France (1 Leek burial)
(Village is 16km south of Valenciennes. Cemetery is on the west side of the village.)

Rossignol Wood Cemetery, Hebuterne, Pas de Calais, France. (1 Leek burial)
(Village is 20km south-west of Arras. Cemetery is lkm outside the village on the D6.)

Salonika (Lembet Road) Military Cemetery, Greece. (1 Leek burial)
(Located on the outskirts of Thessalonika on the road towards Seres.)

Sancourt British Cemetery, Nord, France. (1 Leek burial)
(Village is 5km north-west of Cambrai. Cemetery is sign-posted from Sancourt and is off the main N43 road.)

Shrewsbury General Cemetery, Shropshire, England. (1 Leek burial)

Soissons Memorial, Aisne, France. (1 Leek name commemorated)
(Soissons stands on the left bank of the River Aisne, 100km north-east of Paris. Memorial is in the public square.)

Spoilbank Cemetery, Ypres (Ieper), Belgium. (1 Leek burial)
(Located 4.5km south-east of the town centre, off the N336.)

St Sever Cemetery Extension, Rouen, France. (4 Leek burials)
(Located 3km south of Rouen cathedral off the N138.)

St Aubert British Cemetery, Nord, France.   (1 Leek burial)
(Village is 13km east of Cambrai. Cemetery is on the D97 road outside the village.)

Strand Military Cemetery, Comines-Warneton, Hainaut, Belgium.   (1 Leek burial)
(Located 13km south of Ypres on the N365.)

Sucrerie Cemetery, Ablain-St Nazaire, Pas de Calais, France.   (1 Leek burial)
(Village is 13km north of Arras. Cemetery is off the D57 road.)

Tehran Memorial, Iran.   (1 Leek name commemorated)
(Situated in Tehran War Cemetery at Gulhak, 13km from Tehran.)

Tehran War Cemetery, Iran.   (1 Leek burial)
(Location as for Memorial.)

Terlincthun British Cemetery, Wimille, Pas de Calais, France.   (2 Leek burials)
(Located on the northern outskirts of Boulogne on the D96E.)

Thiepval Memorial, Somme, France.   (39 Leek names commemorated)
(Situated on the D73, off the D929 Albert to Bapaume road.)

Tidworth Military Cemetery, Wiltshire, England.   (1 Leek burial)

Toronto (Mount Pleasant) Cemetery, Ontario, Canada.   (1 Leek burial)

Tourgeville Military Cemetery, Calvados, France.   (1 Leek burial)
(Village adjoins the town of Trouville. Cemetery is to the north of the village.)

Tournai Communal Cemetery Allied Extension, Tournai, Hainaut, Belgium. (1 Leek burial)
(Located in the south west of the town on the N508.)

Twelve Tree Copse Cemetery, Gallipoli.   (1 Leek burial)
(Located in the Helles area, lkm south-west of Krithia.)

Tyne Cot Memorial, Belgium.   (11 Leek names commemorated)
(Located within Tyne Cot Cemetery, 9km north-east of Ypres on the N332.)

Vermelles British Cemetery, Pas de Calais, France.   (1 Leek burial)
(Village is 10km north-west of Lens. Cemetery is off the D75 road.)

Vichte Military Cemetery, Anzegem, Belgium.   (1 Leek burial)
(Situated 40km east of Ypres and 13km east of Kortrijk at Ingooigem on the N36.)

Vielle-Chapelle New Military Cemetery, Lacouture, Pas de Calais, France. (1 Leek burial)
(Situated north-east of Bethune off the main D945 Bethune to Estaires road.)

Villers-Bretonneux Military Cemetery, Somme, France.   (2 Leek burials)
(Village is 16km east of Amiens on the main road to St Quentin. Cemetery is 2km north of village on the road to Fouilly.)

Villers-Bretonneux Memorial, Somme, France.   (1 Leek name commemorated)
(Location as for Cemetery.)

Vimy Memorial, Pas de Calais, France.   (2 Leek names commemorated)
(Situated 8km north-east of Arras on the N17 Lens road.)

Vis-en-Artois Memorial, Pas de Calais, France.   (3 Leek names commemorated)
(Located on the Arras to Cambrai road, 10km south-east of Arras.)

Vlamertinghe New Military Cemetery, Belgium.   (3 Leek burials)
(Located 5km west of Ypres and to the south of Vlamertinge village.)

Vormezeele Enclosure No 3 Cemetery, Belgium.   (3 Leek burials)
(Located 4km south-west of Ypres off the N331 Ypres-Kemmel road.)

Warlincourt Halte British Cemetery, Saulty, Pas de Calais, France.   (2 Leek burials)
(Situated on the N25 Arras to Doullens road 22km from Arras.)

Warloy-Baillon Communal Cemetery, Somme, France.   (1 Leek burial)
(Situated on the D919 Amiens to Arras road, 21km north-east of Amiens.)

White House Cemetery, Ypres (Ieper), Belgium.   (2 Leek burials)
(Located north-east of Ypres on the N313 near the village of St Jan.)

Ypres Reservoir Cemetery, Ypres (Ieper), Belgium.   (2 Leek burials)
(Located north-west of Ypres on the M.Plumerlaan.)

Apendix 3

Buried/Com	Rank	Name	Initial	Number	Unit	Died
Aire Com . Cem.	Pioneer	Walker	A.T.	604982	Royal Engineers	19.12.1919
Albert Com. Cem.	Private	Robinson	A	44112	Essex Reg't.	23.8.1918
Alexandria Cem, Egypt	Private	Biddulph	J	15949	North Staffords	10.1.1916
Amara War Cem, Iraq	Private	Godwin	J.	16535	North Staffords	29.5.1916
Amara War Cem, Iraq	Lieutenant	Green	N.		North Staffords	25.1.1917
Amara War Cem, Iraq	Sergeant	Moss	W	SE/8959	Army Vet. Corps	1.9.1916
Amara War Cem, Iraq	Private	Noble	A	16818	North Staffords	27.1.1917
Amara War Cem, Iraq	Corporal	Wrench	T	8511	North Staffords	12.1.1917
Arras Memorial	Private	Astles	F	201347	Northumberland Fus.	3.5.1917
Arras Memorial	Private	Bailey	I	16995	Bedfordshire Reg't.	15.4.1917
Arras Memorial	Lieutenant	Ball	G.		Sherwood Foresters	21.3.1918
Arras Memorial	Private	Barber	H	202028	North Staffords	1.7.1917

257

Location	Rank	Surname	Initials	Number	Regiment	Date
Arras Memorial	Private	Barnett	A	41210	Suffolk Reg't.	8.6.1917
Arras Memorial	Private	Chawner	J.	14318	North Staffords	21.3.1918
Arras Memorial	Private	Clowes	E.H.	G/44302	Royal Fusiliers	10.5.1917
Arras Memorial	Private	Foster	W	201568	North Staffords	1.7.1917
Arras Memorial	Private	Fowler	J.	G/11094	Royal Fusiliers	24.3.1918
Arras Memorial	Private	Graham	A	42496	South Staffords	15.4.1918
Arras Memorial	L/Corporal	Hill	C.E.	242523	North Staffords	30.6.1917
Arras Memorial	Private	Hudson	A	23352	North Staffords	20.9.1917
Arras Memorial	Private	Johnson	J.J.	200470	North Staffords	21.3.1918
Arras Memorial	Private	Keates	F.W.	41099	Royal Inniskilling Fus.	19.5.1917
Arras Memorial	Private	Lovatt	G	201585	North Staffords	1.7.1917
Arras Memorial	Private	Oakes	W.E.	38536	Northumberland Fus.	9.4.1917
Arras Memorial	Private	Pickford	F	29254	East Lancashire Reg't.	12.5.1917
Arras Memorial	Private	Prince	J	42383	Worcestershire Reg't.	21.3.1918
Arras Memorial	Private	Simpson	H	241995	West Yorkshire Reg't.	3.5.1917
Arras Memorial	Private	Smith	A	200756	Durham Light Infantry	23.4.1917
Arras Memorial	Private	Smith	W.T.	201958	North Staffords	27.6.1917
Baghdad Cem, Iraq	Private	Cheshire	J.	19300	North Staffords	23.7.1917
Baghdad Cem, Iraq	Private	Plant	J.W.	29994	North Staffords	18.5.1918
Bailleul Com. Cem.	Private	Johnson	R	8624	North Staffords	7.6.1916
Bailleul Com. Cem.	Private	Simister	C.R.	4765	Royal Fusiliers	2.5.1915
Bard Cottage Cem. Ypres	Private	Shaw	H	54530	Royal Welsh Fusiliers	22.6.1917
Basra Memorial Iraq	Private	Sharratt	J	17811	North Staffords	20.4.1916
Basra Memorial, Iraq	Private	Fowler	W	14083	North Staffords	25.2.1917
Basra Memorial, Iraq	Private	Keates	J.E.	15575	North Staffords	22.4.1916

Cemetery / Memorial	Rank	Surname	Initials	Number	Regiment	Date
Basra Memorial, Iraq	Private	Lowe	T.E.	18592	North Staffords	25.2.1917
Basra Memorial, Iraq	Private	O'Shaughnessy	W	16108	North Staffords	5.4.1916
Beacon Cem.	Private	Belfield	P	G/15156	Royal Sussex Reg't.	13.8.1918
Becourt Mil. Cem.	Private	Tatton	H.	G/72320	Royal West Surreys	23.8.1918
Bedford House Cem.	Rifleman	Green	D.J.	R/6249	King's Royal Rifle Corps	30.6.1915
Belgrade Cem.	Private	Hibbert	G.A.	S/12563	Seaforth Highlanders	17.2.1919
Bellicourt Cem.	Sergeant	Pickford	P.	805429	Royal Field Artillery	5.10.1918
Berks Cem. Ext.	Rifleman	Trafford	H.S.	BC/12262	King's Royal Rifle Corps	24.6.1916
Bethencourt Cem.	Corporal	Graham	G.H.	8788	Royal Irish Reg't.	26.8.1914
Bethune Town Cem.	Private	Scotton	W	49668	King's (Liverpool) Reg't.	26.7.1917
Bienvillers Mil Cem.	Corporal	Bailey	H	805431	Royal Field Artillery	10.1.1917
Bienvillers Mil Cem.	Private	Birchenough	D	50699	K.O.Y.L.I.	2.6.1918
Bienvillers Mil Cem.	Bombardier	Crabtree	H	805444	Royal Field Artillery	10.1.1917
Bienvillers Mil Cem.	Private	Davies	R	39347	K.O.Y.L.I.	26.5.1918
Bleuet Farm Cem.	Gunner	Hall	F	31405	Royal Field Artillery	10.9.1917
Bois-de-Noilette Brit. Cem.	Private	Wheeldon	E	9800	Machine Gun Corps	25.6.1916
Boulogne Eastern Cem.	Private	Messham	H.J.	467037	Canadian M.G.C.	17.6.1916

Cemetery/Memorial	Rank	Surname	Initial	Number	Regiment	Date
Bouzincourt Com. Cem	Private	Richardson	E	3042	Royal Fusiliers	6.2.1917
Braine Cem.	Private	Drury	J.	9390	South Staffords	20.9.1914
Bralo Brit. Cem. Greece	Driver	Rhead	W.H.	T4/186340	R.A.S.C.	24.12.1918
Brancourt-le-Grand Cem.	Private	Smith	J.T	50134	Essex Reg't.	12.10.1918
Bristol Cem, U.K.	Private	Hampson	S	R4/065741	R.A.S.C.	18.5.1915
Browns Road, Festubert	Sergeant	Arrowsmith	E.	12370	North Staffords	6.11.1915
Bruay Communal Cem.	Private	Carter	P	201623	North Staffords	13.11.1917
Buttes New B/Cem.	Private	Clulow	R	32124	N.Z. Exp. Force	22.11.1917
Caister on Sea Cem.U.K.	Col.Sergeant	Edge	A.E.		Royal Marine L.I.	12.2.1917
Cambrai Memorial	Rifleman	Goodwin	A.W.	A/200236	King's Royal Rifle Corps	30.11.1917
Cambrai Memorial	Private	Lee	J	40900	North Staffords	29.11.1917
Cambrai Memorial	Guardsman	Trafford	G	23899	Grenadier Guards	1.12.1917
Capetown Cem S.A.	Private	Mellor	E.S.	36857	South Lancashire Reg't.	13.12.1917
Caterpillar Valley Cem.	Private	Dickenson	J.	23794	Royal Welsh Fusiliers	20.7.1916
Cement House Cem.	Private	Cope	G	35831	North Staffords	1.3.1918
Cement House Cem.	Private	Hewitt	E	G/68400	Royal Fusiliers	26.10.1917
Cement House Cem.	Private	Lovatt	J	202464	North Staffords	24.10.1918

Cemetery	Rank	Surname	Initials	Number	Regiment	Date
Cheddleton Churchyard	Lieutenant	Boucher	B.E.		Royal Welsh Fusiliers	10.5.1919
Chipping Barnet U.K.	Private	Street	J.H.H	10221	North Staffords	12.4.1917
Choques Mil. Cem.	Private	Winckle	J.G.	G/4583	Royal Sussex Reg't.	11.5.1915
Cite Bonjean Mil. Cem.	Corporal	Lillie-Mitchell	J.E.	93175	Royal Garrison Artillery	20.6.1917
Cologne Southern Cem.	Private	Hulme	W	42035	South Staffords	1.2.1918
Cologne Southern Cem.	L/Corporal	Hunt	S	201850	North Staffords	12.7.1918
Connaught Cem.	Private	Atkinson	J	40559	North Staffords	18.11.1916
Connaught Cem.	R.S.M.	Wilson	A	9274	North Staffords	18.11.1916
Couin New Brit. Cem.	Gunner	Salt	S	174175	Royal Field Artillery	7.4.1918
Curragh Mil. Cem. Ireland.	Sergeant	Walwyn	P	TT/02467	Royal Army Vet. Corps	6.12.1916
Daours Com. Cem.	Private	Leckenby	S.W.	M/274359	R.A.S.C.	31.5.1918
De Cusine Ravine Cem.	Private	Doxey	J	5011	North Staffords	26.8.1916
De Cusine Ravine Cem.	Sergeant	Salt	C	5331	North Staffords	4.8.1916
Delsaux Farm Cem.	Private	Ball	G	241725	North Staffords	17.10.1918
Dickebusch New Cem.	Private	Mycock	H	11182	Royal Fusiliers	24.4.1917
Div Collecting Post Cem	Private	Nowland	H	25602	Lincolnshire Reg't	14.8.1917
Divisional Cem.	Private	Bostock	E	8470	North Staffords	21.2.1916

Location	Rank	Surname	Initial	Regiment	Number	Date
Doiran Mem. Greece	Private	Goodfellow	P.	Cheshire Reg't.	25898	15.4.1918
Douchy-Les-Ayette Cem.	Private	Fleet	J.	Royal Fusiliers	81525	10.6.1918
Douchy-Les-Ayette Cem.	Guardsman	Slater	H	Grenadier Guards	28809	28.3.1918
Douchy-Les-Ayette Cem.	Private	Yates	T.C.	South Staffords	235395	1.8.1918
Doullens Com. Cem.	Private	Bond	W.E.	Lancashire Fusiliers	20829	11.6.1918
Doullens Com. Cem.	Private	Hulme	H.P.	R.A.S.C. and R.G.A.	T4/219384	11.2.1919
Dover Cem. U.K.	W/Officer	Walker	J.E	R.C.A.S.		29.8.1914
Dozinghem Cem.	Gunner	Birch	A	Royal Garrison Artillery	151379	9.11.1917
Dozinghem Cem.	Private	Nelson	F	Royal Sussex Reg't.	G/15122	14.8.1917
Dranouter Churchyard	Lieutenant	Nicholson	B.L.	Royal Field Artillery		24.7.1915
Dranouter Mil. Cem.	Private	Hulme	J.J.	North Staffords	7445	27.4.1916
Duisans Brit. Cem.	Gunner	Harrod	W	Royal Field Artillery	L/23563	18.5.1917
East London Cem.	A.B.	Mitchell	T	Royal Navy	172225	6.5.1918
Estaires Com. Cem.	Private	Graham	A	Worcestershire Reg't.	13590	12.3.1915
Etaples Mil Cem.	Private	Ainsworth	J.	North Staffords	12065	31.8.1918
Etaples Mil Cem.	Private	Bishop	J	South Staffords	32374	8.12.1917
Etaples Mil Cem.	Private	Osbourne	P	R.A.S.C.	M2/031683	12.11.1918
Etaples Mil Cem.	Private	Sims	S	R.A.M.C.	2960	16.7.1915
Etaples Mil Cem.	Guardsman	Smith	H.	Grenadier Guards	20793	16.10.1916

Cemetery	Rank	Surname	Initials	Number	Regiment	Date
Favreuil Brit. Cem.	Private	Cannon	T.A.	235127	King's Liverpool Reg't.	12.12.1917
Favreuil Brit. Cem.	Private	Brindley	H.	93549	Sherwood Foresters	16.3.1918
Fins New Brit. Cem.	Private	Hulme	E.	28585	K.O.S.B.	23.1.1918
Flatiron Copse Cem.	Private	Astles	A	11009	North Staffords	13.8.1916
Flatiron Copse Cem.	Private	Goldstraw	B	12140	North Staffords	13.8.1916
Flatiron Copse Cem.	Private	Turner	J	12262	North Staffords	13.8.1916
Fld amb Cem, Gallipoli	Private	Barks	W	10995	North Staffords	9.8.1915
Flesquireres Hill Cem.	Gunner	Hunt	H	69979	Tank Corps	20.11.1917
Fosse No: 10 Cem.	Sergeant	Bestwick	G	805420	Royal Field Artillery	8.6.1917
Fosse No: 10 Cem.	Lieutenant	Lewthwaite	C.G.		Royal Field Artillery	29.7.1917
Fosse No: 10 Cem.	Lieutenant	Watson	C.C.		Royal Field Artillery	1.6.1917
Fouquieres Cem.	Gunner	Ball	C.O.	805468	Royal Field Artillery	12.6.1918
Fouquieres Cem.	Private	Clay	F.W.	93551	Sherwood Foresters	3.9.1918
Fouquieres Cem.	Gunner	Malkin	T.W.	86286	Machine Gun Corps	24.7.1918
Gaza War Cem, Israel	Private	Birch	H	201366	Norfolk Reg't.	19.4.1917
Ghissignies Brit. Cem.	Private	Fowell	T	103698	Sherwood Foresters	4.11.1918
Gommecourt Wood Cem	Corporal	Ford	R	9399	South Staffords	26.6.1916
Gonnehem Brit. Cem.	Private	Brindley	G	42784	Essex Reg't.	29.5.1918

263

Cemetery/Memorial	Rank	Surname	Initials	Number	Regiment	Date
Grand Ravine Cem.	Private	Collins	J	22334	West Riding Reg't.	29.9.1918
Grevillers Cem.	Private	Gilman	J.	2154	Coldstream Guards	30.9.1918
Grevillers Cem.	Private	Partridge	C	305334	West Riding Reg't.	11.8.1917
Grevillers N.Z. Memorial	L/Corporal	Mansell	F	23/1513	N.Z. Rifle Brigade	27.9.1918
Grove Town Cem.	Lieutenant	Mellor	F.G.		Sherwood Foresters	19.9.1916
Guillemont Road Cem.	Private	Goodwin	G	16993	Bedfordshire Reg't.	3.9.1916
Habarcq Com. Cem.	Gunner	Hill	G.T.	65876	Royal Garrison Artillery	22.3.1917
Haidar Pasha Mem. Turkey	Captain	Spink	E.M.		North Staffords	14.9.1918
Hamburg Cem.	Corporal	Goldstraw	R	PO/16513	Royal Marine L.I.	23.12.1918
Hamel Mil. Cem.	Corporal	Robinson	C.W.	16948	Hampshire Reg't.	12.9.1915
Hargicourt Brit. Cem.	Private	Wardle	J.T.	242673	North Staffords	9.5.1917
Haringhe Cem, Ypres	Gunner	Baddeley	W	64242	Royal Garrison Artillery	25.4.1918
Haringhe Cem, Ypres	L/Corporal	Morris	A	106196	Sherwood Foresters	21.4.1918
Helles Memorial	L/Corporal	Brennan	J.J.	10469	North Staffords	14.8.1915
Helles Memorial	Private	Eaton	A	10515	North Staffords	10.8.1915
Helles Memorial	L/Corporal	Farnell	W	G/11342	Royal Fusiliers	23.9.1915
Helles Memorial	Private	Hall	J.	1545	Manchester Reg't.	5.6.1915
Helles Memorial	Private	Quinn	P	11037	North Staffords	10.8.1915

Cemetery/Memorial	Rank	Surname	Initials	Number	Regiment	Date
Helles Memorial	Q.M.S.	Rider	W	8728	North Staffords	7.1.1916
Helles Memorial	Private	Smith	W	27114	Royal Welsh Fusiliers	8.8.1915
Helles Memorial	Private	Trafford	H.E.	15126	North Staffords	21.10.1915
Helles Memorial	Corporal	Wood	F	41826	Royal Garrison Artillery	14.8.1915
Hermies Hill Cem.	Private	Ball	J.,W.	39547	Hertfordshire Reg't.	4.9.1918
Hermies Hill Cem.	L/Corporal	Elkin	G	R/39530	King's Royal Rifle Corps	22..11.1917
Hoogstade Mil. Cem.	Gunner	Malkin	H.	46613	Royal Garrison Artillery	16.6.1918
Kantara Cem, Egypt	Trooper	Atkinson	W	300843	Staffs Imp. Yeomanry	7.10.1918
Kemmel No: 1 Cem.	Private	Booth	F	29119	Machine Gun Corps	23.9.1917
Kirkee Memorial, India	Private	Smith	S	4438	R.A.M.C.	29.6.1916
Kortrijk Com. Cem.	Private	Murfin	C		Hampshire Reg't.	27.11.1918
La Brique Mil. Cem.	Private	Salt	S	8423	North Staffords	25.9.1915
La Chapelle Com. Cem.	Private	Higginbotham	W	9116	Royal Fusiliers	10.5.1915
La Ferte-S-J Mem.	Private	Merriman	E	8282	Royal Irish Reg't.	23.8.1914
La Laiterie Mil. Cem.	Lieutenant	Dale	A.W.	-	Northumberland Fusiliers	1.7.1916
La Neuville Cem.	Private	Thornton	T	10551	Royal Fusiliers	14.9.1916
Lapugnoy Mil. Cem.	Private	Yates	H	12107	Royal Fusiliers	19.10.1915

	Rank	Surname	Initials	Number	Regiment	Date
Laventie Mil. Cem.	Rifleman	Sales	V	267778	West Yorkshire Reg't.	3.7.1917
Le Touret Memorial	Private	Bloore	F	G/4584	Royal Sussex Reg't.	9.5.1915
Le Touret Memorial	Private	Smethurst	J.V.	G/4585	Royal Sussex Reg't.	9.5.1915
Leek Cemetery	Private	Booth	T	21338	Canadian Infantry	30.9.1915
Leek Cemetery	Private	Bowyer	W	8555	Royal Defence Gorps	10.5.1917
Leek Cemetery	Gunner	Broome	J.	RMA/7422	Royal Marine Artillery	8.11.1915
Leek Cemetery	Private	Chappells	E.C.	-	Sherwood Foresters	3.12.1917
Leek Cemetery	L/Corporal	Doxey	J.	-	Machine Gun Corps	23.11.1920
Leek Cemetery	Sergeant	Doxey	W	12463	Royal Defence Corps	27.9.1917
Leek Cemetery	Private	Fenton	C.V.	60515	Northamptonshire Reg't.	2.10.1918
Leek Cemetery	Private	Flanagan	G	20088	South Staffords	1.10.1915
Leek Cemetery	Corporal	Gee	J.E.	-	Royal Welsh Fusiliers	9.2.1920
Leek Cemetery	Bombardier	Goodfellow	N	204949	Royal Field Artillery	12.11.1918
Leek Cemetery	Sapper	Heath	G.W.	5927	Royal Engineers	27.1.1917
Leek Cemetery	Gunner	Johnson	J.A	240571	Royal Field Artillery	28.5.1918
Leek Cemetery	Air Mechanic	Keates	H.	21953	Royal Air Force	23.10.1918
Leek Cemetery	Private	Kirby	L.	196392	Labour Corps	10.9.1917
Leek Cemetery	Private	Kirkham	J.	8809	Royal Irish Fusiliers	9.4.1918
LeekCemetery	Sergeant	Lear	J.W.	23117	South Lancashire Reg't.	12.2.1916
Leek Cemetery	L/Corporal	Malkin	F	33402	Royal Engineers	17.5.1918
Leek Cemetery	Private	McLeavy	E.	-	Royal Defence Corps	5.7.1918
Leek Cemetery	Driver	Peacock	H	-	Royal Field Artillery	7.3.1919
Leek Cemetery	C/Sgt-Maj	Pickford	D	9031	Sherwood Foresters	23.10.1916
Leek Cemetery	Sergeant	Pickford	D	-	Royal Field Artillery	2.b.1Ylt
Leek Cemetery	Private	Pickford	J.J.	11162	Labour Corps	6.2.1919
Leek Cemetery	Corporal	Poole	E	-	West Yorkshire Reg't.	26.11.1918
Leek Cemetery	Private	Riches	R.C.	M/321671	R.A.S.C.	2.7.1919

Cemetery	Rank	Surname	Initials	Number	Regiment	Date
Leek Cemetery	Driver	Rider	C	-	R.A.S.C.	15.5.1919
Leek Cemetery	Private	Riley	N	TRG/51569	Sherwood Foresters	7.7.1918
Leek Cemetery	Private	Simpson	S	15561	R.A.M.C.	5.7.1918
Leek Cemetery	Corporal	Stanmore	F.E.	-	Ox and Bucks L.I.	14.3.1919
Leek Cemetery	Corporal	Stretch	S	3/16255	West Riding Reg't.	21.5.1918
Leek Cemetery	Private	Swarbrook	J	-	Royal Fusiliers	6.12.1922
Leek Cemetery	Private	Tatton	R	11342	Labour Corps	9.7.1919
Leek Cemetery	L/Corporal	Trafford	W.R.	7970	K.S.L.I.	5.11.1914
Leek Cemetery	Private	Vernon	R	TT/0936	Royal Army Vet. Corps	12.11.1918
Leek Cemetery	Sergeant	Vigrass	S.B.	22748	R.A.O.C.	2.12.1918
Leek Cemetery	Private	Weaver	J	-	Royal Defence Corps	12.4.1921
Leek Cemetery	Private	Whitehouse	J.D	330122	Sherwood Foresters	11.12.1917
Leek Cemetery	Private	Willmer	H.D.	47159	Manchester Regt.	30.11.1917
Leek Cemetery	Private	Wilson	V.H.	106658	Durham Light Infantry	13.11.1918
Leek Cemetery	Private	Yates	S	S/8190	Rifle Brigade	23.12.1916
Lijssenhoek Cem.	Sergeant	Birch	T.R	12907	Royal Berkshire Reg't.	2.8.1917
Lijssenhoek Cem.	Private	Hambleton	G	123015	Canadian Infantry	7.11.1917
Lijssenhoek Cem.	Gunner	Keates	G	151089	Royal Garrison Artillery	16.9.1917
Lijssenhoek Cem.	Sergeant	Kelly	S.G.	C/395	King's Royal Rifle Corps	29.9.1917
Lijssenhoek Cem.	Gunner	Pickford	E	152263	Royal Field Artillery	23.7.1917
Lijssenhoek Cem.	Private	Tomlinson	W	14115	Royal Fusiliers	1.7.1917
Lillers Com. Cem.	Private	Prosser	W	3971	North Staffords	17.10.1915
Lindenhoek Chalet Cem.	Private	Sigley	F	23189	Royal Welsh Fusiliers	30.4.1916
Longuenesse Cem.	Private	Holden	C.V	91868	R.A.M.C.	1.10.1917
Longuenesse Cem.	Gunner	Howard	W.S	844	Royal Field Artillery	7.4.1915

Location	Rank	Surname	Initials	Number	Regiment	Date
Loos Memorial	L/Corporal	Dunn	C	8826	Royal Fusiliers	29.9.1915
Loos Memorial	Private	Glenn	H	57187	King's (Liverpool) Reg't.	9.4.1918
Loos Memorial	Private	Hammersley	H.	3911	Royal Fusiliers	18.2.1916
Loos Memorial	Captain	Johnson	R.T.	-	North Staffords	13.10.1915
Loos Memorial	Private	Mellor	T	16584	South Staffords	25.9.1915
Loos Memorial	Guardsman	White	H.G.	13231	Grenadier Guards	27.9.1915
Loos Memorial	Private	Wilson	R	16600	Scottish Rifles	27.1.1916
Loos Memorial	Corporal	Wood	R	60480	M.G.C.	6.5.1918
Menin Gate Memorial	Gunner	Biddulph	E	127598	Royal Garrison Artillery	3.8.1917
Menin Gate Memorial	Private	Cartlidge	J.	7647	North Staffords	8.11.1915
Menin Gate Memorial	Private	Cox	F.W.	36193	Sherwood Foresters	31.7.1917
Menin Gate Memorial	Private	Goldstraw	G.O.	12113	Royal Fusiliers	26.4.1915
Menin Gate Memorial	Private	Greatbatch	J.J.	12788	Ox and Bucks L.I.	17.10.1915
Menin Gate Memorial	L/Corporal	Higginbotham	F.L.	46667	Northumberland Fus.	19.6.1917
Menin Gate Memorial	Private	Lees	E	23431	Durham Light Infantry	31.7.1917
Menin Gate Memorial	Private	Lowe	W	8018	North Staffords	8.11.1915
Menin Gate Memorial	Private	Machin	J.	9041	South Staffords	7.11.1914
Menin Gate Memorial	Rifleman	Malkin	H	R/15158	King's Royal Rifle Corps	10.8.1917
Menin Gate Memorial	Private	Malkin	P	2941	East Surrey Reg't.	8.5.1915
Menin Gate Memorial	Gunner	Phillips	J.	837268	Royal Field Artillery	11.8.1917
Menin Gate Memorial	Private	Poyser	J.W	3640	East Surrey Reg't.	27.4.1915
Menin Gate Memorial	Private	Rushton	G.A.	60955	Machine Gun Corps	4.8.1917
Menin Gate Memorial	Private	Rushton	J	16443	Bedfordshire Reg't.	2.6.1915
Menin Gate Memorial	Private	Sillito	M	16391	Royal Fusiliers	26.4.1915
Mericourt L'Abbe Cem.	Sapper	Tomkinson	H	10692	Royal Engineers	15.7.1916
Merville Com. Cem.	Private	Smith	T	13584	East Lancashire Reg't.	22.8.1915

Cemetery/Memorial	Rank	Surname	Initials	Number	Regiment	Date
Mikra Cem, Greece	Private	Cantrell	R	20686	K.S.L.I.	30.9.1918
Nechin Com. Cem.	Corporal	Prime	C	805739	Royal Field Artillery	6.11.1918
Neiderzwehren Cem.	Private	Pointon	F	43694	Yorkshire Reg't.	22.6.1918
New Irish Farm Cem.	Gunner	Read	H	101586	Royal Field Artillery	5.8.1917
N'ham Rd Cem. Derby.	C.S.M.	Smith	E	5924	King's Royal Rifle Corps	11.10.1917
Nieuport Memorial	Lieutenant	Boucher	A.G.	-	King's Royal Rifle Corps	10.7.1917
Nine Elms Mil. Cem.	Bombardier	Shute	H	76684	Royal Field Artillery	12.4.1917
Noeux-le-Mines Cem.	Private	Warbrick	J.E.	201644	North Staffords	15.6.1917
Not Known	Private	Peacock	H	-	Cheshire Reg't.	2.9.1918
Pernes Brit. Cem.	Private	Goldstraw	J.W.	241597	North Staffords	24 5.1918
Perth Cem. U.K.	Sergeant	Robinson	C.C.	3/3957	Black Watch	2.12.1916
Philosophe Brit. Cem.	Lieutenant	Swindells	H.	-	South Staffords	15.8.1917
Ploegsteert Memorial	Private	Goodwin	J	11031	Scotish Rifles	5.11.1914
Plymouth Memorial	Boy	Johnson	R	J/37132	HMS Barham, R.N.	31.5.1916
Poelcapelle Brit. Cem.	Lieutenant	Wagstaffe	J.C.	-	South Staffords	12.10.1917

Cemetery	Rank	Surname	Initials	Number	Regiment	Date
Pont du Hem Mil. Cem.	Lieutenant	Ellis	P.C.	-	H.L.I./ Royal Flying Corps	17.10.1916
Pont-Remy Cem.	Private	Geston	H	368819	Labour Corps	22.2.1919
Poperinge New Cem.	Bombardier	Hilton	W.T.	78822	Royal Field Artillery	16.7.1915
Portsmouth Memorial	A.B.	Billing	A	J/26661	HMS Invincible, R.N.	31.5.1916
Portsmouth Memorial	Boy	Bloor	T	J/35047	HMS Hampshire, R.N.	5.6.1916
Portsmouth Memorial	A.B.	Tomkinson	G	SS/805	HMS Good Hope. R.N.	1.11.1914
Pozieres British Cem.	L/Corporal	Ashworth	H.	11138	Royal Fusiliers	16.7.1916
Pozieres British Cem.	Private	Meakin	T	14473	Loyal North Lancs Reg't.	7.7.1916
Pozieres Memorial	L/Corporal	Ashley	W.	242014	Gloucesters	31.3.1918
Pozieres Memorial	Private	Barber	H	G/15150	Royal Sussex Reg't.	26.3.1918
Pozieres Memorial	Private	Bishop	C	201344	Northumberland Fus.	26.3.1918
Pozieres Memorial	Private	Carter	E	2919	East Lancashire Reg't.	21.3.1918
Pozieres Memorial	Private	Goodwin	S.A.	43416	Royal Fusiliers	27.3.1918
Pozieres Memorial	Private	Owen	J.W	204459	Royal West Kent Reg't.	28.3.1918
Pozieres Memorial	Private	Prince	W	7738	North Staffords	21.3.1918
Premont Brit. Cem	Private	Smith	G	53167	Sherwood Foresters	12.6.1918
Puchevillers Cem.	Private	Fogg	T	31192	South Lancashire Reg't.	18.2.1917
Queens Cem, Puisieux	Private	Mayers	J.W.	40745	Worcestershire Reg't.	11.2.1917
Ramleh War Cem. Israel	Lieutenant	Gould	E.W.	-	South Lancashire Reg't.	11.4.1918
Ramparts Cem, Ypres	Gunner	Goodfellow	A	66889	Royal Field Artillery	9.8.1915

Cemetery/Memorial	Rank	Surname	Initials	Number	Regiment	Date
Raperie Brit. Cem.	Private	Pickford	H	352859	Royal Scots	1.8.1918
Ration Farm Mil. Cem.	Private	Edge	H.	46000	Northumberland Fus.	19.1.1917
Red Cross Corner Cem.	Corporal	Marren	J	9705	Royal Fusiliers	21.8.1917
Regina Trench Cem.	Private	Cheshire	S	15498	Cheshire Reg't.	1.10.1916
Regina Trench Cem.	Private	Crombie	R	24158	Manchester Reg't.	26.9.1916
Ribecourt Road Cem.	Sapper	Goldstraw	P.	486861	Royal Engineers	9.12.1917
Rocquigny-Eq'crt Rd. Cem.	Private	Booth	P	G/42640	Middlesex Reg't.	7.1.1918
Rocquigny-Eq'crt Rd. Cem.	Private	Robinson	S.W.	201841	Argylls	24.11.1917
Rocquigny-Eq'crt Rd. Cem.	Rifleman	Rogers	G	R/38033	King's Royal Rifle Corps	3.12.1917
Roisel Com. Cem.	Private	Lowe	W	49527	Lincolnshire Reg't.	1.4.1918
Romeries Com. Cem.	Private	Wood	C.M.	57107	Lancashire Fusiliers	23.10.1918
Rossignol Wood Cem.	Private	Travis	J	201567	North Staffords	14.3.1917
Salonika Cem, Greece	Private	Hammond	W	25915	Cheshire Reg't.	12.8.1916
Sancourt Brit. Cem.	Corporal	Knowles	J	2378440	Canadian Infantry	27.9.1918
Shrewsbury Cem. UK	Private	Connolly	W.P.	372029	London Reg't.	11.2.1919
Soissons Memorial	Sergeant	Birchenough	H	91909	Durham Light Infantry	27.5.1918
Spoilbank Cem.	Private	Murray	P.V.	10578	Royal Fusiliers	4.11.1915

Cemetery/Memorial	Rank	Surname	Initials	Number	Regiment	Date
St Sever Cem.	Private	Bould	H	19323	Bedfordshire Reg't.	26.8.1918
St Sever Cem.	Private	Bratt	J.H.	202034	North Staffords	15.5.1918
St Sever Cem.	Private	Peach	G.W.	241596	North Staffords	5.12.1917
St Sever Cem.	L/Corporal	Stockton	H.	12244	North Staffords	22.5.1918
St. Aubert Cem.	Corporal	Golby	H.	S/32302	Rifle Brigade	11 10.1918
Strand Mil. Cem.	L/Corporal	Doody	C.H.	9171	Royal Lancaster Reg't.	19.3.1915
Sucrerie Cem.	L/Corporal	Dean	R.J	201926	North Staffords	18.10.1917
Tehran Memorial	L/Corporal	Birch	E	13052	North Staffords	14.9.1918
Tehran War Cem. Iran	Corporal	Davenport	A	15726	North Staffords	12.1.1919
Terlincthun Cem.	Private	Hambleton	A	82138	Durham Light Infantry	29.10.1918
Terlincthun Cem.	Gunner	Lazenby	J.W.	25903	Royal Field Artillery	25.10.1918
Thiepval Memorial	Private	Alcock	U.	G/15134	Royal Sussex	21.10.1916
Thiepval Memorial	Private	Allard	S.	16810	Sherwood Foresters	1.7.1916
Thiepval Memorial	Private	Bestwick	R	4648	Durham Light Infantry	16.9.1916
Thiepval Memorial	L/Corporal	Billing	H	200680	South Staffords	1.7.1916
Thiepval Memorial	Guardsman	Booth	W	23044	Grenadier Guards	15.9.1916
Thiepval Memorial	Private	Bowyer	S	23565	D.C.L.I.	18.8.1916
Thiepval Memorial	Private	Brookes	J.	201584	North Staffords	14.3.1917
Thiepval Memorial	Driver	Cade	H.E.	810184	Royal Field Artillery	1.7.1916
Thiepval Memorial	Private	Clarke	J.	11141	Royal Fusiliers	16.7.1916
Thiepval Memorial	Private	Desborough	J.J.	27356	Loyal North Lancs	25.10.1916
Thiepval Memorial	Private	Flower	E	8999	Manchester Reg't.	1.7.1916
Thiepval Memorial	Private	Fogg	J.	43232	Bedfordshire Reg't.	16.11.1916

Memorial	Rank	Surname	Initial	Number	Regiment	Date
Thiepval Memorial	Private	Gibson	E	9180	Royal Fusiliers	7.7.1916
Thiepval Memorial	Private	Giddings	J.	16992	Bedfordshire Reg't.	28.9.1916
Thiepval Memorial	Lieutenant	Green	C.E.	-	K.S.L.I.	15.7.1916
Thiepval Memorial	Lieutenant	Gwynne	H.L.	-	North Staffords	18.11.1916
Thiepval Memorial	Private	Hollinshead	S	19322	North Staffords	18.11.1916
Thiepval Memorial	Private	Hudson	J.J.	16444	Bedfordshire Reg't.	4.9.1916
Thiepval Memorial	Corporal	Hulme	J A	G/4581	Royal Sussex Reg't.	3.10.1916
Thiepval Memorial	Private	Johnson	H.P.	15247	North Staffords	22.7.1916
Thiepval Memorial	Private	Kelk	J.H.	12/1481	York and Lancs Reg't	1.7.1916
Thiepval Memorial	Private	Kirkham	E	4021	Northumberland Fus.	15.9.1916
Thiepval Memorial	Private	Moorcroft	F	41731	Sherwood Foresters	12.5.1917
Thiepval Memorial	Private	Nowland	A	8851	East Surrey Reg't.	16.8.1916
Thiepval Memorial	Private	Plant	H.	26584	Sherwood Foresters	3.9.1916
Thiepval Memorial	Private	Plant	W	16854	Bedfordshire Reg't.	27.7.1916
Thiepval Memorial	Gunner	Prime	G.V.	398	Royal Field Artillery	1.7.1916
Thiepval Memorial	Private	Prince	E	16994	Bedfordshire Reg't.	27.7.1916
Thiepval Memorial	Private	Rhead	F	14761	Royal Fusiliers	7.10.1916
Thiepval Memorial	Private	Robinson	J.H.	G/6849	East Kent Reg't.	25.9.1916
Thiepval Memorial	Private	Shenton	H	5251	North Staffords	24.6.1916
Thiepval Memorial	Private	Sigley	RJ.	18297	K.O.Y.L.I.	18.11.1916
Thiepval Memorial	Private	Slater	J.T	11095	Royal Fusiliers	9.7.1916
Thiepval Memorial	Gunner	Spearing	J	119389	Royal Field Artillery	8.11.1916
Thiepval Memorial	Private	Sweetmore	H.	11196	Royal Fusiliers	9.8.1916
Thiepval Memorial	Private	Tatton	A	11120	Royal Welsh Fusiliers	20.7.1916
Thiepval Memorial	Private	Taylor	T	201621	North Staffords	1.7.1916
Thiepval Memorial	Private	Wallis	R	16991	Bedfordshire Reg't.	5.9.1916
Thiepval Memorial	L/Corporal	Wheeldon	W.F.	4783	Manchester Reg't.	7.7.1916
Tidworth Cem, U.K.	Sergeant	Hill	R	171347	Royal Army Vet. Corps	25.2.1919

Cemetery/Memorial	Rank	Surname	Initial	Number	Regiment	Date
Toronto Cem. Canada	Air Mechanic	Irwin	T	70646	Royal Air Force	26.8.1921
Tourgeville Mil. Cem.	Private	McKenzie	H	94258	Alias Kinzey. R.A.M.C.	2.11.1918
Tournai Cem.	Private	Constantine	W	241784	North Staffords	8.6.1917
Twelve Tree Cps, G'poli	Private	Baskerville	W	G/11021	Royal Fusiliers	25.6.1915
Tyne Cot Memorial	L/Corporal	Astles	J	2111B	Bedfordshire Reg't.	25.10.1917
Tyne Cot Memorial	Private	Bintcliffe	C	20208	Border Reg't.	4.10.1917
Tyne Cot Memorial	Lieutenant	Conley	W.C.	-	South Staffords	26.10.1917
Tyne Cot Memorial	Private	Cotterill	J.A.	32321	South Staffords	12.10.1917
Tyne Cot Memorial	Private	Nelson	E	51326	West Yorkshire Reg't.	25.4.1918
Tyne Cot Memorial	Private	Renshaw	V	43011	South Staffords	4.10.1917
Tyne Cot Memorial	Private	Robinson	T	50793	Lancashire Fusiliers	20.4.1918
Tyne Cot Memorial	Private	Sheldon	J	41473	South Staffords	12.10.1917
Tyne Cot Memorial	Private	Smith	E	352863	Royal Scots	20.9.1917
Tyne Cot Memorial	Private	Wheatley	B	28513	Loyal North Lancs Reg't	26.10.1917
Tyne Cot Memorial	Private	Wood	T.H.	G/96300	Middlesex Reg't.	28.9.1918
Vermelles Brit. Cem.	Private	Tudor .	H.A.	2767	North Staffords	13.10.1915
Vichte Mil. Cem.	Private	Clayton	W.H.,	54017	Lancashire Fusiliers	30.9.1918
Vielle-Chapelle Cem.	L/Corporal	Richards	J.	31869	K.S.L.I.	22.8.1918
Villers-Bretonneux Cem	Private	Ball	H	44768	Royal Berkshire Reg't.	22.10.1918
Villers-Bretonneux Cem	Driver	Missen	T.M.	59650	Royal Field Artillery	22.8.1918
Villers-Bretonneux Mem.	Captain	Leadbeater	J.	-	Australian Infantry	25.7.1916
Vimy Memorial	Private	Robinson	J	808287	Canadian Infantry	9.4.1917

Cemetery/Memorial	Rank	Surname	Initial	Number	Regiment	Date
Vimy Memorial	Private	Stannard	H	234936	Canadian Infantry.	9.5.1917
Vis-en-Artois Memorial	Private	Hammersley	P.	38036	Gloucestershire Reg't.	22.8.1918
Vis-en-Artois Memorial	Private	Keates	H.M.	202193	K.O.S.B.	20.9.1918
Vis-en-Artois Memorial	Private	Robinson	T	41060	South Staffords	28.9.1918
Vlamertinghe Cem.	Gunner	Carter	J.A.	1526828	Royal Field Artillery	21.10.1917
Vlamertinghe Cem.	L/Corporal	Hudson	W	241732	North Staffs	30.9.1917
Vlamertinghe Cem.	Private	Hulme	H.	15741	Royal Sussex Reg't.	22.4.1917
Voormezeele Cem.	Gunner	Brandrick	W.E	2660	Machine Gun Corps	16.4.1918
Voormezeele Cem.	Private	Carter	W.H.	16301	West Riding Reg't.	27.6.1915
Voormezeele Cem.	Lieutenant	Price	C.H.	-	Canadian Light Infantry	24.1.1915
Warlincourt Halte Cem.	Sapper	Fogg	J.	1165	Royal Engineers	5.1.1917
Warlincourt Halte Cem.	Private	Trafford	A	5500	North Staffs	11.8.1916
Warloy-Baillon Cem.	Private	Sproson	A	17066	Lincolnshire Reg't.	21.5.1916
White House Cem.	Major	Breton	W.G.	-	Royal Garrison Artillery	14.9.1917
White House Cem.	Gunner	Plant	S	151494	Royal Garrison Artillery	6.7.1917
Ypres Reservoir Cem.	Major	Davenport	F.	-	Royal Field Artillery	25.9.1917
Ypres Reservoir Cem.	Guardsman	Robinson	E	22313	Grenadier Guards	9.5.1916

Appendix 4

SERVICEMEN LISTED ON THE NICHOLSON WAR MEMORIAL WHO CANNOT BE LINKED TO OFFICIAL RECORDS. IN EACH CASE, THE DATE OF DEATH AND PLACE OF BURIAL IS UNKNOWN.

Name	Unit believed to belong to.
Lieutenant G. Hambleton	Canadian Contingent
Private H. Beard	Royal Scots
Private W. Beresford	King's Own Scottish Borderers
Private H. Birchenough	Royal Engineers
Private J. Dutton	North Staffordshire Regiment
Sapper H. Goldstraw	Royal Engineers
Trooper A. Goodfellow	Staffordshire Imperial Yeomanry
Private J. Goodwin	North Staffordshire Regiment
Private A. Grimes	Lancashire Fusiliers
Private F. Hodgkinson	Royal Defence Corps
Corporal F. Malkin	North Staffordshire Regiment
Driver E. Noble	Royal Army Service Corps
Private C. Pointon	Royal Fusiliers
Corporal J. Ratcliffe	Cheshire Regiment
Gunner E. Rider	Royal Field Artillery or Royal Garrison Artillery
Bandsman H.L. Robinson	Not Known
Private G.A. Ryder	Royal Fusiliers
Private J. Sigley	Labour Corps
Pioneer E.S. Smith	Royal Engineers
Corporal W.L. Smith	Cheshire Regiment
L/Corporal A. Unsworth	North Staffordshire Regiment
L/Corporal A. Walters	Gloucestershire Regiment
Private R. Wheatley	Loyal North Lancashire Regiment
Sergeant V. Wheeldon	Royal Field Artillery

The following names are also listed but have no rank or unit recorded against them.

H.Barnett	J.Cotterill	A.Hassall	C.Hibbert	F.High	A.Hulme	A.Johnson
R.Johnson	A.Perkin	E.W.Salt	E.H.Smith	H.Spencer	J.Tatton	A.Vernon
S.Wardle	H.Woodcock					

Order form overleaf for other books published by
Three Counties Publishing (Books) Limited.

Roll of Honour

Other Books published by THREE COUNTIES PUBLISHING (Books) LTD, which are all available by mail order from the publishers are: -

Roll of Honour	by C. W. Sheldon ISBN 0 9544080 - 3 - 9	*Price £ 15.95*
Policing The Potteries	by Alf Tunstall & Jeff Cowdell ISBN 0-9535239-9-3	*Price £ 17.95*
Hanley Wakes	by Derrick Woodward ISBN 0 9535239 - 8 - 5	*Price £ 7.95*
Where Have all the Years Gone	by Reg. Harvey ISBN 0 9544080 - 1 - 2	*Price £ 9.95*
A History of Longton	by Prof. J. H. Y. Briggs ISBN 0 9535239 - 1 - 8	*Price £14.95*
The Spirit of the Place	by M. J. W. Rogers ISBN 0 9535239 - 3 - 4	*Price £16.95*
In Name Only	by C. W. Sheldon ISBN 0 9535239 - 5 - 0	*Price £ 13.95*
Gently Thru' Life	by David Whitmore ISBN 0 9535239 - 4 - 2	*Price £ 12.95*
A Victorian Pottery	by Peter Beckett ISBN 0 9535239 - 6 - 9	*Price £ 8.95*
In Search of Fenton Castle	by Barbara Maddox ISBN 0 9535239 - 7 - 7	*Price £ 7.95*

If you do not wish to order any books but would like to be sent our twice yearly newsletter on new publications please complete the address panel below and send it to us marked NEWSLETTER PLEASE

POSTAGE - PLEASE NOTE:

ORDER ONE BOOK — POSTAGE & PACKAGE ADD £ 2.00
ORDER TWO BOOKS — POSTAGE & PACKAGE ADD £ 3.00
ORDER ANY THREE BOOKS OR MORE — POSTAGE & PACKAGE **FREE**

TOTAL REMITTANCE Incl. POSTAGE   £   .   p

Your Name ....

Address ....

....

Post Code .... Tel. No. ....(for use only if difficulty with delivery)

Cheques should be made payable to **Three Counties Publishing (Books) Ltd**
and sent to **P.O. Box 435, Leek, Staffs, ST13 5TB**
Please allow up to 10 - 21 days for delivery of books in stock.
This Order Form may be photocopied if you require more or would like to pass one to a friend

Roll of Honour